The Internal Impact and External Influence of the Greek Financial Crisis

John Marangos
Editor

The Internal Impact and External Influence of the Greek Financial Crisis

palgrave
macmillan

Editor
John Marangos
University of Macedonia
Thessaloniki, Greece

ISBN 978-3-319-60200-4   ISBN 978-3-319-60201-1   (eBook)
DOI 10.1007/978-3-319-60201-1

Library of Congress Control Number: 2017948396

Cover image © PeskyMonkey / Getty Images
Cover design by Ran Shauli

Printed on acid-free paper

This Palgrave Macmillan imprint is published by Springer Nature
The registered company is Springer International Publishing AG
The registered company address is: Gewerbestrasse 11, 6330 Cham, Switzerland

Prologue

"If we restrict ourselves to the rationality postulate, if we make that assumption and that assumption alone, the results in terms of operational meaningful theorems will be very puny indeed." (Papandreou 1950)

The words of Andreas Papandreou are echoed throughout the world suffering the Global Financial Crisis (GFC), constantly reminding us of the inadequacy of orthodox theory. The orthodox theorems are "very puny indeed", as Andreas, the economist, told us some 70 years ago. The economist Andreas, a stern critic of the orthodox postulates, would not have had been surprised of the GFC and the consequences of the crisis, especially for Greece. The assumption of the rationality postulate of the orthodox economics requires revision or even better abandonment to develop theorems that are realistic and practical. The book by John Marangos as an editor, providing us with a collection of chapters by international, well-respected authors, actually attempts implicitly in the spirit of Andreas Papandreou to achieve this goal set forth. The chapters published are able to explain, evaluate and reorganize economic theory. The consequences and the international impact of the Greek financial crisis, as analyzed by the authors in this book, provide a framework to accurately scrutinize the crisis beyond the "rationality postulate". I have no doubt that the book by John Marangos as an editor is a contribution to both economic and social theory, and I wholeheartedly recommend the book without any hesitation.

Panagiotis Roumeliotis
Emeritus Professor, Panteion University
Chairman of Attica Bank

REFERENCE

Papandreou, A. G. (1950). Economics and Social Sciences. *The Economic Journal, 60*(240), 715–723.

CONTENTS

LIST OF FIGURES

List of Tables

CHAPTER 1

Introduction

John Marangos

Dear Reader,

It is a great pleasure that you are holding our book, hopefully, with the intention to read. The Greek Financial Crisis (GRFC) which unfolded because of the mid-2008 Global Financial Crisis had internal economic and social outcomes and external consequences. The current study of the GRFC is limited mainly to the reasons of the crisis, without adequate determination of the economic and social results to the domestic economy. The GRFC initiated the establishment of new European Union (EU) institutions to deal with the crisis, which have not been assessed for their effectiveness. Subsequently, the internal and external reactions to the crisis are imperative in determining the current situation. As well, commonalities of the GRFC with other financial crises are not investigated in the literature, which is an important issue addressed in this book. The edited book that you are holding in your hands is a collection of chapters by international experts with the scope of exploring the impact of the GRFC adding to our concise understanding and domestic and international impact of the crisis.

The chapters examine and explicitly deal with issues that have been ignored by the dominant socio-economic theory and practice. The authors

J. Marangos (✉)
Department of Balkan, Slavic and Oriental Studies, University of Macedonia, Thessaloniki, Greece

© The Author(s) 2017
J. Marangos (ed.), *The Internal Impact and External Influence of the Greek Financial Crisis*, DOI 10.1007/978-3-319-60201-1_1

1

aim to use alternative perspectives in ways that go beyond traditional dominant socio-economic theories. The chapters examine and question the prevailing consensus and as such illustrate alternative responses to the crisis for the benefit of the people. The methodology adopted is holistic, historical, dynamic and comparative in nature.

In Chap. 2 titled "The 'Greek Crisis' and the Austerity Controversy in Europe" by John G. Milios, Spyros Lapatsioras and Dimitris P. Sotiropoulos, the authors maintain that shortly after the outbreak of the 2008 global economic crisis, Greece functioned as a "guinea pig" for shaping the second phase of the project of European Unification. The strategic target of European economic and political elites is to deepen and render irreversible the neoliberal policy framework all over Europe. European authorities argue that this policy framework will promote "competitiveness", which shall reflect in a positive current account balance and a process of export-oriented growth. However, the authors argue many prominent economists see austerity-led European current account surpluses as the main mechanism creating global imbalances and retarding growth. Nevertheless, these criticisms can hardly explain why neoliberal strategies persist, despite "failures". In this chapter, the authors attempt to formulate an answer to this discrepancy on the basis of a Marxist analysis.

In Chap. 3, "Troika's Economic Adjustment Programmes for Greece: Why Do They Systematically Fail?", Stavros Mavroudeas states that the current Greek crisis—together with crises of the other euro-periphery economies—is at the epicenter of EU's structural problems. To overcome this crisis, the EU in agreement with successive Greek governments has applied three Economic Adjustment Programs (EAPs), entailing successive loans to Greece in order to avoid default and linked to conditionality delineating the recipient's obligations. These programs despite their successive reviews and modifications failed dismally to overcome the Greek crisis and achieve their own milestones. This chapter explores the causes of this blatant failure. The first part presents the historical timeline of the Greek EAPs and pinpoints their failures. The next part analyzes the origins of these programmes and the peculiarities of the Greek EAPs. The last part explains the political economic reasons of their systematic failures.

Chapter 4, "The ECB's Non-standard Monetary Policy Measures and the Greek Financial Crisis", by Marica Frangakis examines and assesses the relation between the ECB's non-standard monetary policy measures and the GRFC. The initial non-standard monetary policy measures were taken in the context of the GRFC. However, Greece has been excluded from the renewed versions of the ECB's non-standard measures on non-monetary grounds. The Greek experience points to the inadequacies and weaknesses of the ECB monetary policy, which limit its role as a lender-of-last-resort and its potential for crisis resolution.

Chapter 5, the "Social Dialogue in Post-crisis Greece: A Sisyphus Syndrome for Greek Social Partners' Expectations", by Theodore Koutroukis argues that due to a large public debt, Greece has been obliged to ask for external financing and to implement measures of reform (Memoranda). The evidence of the years 2010–2016 indicates: (a) higher flexibility in the labor market, (b) reduction of minimum wages at the national and the sectoral level, (c) decentralization of the collective bargaining procedures and (d) abandonment or extreme limitation of the arbitration procedure for several years. The aim of this chapter is to assess the impact of joint EC-ECB-IMF programs on the Greek industrial relation system, using an analysis of the institutional changes in labor market and social dialogue. In the years to come, a new response to the crisis is likely to appear, an "organized decentralization" shift in which higher-level agreements set the parameters and the procedures for collective bargaining at the company level. This process allows for adaptation to firm-specific circumstances but put limit on the labor flexibility avoiding extreme solutions.

Chapter 6, "Unregistered Economic Activities During the Greek Multidimensional Crisis", by Aristidis Bitzenis and Vasileios Vlachos states that the political, economic and social dimensions of the Greek multifaceted (economic, banking, social and sovereign debt) crisis have turned attention to the size and impact of the unofficial to the official economy. The relation between corruption and the unofficial economy in Greece and their role in the Greek crisis have stimulated discussion at an international level about the potential of unregistered economic activities to provide economic succor in times of crisis. This chapter builds on this discussion and explores whether the unofficial economy is a substitute for the official economy in economic downturns and by what means there can be a transfer of a part of the unofficial to the official economy (i.e. to register unregistered economic activities which deliver lawful goods and/or services). The exploration is based on data from an EU THALES research project about the size, causes and impact of the shadow economy in Greece. The focus of the research is on the least explored aspect of tax compliance in Greece, namely, tax morale. The findings on the level of tax morale amid the crisis contribute to the ongoing international debate on enforced versus voluntary tax compliance (slippery slope framework) and highlight the factors favoring the transfer of unregistered economic activities to the official economy in Greece.

Chapter 7, headed "The Impact of the Financial Crisis on Greece's Defense Diplomacy", by Fotini Bellou explores the implications of the GRFC on the country's defense diplomacy. Although defense budgets have been reduced in recent years almost in all European countries, Greece's defense expenditures have experienced a dramatic reduction prompting Athens to reconsider its defense priorities, including its defense diplomacy. For this reason, Greece started to fashion the triptych of rationalization, optimization and prioritization in filtering its policies related to defense diplomacy, including its participation in peace support operations or other cooperative military initiatives. Emphasis is given to augmenting its training and operational military cooperation in the context of the evolving commitments as a member of NATO and the EU. Yet, the recent strategic regional environment, including the need for managing the migration crisis, has revealed the importance of defense diplomacy and its credentials, which were previously not fully appreciated.

Chapter 8, "Hierarchies, Civilization and the Eurozone Crisis: The Greek Financial Crisis", by Kyriakos Mikelis and Dimitrios Stroikos asserts that one of the most important aspects of the EU has been the complex and often ambiguous power politics of conditionality. However, less attention has been paid to the ways in which the management of the Eurozone crisis, especially with regard to the case of Greece, has been embedded in practices that construct distinctions between insiders and outsiders within the Eurozone. Drawing on the concept of the "standard of civilization" and postcolonial approaches to the study of the EU, the aim of this chapter is to examine the transformation of Greece into a negative signifier and to illustrate the relevance of civilizational practices and narratives to the GRFC. In this respect, the chapter provides a reflective critique to exclusionary practices engrained in the management of the crisis. It also highlights the enduring importance of hierarchy and civilization within the Eurozone.

Chapter 9, "Greece in the Aftermath of the Economic Crisis Needs to Change Its Strategy in the International System: Choosing Between Melians and David", by Revecca Pedi provides a new narrative about Greece's inefficiency to respond effectively to challenges and pressures posed by the international system. It considers the hypothesis that had Greece followed a "small but smart" state strategy during the economic crisis, it would have avoided costly miscalculations. It focuses on the way that Greece dealt with its partners and creditors in the negotiations from January 2015 to July 2015 and examines a series of factors such as Greek government's ability to estimate the state of the international system, the arguments and mind-set of the Greek side, its level of preparation, experience and understanding of the negotiations' context, and existence of allies and other resources such as reputation, unity, its geography and leadership. It concludes that Greece should abandon its victimhood mind-set and "Melians' narrative" and understand that the international system is first and foremost a self-help system.

Chapter 10, "A Comparative Analysis of the Greek Financial Crisis and the IMF's Bailout Programs: An East Asian View", by Hee-Young Shin examines the current financial and economic crisis in Greece from a perspective of the East Asian Financial Crisis. The chapter traces some of the distinctive features of the ongoing economic crisis in Greece, comparing them with those of the financial crisis in East Asia in the late 1990s. This comparative analysis of the two crises shows that the aggravation in the Greek economic situation is primarily due to the IMF and the Troika's misguided bailout conditionality, just as the IMF's failed bailout programs in East Asia severely damaged many East Asian economies. Drawing upon this observation, the chapter proposes a series of applicable reform agendas in the domain of regional and international financial arrangement. These proposals include (1) a need of reversing myopic financial liberalization and premature relegation of fiscal and monetary authorities to a supranational entity, (2) a need of extending the US Chapter 11 bankruptcy provision to sovereign states at the regional and international arena, (3) a need of creating an effective international lender of last resort and (4) a need of overhauling the existing austerity-oriented bailout conditionality in favor of aggregate demand-enhancing inclusive economic development.

Chapter 11, written by Jesús Muñoz, with the title "Commonalities Between the 'Bookends' Financial Crises of Mexico 1994 and Greece 2007", is a historical and theoretical investigation on the theme of "modern" financial crises focused on contrasting the "bookends" cases of Mexico 1994 and of Greece 2007 for improving the understanding of these two cases. The great Latin American financial crisis with an epicenter in Mexico occurred in the developing world. On the other hand, the Global North Crisis with an epicenter in Greece occurred in 2007 in the developed world. Thus, these crises are different, but the hypothesis offered hereby is that all modern financial crises possess a common pattern in terms of causes, interrelations, mobiles, consequences and remedies. In an attempt to prove this qualitative hypothesis, the effects of mismanaged economies, coupled with volatile financial markets in these selected financial crises, are reanalyzed. The central idea is that the mechanics of crises involves mismatches between investment and debt generating busts. Then, pegged currencies attract speculation. Thereafter, deregulation, desupervision and financial instruments proliferation speed up the crises, whereas misguided policies aggravate the crisis especially in the case of fragile economies. At the end, only comprehensive international remedies avoid the "socialization" of effects. The central idea of the chapter is based on the comparison of financial crises models: Orthodox, Heterodox (Minskyan) and a complex system framework, advocating heterodox models as the best explication for the case in point. Then, some guidelines for mitigating the impact of crises are proposed, and thereafter some general conclusions are offered, both of them considering the selected cases on the basis of a pragmatic selection of parts of these explications including the historical perspective.

The final chapter (Chap. 12) titled "Restructuring Accounting Education: The Key to Avoiding Another Financial Crisis in Greece", by Dimitrios Siskos and John Marangos, contends that accounting education is strongly related to the recent financial crisis in Greece, since some of the main root causes of the crisis were accounting, omissions and manipulations in financial statements all embraced by unethical actions. The global financial crisis in Greece epitomized by the recession of 2009 raised the question of whether and how should accounting educators respond. The purpose of this chapter is to understand the role of accounting education in the efforts made to prevent another financial crisis in Greece. The study explored the individual lived experiences of 10 accounting professionals and 15 accounting professors in Greece. The results revealed that accountancy programs of Greek universities as currently structured are outdated and inappropriate in terms of assisting graduates acquire the skills and competencies needed in the real world. The study recommends a new educational framework along with a reorientation of accounting education, both in regard to students' deliveries and learning approaches.

Every effort would be made so the book be translated into Greek and will be made available in the Greek market in both the Greek and English versions.

Thank you, and may your reading be challenging and thought provoking.

John Marangos
Fort Collins, Colorado, USA
Thessaloniki, Greece
April 2017

CHAPTER 2

The 'Greek Crisis' and the Austerity Controversy in Europe

John G. Milios, Spyros Lapatsioras, and Dimitris P. Sotiropoulos

INTRODUCTION: THE GLOBAL CRISIS AS A POINT OF DEPARTURE FOR CONSOLIDATING AUSTERITY POLICIES IN EUROPE—THE GREEK CASE

The 2008 global economic crisis is without precedent in the post-war period, a fact acknowledged by the majority of economists. In Greece, the crisis has become devastating for the working classes after implementing the 'Measures of Fiscal Adjustment' contained in the bailout programme, known as 'Memorandum of Understanding' (MoU), which was signed

J.G. Milios (✉)
Department of Humanities, Social Sciences and Law, National Technical University of Athens, Athens, Greece

S. Lapatsioras
Department of Economics, University of Crete, Crete, Greece

D.P. Sotiropoulos
The Open University Business School, Milton Keynes, UK

© The Author(s) 2017
J. Marangos (ed.), *The Internal Impact and External Influence of the Greek Financial Crisis*, DOI 10.1007/978-3-319-60201-1_2

between the Greek government and the Troika (International Monetary Fund [IMF], EU, European Central Bank [ECB]) in May 2010. In fact, Greece can be seen as a 'guinea pig' for shaping the second phase of the project of European Unification, the cornerstones of which are on the one hand austerity policies and on the other institutional reforms aiming at significantly increasing the power of employers over workers and dismantling the welfare state. These policies, in the framework of the so-called European 'economic governance', constitute an attempt to place all the fallout of the systemic capitalist crisis on the shoulders of the working people.

These extreme austerity policies were not left undisputed. A series of mass demonstrations and strikes ensued in Greece, soon after the bailout agreement. The most important result of these mass movements was the unravelling of the Socialist Party (PASOK) that has stayed in power for more than 20 years in the last three decades and which negotiated the 'stabilization program'. Mass movements and popular demonstrations finally led to national elections in May and June 2012, through which the Coalition of the Radical Left (SYRIZA) became the major opposition party in Parliament. SYRIZA was until then a small radical left party (4.6% in the national elections of 2009). In the early national elections on January 25, 2015, SYRIZA achieved a stunning victory with 36.3%, as compared to 27.8% of conservative New Democracy and 4.7% of PASOK, the two government coalition partners, until that time. This electoral result was translated to 149 parliamentary seats for SYRIZA, out of the total 300, and led to a coalition government with the 'Independent Greeks' (ANEL), an anti-austerity party stemming from the conservative political camp (4.75%, 13 seats). New Democracy elected 76 MPs and PASOK 13 MPs. Other parties in the Parliament were as follows: Golden Dawn (Nazis) 6.3% and 17 seats, To Potami (liberals) 6% and 17 seats, and KKE (Communist Party of Greece) 5.5% and 15 seats.

However, after six months in office, the SYRIZA-ANEL government agreed on a third financing programme by the European Stability Mechanism (ESM), connected to a new austerity memorandum. The IMF retained its consultative role, as part of a still in force MoU programme with the Greek government. The secession of 25 SYRIZA MPs, who soon after formed a new anti-austerity parliamentary group called Popular Unity (LAE), led to the resignation of the government and to new national elections on September 20, 2015. SYRIZA won again with 35.4% and 145 seats, as compared to 28.10% and 75 seats of New Democracy, and formed a new coalition government with ANEL (3.69%, 10 seats). LAE, with only 2.86% of the vote, did not reach the 3% electoral threshold and remained without any representation in Parliament (Milios 2016).

After the capitulation of SYRIZA and the Greek government, who had promised to 'end with austerity' and, by 'changing Greece', to initiate a 'democratic chain reaction' that would re-establish the 'European social model', neoliberal austerity policies remained undisputed all over the EU. Both the 'Treaty on Stability, Coordination and Governance' (March 2012) and the planning of 'National Competitiveness Boards', which shall be established in all Eurozone member states in the time span July 2015–June 2017, are typical. They signify the strategic target of European economic and political elites to deepen and render irreversible the neoliberal policy framework all over Europe (Kennedy 2016).

By the word 'neoliberalism', in this chapter, we mean a form of capitalist governmentality that reshapes the relations between capitalist states, individual capitals and 'liberalized' financial markets. This recomposition presupposes a reforming of all components involved, in a way that secures the reproduction of the dominant capitalist paradigm. From this point of view, with the term 'neoliberalism' we denote a historically specific form of organization of capitalist power on a social-wide scale. For further elaboration, see Sotiropoulos et al. (2013, pp. 201–3).

European Austerity Policies and Global Imbalances

The 2008 global economic crisis had hit not only Greece, but also the EU as a whole. The European Unification project has entered its second, less optimistic phase. Cross-country differentials in growth and inflation, persistent current account (or financial account) imbalances, real effective rate appreciation (mostly for countries with current account deficits), a sharp rise in the sovereign debt overhang of several European countries, culminating in a European debt crisis and the setting up of a leveraged and highly integrated banking system were the most striking developments.

Political authorities in the EU and the Euro-area (EA) argued that only austerity policies were in a position to tame the crisis and to promote 'competitiveness' and a process of export-oriented growth. In the EA, where currency devaluations are not possible, austerity is considered to be a mechanism of 'internal devaluation' of wages and, consequently, of prices of tradable goods. A positive current account balance and a process of export-oriented growth shall thus be put in motion through austerity policies.

According to the *European Economic Forecast*, of Winter 2016 (European Commission 2016), the current account balance of both the EU and the EA has been improved for all countries during recent years, and it is expected to exceed 3.0% of the GDP of the EA in 2016, with Germany keeping the lead with a current account surplus of 8.5% of the GDP.

This apparently positive outcome coincides, though, with a negative performance as regards other crucial indexes of economic and social development:

Unemployment has risen since the 2008 financial meltdown in the EU and the EA more than in other regions of the developed capitalist world, still remaining above 10% (as compared to 5.0% in the USA and 3.3% in Japan), despite some mild improvement since 2013.

The output gap related to potential GDP was −1.1% in 2016 (as compared to 0.4% in the USA).

The inflation rate (Harmonized Index of Consumer Prices) reached near to zero values in recent years, trapping investment and growth.

Last but not least, the sovereign debt overhang in the EA cannot be contained by the methods implicit in the austerity strategy, that is, increasing primary surpluses and privatizations. The debt ratio of the EA increases in recent years, and this is especially the case for the higher indebted EA countries like Greece, Italy, Portugal, Cyprus, Belgium, Spain and France (Eurostat 2016).

Austerity has been criticized by many prominent economists as an irrational policy, which further deteriorates the economic crisis by creating a vicious cycle of falling effective demand, recession and over-indebtedness. Moreover, European austerity policies have been accused of dragging the global economy into recession and a liquidity trap, by exacerbating global imbalances.

Given that since the 2008 financial meltdown, the US current account deficit was reduced by almost 50%, while China's current account surplus was considerably reduced (Caballero et al. 2015; OECD 2016), austerity-led European current account surpluses are seen as the main mechanism creating global imbalances.

HETERODOX CRITICAL APPROACHES TO NEOLIBERALISM AND AUSTERITY

A crucial aspect of many heterodox critiques to austerity policies, which are being attributed to modern capitalism, crisis and the prevalence of the financial sphere, is the idea that the domination of neoliberalism and of the globalized financial sector of the economy produces a predatory version of capitalism, a capitalism that inherently tends towards crisis.

Recent heterodox literature is dominated by a persistent argument, according to which contemporary financial liberalization should be approached as a process in which the financial elites and financial inter-mediaries, that is, contemporary *rentiers* in the Keynesian terminology, have a leading role in working out the details of the neoliberal form of capitalism. According to Epstein (2001, p. 1), *financialization* denotes 'the increasing importance of financial markets, financial motives, finan-cial institutions, and financial elites in the operation of the economy and its governing institutions, both at the national and international level'. Writing in the mid-1930s, Keynes (1973, p. 377) predicted the even-tual extinction ('euthanasia') of the rentiers 'within one or two genera-tions'. Many present-day Keynesians portray the developments of the last decades as the 'revenge of the rentiers'—a phrase coined by Smithin (1996, p. 84)—who are said to have shaped the contemporary political and economical agenda in accordance with their own vested interests.

In this quasi-Keynesian discourse, the economic and political strength-ening of rentiers entails: (a) an increase in the economic importance of the financial sector as opposed to the 'real' industrial sector of the economy, (b) the transfer of income from the latter to the former, thereby increas-ing economic inequalities, promoting austerity and depressing effective demand and (c) the exacerbation of financial instability, transforming it into a central aspect of modern capitalism.

According to these approaches, industrial corporations have ceased to be the 'steam-engine of the economy' as Keynes and Schumpeter por-trayed them in the past. Their priority is to serve the interests of rent-iers (i.e. of major shareholders and the financial institutions representing them): to increase remuneration for major shareholders, enhancing their influence over company decision-making at the expense of the interests of other stakeholders (viz. workers, consumers and managers).

It appears that two relevant changes have taken place in enterprises. Firstly, joint-stock companies are now conceived of as portfolios of liquid subunits that home-office management must continually restructure to maximize their stock price at every point in time. Secondly, and as a consequence of the first change, there is a fundamental (forced) change in the incentives of top managers who now think rather in terms of maximization of short-term stock prices. The end-product of the whole process is anti-labour business policies on the one hand and on the other a focus on short-term (speculative) gains rather than on long-term economic development, stability and employment.

These analyses are all more or less variations on the same theme and within the same problematic. Shareholders and the managers they hire are conceptualized as *collective economic agents* with distinct economic behaviours and objectives. Managers are supposedly interested in promoting their personal power and status through an infinite expansion in the size of the firm, but not interested in increasing dividends to shareholders. The renewed dominance of rentiers that has come with the resurgence of neoliberalism has forced managers to comply with shareholder demands. They were obliged to abandon the long-term policy of 'retain and reinvest' in favour of a short-sighted practice of 'downsize and distribute'.

Hence, neoliberalism is conceived as an 'unjust' (in terms of income distribution), unstable, anti-developmental variant of capitalism whose direct consequence is contraction of workers' incomes and the proliferation of speculation. To put matters schematically, the rentier owners of financial securities induce a fall in the 'price' of labour so as to increase the value of their stocks (bonds and shares) at the same time engaging in speculation so as to obtain short-term advantages vis-à-vis rival *rentiers*.

This general conception seems to be prevalent in the realm of Marxist discussion also. For a number of theoreticians, neoliberal capitalism has not succeeded (at least to date) in restoring the profitability of capital (the rate of profit) to high levels, that is to say to levels satisfactory for dynamic capitalist accumulation. It appears to be entrapped (since the mid-1970s) in a perennial crisis, the end of which is not readily visible. The result of this is that large sums of capital are unable to find outlets for investment. This has two probable consequences. Firstly, this 'surplus' capital stagnates in the money markets, creating 'bubbles', or is used to underpin ineffective policies of forced accumulation that depend on lending and debt (Brenner 2001, 2008; Wolff 2008). Secondly, this capital circulates internationally in pursuit of *accumulation by dispossession* (Harvey 2010), even profiting, that is to say, not from exploitation of labour but from direct appropriation of income chiefly from those who are not financially privileged or do not occupy an appropriate *position* in the market for credit.

The basic weakness of these approaches—and at the same time the link that holds them together—is that they represent the neoliberal formula for securing profitability of capital not as a question of producing surplus value but as a question of income redistribution pertaining essentially to the sphere of circulation. It thus appears that the developmental 'ineptitude' and the instability of present-day capitalism are the result of a certain 'insatiability', or at any rate of bad regulation, in the relations governing income.

In other words, these approaches understand extreme austerity policies, which prevailed in many parts of the developed capitalist world and especially in the EU and the EA, after the outbreak of the 2008 global economic crisis, as *irrational*. This supposed irrationality further deteriorates the economic crisis by creating a vicious cycle of falling effective demand, recession and over-indebtedness (Sotiropoulos et al. 2015).

However, these criticisms can hardly explain why this 'irrational' or 'wrong' policy persists, despite its 'failures' (for a critique of these approaches, see Sotiropoulos et al. (2013), Chaps. 9 and 10). In reality, economic crises express themselves not only in a lack of effective demand, but above all in a reduction of profitability of the capitalist class. As it will be argued in the next section of this chapter, austerity constitutes a strategy for raising capital's profit rate.

Karl Marx has clearly illustrated this point. Criticizing underconsumptionist approaches, according to which the cause of crises is a lack of effective demand, he notes that it is exactly when the purchasing power of the working people reaches a relatively high level that crises erupt. A crisis means rather a 'lack of surplus value', not of demand:

> It is sheer tautology to say that crises are caused by the scarcity of effective consumption, or of effective consumers. The capitalist system does not know any other modes of consumption than effective ones, except that of sub forma pauperis or of the swindler. That commodities are unsaleable means only that no effective purchasers have been found for them, i.e., consumers (since commodities are bought in the final analysis for productive

or individual consumption). But if one were to attempt to give this tautology the semblance of a profounder justification by saying that the working-class receives too small a portion of its own product and the evil would be remedied as soon as it receives a larger share of it and its wages increase in consequence, one could only remark that crises are always prepared by precisely a period in which wages rise generally and the working-class actually gets a larger share of that part of the annual product which is intended for consumption. From the point of view of these advocates of sound and 'simple' (!) common sense, such a period should rather remove the crisis. It appears, then, that capitalist production comprises conditions independent of good or bad will, conditions which permit the working-class to enjoy that relative prosperity only momentarily, and at that always only as the harbinger of a coming crisis. (Marx 1992, pp. 486–87)

As a cure to the vicious cycle of austerity–recession–indebtedness–global imbalances, the proponents of these heterodox approaches propose a shift in European economic policies, through abandoning austerity, increasing public spending and curtailing German and European current account surpluses. A raise in wages in Germany (and Europe) should be the starting point of this policy shift. As former Chairman of the Board of Governors of the Federal Reserve System (Fed), Ben Bernanke (2015, p. 4), put it:

German workers deserve a substantial raise, and the cooperation of the government, employers, and unions could give them one. Higher German wages would both speed the adjustment of relative production costs and increase domestic income and consumption. Both would tend to reduce the trade surplus.

Many economists share exactly the same view. For example:

The eurozone needs to address its internal and external imbalances more seriously. This can't be achieved by fiscal consolidation, structural reforms and devaluations. It has to involve not only fiscal expansion in countries that can afford it most, but also a sustained rise in wages across the euro area to boost domestic demand. (Vallée 2015; see also Krugman 2015)

However, the question remains: What holds austerity policies together despite all criticisms? In the next section of this chapter, we will try to formulate a first answer to this discrepancy.

The Causal Interdependence Between Economic Crisis and Austerity

Austerity is a policy neither 'false' nor 'correct'. In reality, it is a policy promoting the (economic, social and political) interests of certain social groups, as opposed to others, especially after the outbreak of the global financial crisis. In this chapter, we mainly deal with European austerity policies.

Austerity as a Cost-Saving Capitalist Strategy

Economic crises express themselves above all in a reduction of profitability of the capitalist class. Austerity constitutes a strategy for raising again capital's profit rate.

Austerity constitutes the cornerstone of neoliberal policies. On the surface, it works as a strategy of reducing entrepreneurial cost. Austerity reduces labour costs of the private sector, increases profit per (labour) unit cost and thereon boosts the profit rate. It is complemented by economy in the use of 'material capital' (alas, another demand curtailing strategy!) and by institutional changes that on the one hand enhance capital mobility and competition and on the other strengthen the power of managers in the enterprise and share and bondholders in society. As regards to fiscal consolidation, austerity gives priority to budget cuts over public revenue, reducing taxes on capital and high incomes, and downsizing the welfare state.

However, what is cost for the capitalist class is the living standard of the working majority of society. This applies also to the welfare state, whose services can be perceived as a form of 'social wage'.

It is clear therefore that austerity is primarily a class policy: It constantly promotes the interests of capital against those of the workers, professionals, pensioners, unemployed and economically vulnerable groups. On the long run, it aims at creating a model of labour with fewer rights and less social protection, with low and flexible wages and the absence of any substantial bargaining power for wage earners.

Austerity does lead, of course, to recession; however, recession puts pressure on every individual entrepreneur, both capitalists and middle bourgeoisie, to reduce all forms of costs, that is, to try to consolidate her/his profit margins through wage cuts, intensification of the labour process, infringement of labour regulations and workers' rights, massive redundancies and so on.

Marx's analysis shows that the restructuring the enterprise, above all, means restructuring a set of social (class) relations and aims at increasing the rate of exploitation. It is thus a process which presupposes on the one *hand an increasing power of the capitalist class over the production process itself*, and on the other *a devalorization of all inadequately valorized capital* (downsizing or liquidating enterprises) and thus economizing on the utilization of constant capital (Marx 1990, p. 799).

From the perspective of big capital's interests, recession gives thus birth to a 'process of creative destruction': redistribution of income and power to the benefit of capital and concentration of wealth in fewer hands (as small and medium enterprises, especially in retail trade, are being 'cleared up' by big enterprises and shopping malls).

This strategy has its own rationality which is not completely obvious at a first glance. It perceives the crisis as an opportunity for a historic shift in the correlation of forces to the benefit of the capitalist power, subjecting (European) societies to the conditions of the unfettered functioning of financial markets, attempting to place all consequences of the systemic capitalist crisis on the shoulders of the working people.

This is the reason why, in a situation of such an intensification of social antagonisms like today, any government that wants to side with labour and social majority cannot even imagine to succumb to pressures to continue implementing austerity policies.

Austerity and Financialization

Neoliberalism is a form of capitalist governmentality, that is, of organizing the power of capital over the working classes and the social majority. It is based on the one hand on austerity, as already argued, and on the other on the crucial regulatory role of the globalized financial markets.

The financial sphere is not simply the reign of speculation or a casino; it is much more an overseeing mechanism. In his analysis in Volume 3 of *Capital*, Karl Marx illustrates that *the social camp of capital* is being occupied by two 'subjects': a *money capitalist* and a *functioning capitalist*. In the course of a lending process, the money capitalist becomes the recipient and proprietor of a *security*, that is to say a written *promise* of payment from the functioning capitalist, the manager.

In Marx's (1991, p. 504) own words: 'in the production process, the functioning capitalist represents capital against the wage-labourers as the property of others, and the money capitalist participates in the exploitation of labour as represented by the functioning capitalist'. Secondary contradictions between the managers and the big financial investors certainly do exist, but they are minor in comparison to the primary contradiction between capital and labour.

Every enterprise is a Janus-faced structure, comprising on the one hand the production apparatus *per se*, and on the other its financial existence, its shares and bonds, which are being traded on the global financial markets.

The production of surplus value constitutes a battlefield situation where resistance is being encountered, meaning that the final outcome can never be taken for granted. Techniques of risk management, organized within the very mode of functioning of the 'deregulated' money market, are a critical point in the management of resistance from labour, thus promoting and stabilizing austerity.

Financial markets generate a structure for overseeing the effectiveness of individual capitals, that is to say a type of supervision of capital movement. The demand for high financial value *puts pressure on individual capitals (enterprises) for more intensive and more effective exploitation of labour, for greater profitability.* This pressure is transmitted through a variety of different channels.

To give one example, when a big company is dependent on financial markets for its funding, every suspicion of inadequate valorization increases the cost of funding, reduces the capability that funding will be available and depresses share and bond prices. Confronted with such a climate, the forces of labour within the politicized environment of the enterprise face the dilemma of deciding whether to accept the employers' unfavourable terms, implying loss of their own bargaining position, or face the possibility to lose their job: *accept the 'laws of capital' or live with insecurity and unemployment.*

This pressure affects the whole organization of the production process. *It therefore presupposes not only increasing 'despotism' of managers over workers but also flexibility in the labour market and high unemployment.* Hence, *'market discipline' must be conceived as synonymous with 'capital discipline'.*

The theoretical sketching that we tried to present above apprehends austerity, neoliberalism, capitalist globalization and financialization as a complex technology of power, the main aspect of which is the organization of capitalist power relations. It is a technology of power formed by different institutions, procedures, analyses and reflections, calculations, tactics and embedding patterns that allow for the exercise of this specific, albeit very complex, function that organizes the efficiency of capitalist power relations through the workings of economic policies and financial markets.

Austerity and the Euro-Area

The working majority in practically every capitalist country will always be opposed to shrinking wages and precarious employment, degeneration and cut-back of public services, raising the cost of education and healthcare, weakening of democratic institutions and strengthening of repression. They will always conceive the 'crisis of labour' (i.e. unemployment, precarious and underpaid work etc.) as a social illness that shall be tackled by itself, not as a prerequisite of 'growth' or a side effect of the recovery of profits.

The continuation of austerity is therefore a matter of the social relation of forces. As Marx (1990, p. 334) commented on the limits of the working day: 'The capitalist maintains his rights as a purchaser when he tries to make the working-day as long as possible [...] On the other hand, [...] the labourer maintains his right as seller when he wishes to reduce the working-day to one of definite normal duration. There is here therefore an antinomy, of right against right, both equally bearing the seal of the law of exchange. Between equal rights force decides'.

Beyond certain limits, the subjection of all parts of social life to the unfettered function of markets and the dictate of profitability may function as 'political risk' for the neoliberal establishment, since it can easily trigger uncontrolled social outbreaks. In the EA, political risk is supposedly being minimized through the introduction of an institutional framework in which austerity is the only way to deal with economic and financial instability.

In the usual nation state setting, a single national fiscal authority stands behind a single national central bank. As we have already mentioned (see also Sotiropoulos et al. 2015), this is not the case with the EA: There is no solid and uniform fiscal authority behind the ECB. Member states issue debt in a currency which they do not control in terms of central banking (they are not able to 'print' euros or any other type of currency, at least not for a considerably long period of time).

Member states will not always have the necessary liquidity to pay off bondholders. This will make the downsizing of the welfare state a precondition for financial solvency.

The ruling European elites have thus voluntarily subjected themselves to a high degree of sovereign default risk in order to consolidate the neo-liberal strategies. In other words, they have jointly decided to exploit the crisis as a means to further neo-liberalize state governance. Member states are faced with the dilemma: austerity-cuts-privatizations or default risk. By and large, these are commensurate choices. Even in the latter scenario, member states, like in the case of Greece, Portugal, Ireland and Cyprus, would accept a rescue package, the content of which is again austerity-cuts-privatizations.

This conservative perspective recognizes as 'moral hazard' any policy that supports the interests of the working class, expands the public space, supports the welfare state and organizes the reproduction of society beyond and outside the scope of markets.

In this framework, the strategic question for the EU neoliberalism is to define the level of austerity that targets an 'optimal' balance between 'political risk' and 'moral hazard'.

Generally speaking, these two risks, the 'moral' and the 'political' one, move in opposite directions due to their consequences in the political conjuncture. When moral hazard increases, political risk declines and vice versa. Therefore, the tension (when they encounter each other) results in an appropriate balance between them. The 'independent authorities,' being immunized against any democratic control, especially on issues related to the economy (the main example here is the 'independence' of the ECB), create a mechanism for detecting the balance between these two 'risks'. Nevertheless, this mechanism will always remain incomplete.

In Greece, the increasing 'political risk' of the period 2010–2015 was a strong weapon in the hands of the Greek working class, SYRIZA and the first left government that was formed after the January 25, 2015, elections, in order to stop austerity and guarantee an agreement with the lenders that would not violate the mandate of the Greek electorate. Under one prerequisite, which was though soon abandoned: that SYRIZA and the government would stick to the class partisanship of its programme, the strategy of 'people before profits', that is, a strategy with an anti-capitalist direction—redistribution of income and power in favour of labour, to re-found the welfare state, democracy and participation in decision-making; a radical reform of the tax system (so that capital and the wealthy strata of the society finally bear the appropriate burden); a wave of radical domestic institutional changes in order to build the allegiance of the subordinate classes on a new basis.

This programme was abandoned. However, class struggle will always create contingent events.

CONCLUSION

Extreme austerity policies implemented by Greek and European governments after the outbreak of the 2008 global economic crisis constitute neither a 'correct' strategy for economic reform and development nor an 'erroneous' strategy, which could be amended through reasonable argumentation and discussion. Austerity is a class strategy, aiming at reshuffling the relation of forces between capital and labour on all social levels to the benefit of capital; it is a class offensive of capital against labour. It is clear then that an anti-austerity agenda cannot be implemented unless a radical shift in the present balance of forces between capital and labour takes place. However, in order to establish a new distribution of the social balance of forces, the working classes must once again elaborate their own autonomous class objectives, independently of the capitalist imperative of labour discipline and profit maximization. For this to be possible, labour must recreate its anti-capitalist strategy of social transformation.

REFERENCES

Bernanke, B. (2015). Germany's trade surplus is a problem. *Brookings Institution*, April 3. Retrieved from http://www.brookings.edu/blogs/ben-bernanke/posts/2015/04/03-germany-trade-surplus-problem

Brenner, R. (2001). The world economy at the turn of the millennium toward boom or crisis? *Review of International Political Economy, 8*(1), 6–44.

Brenner, R. (2008). Devastating crisis unfolds. *IV Online Magazine: IV396*, January. Retrieved from http://www.internationalviewpoint.org/spip.php?article1417

Caballero, R. J., Farhi, E., & Gourinchas, P.-O. (2015). Global imbalances and currency wars at the ZLB. Draft Paper, October 22. Retrieved from http://economics.mit.edu/files/10839

Epstein, G. (2001). *Financialization, rentier interests, and Central Bank policy*. Paper presented at PERI conference on "Financialization of the World Economy", December 7–8. Retrieved from http://www.umass.edu/peri/pdfs/fin_Epstein.pdf

European Commission. (2016). *European economic forecast, Winter 2016.* Retrieved from http://ec.europa.eu/economy_finance/eu/forecasts/2016_inter_forecast_en.htm

Eurostat. (2016). *Eurostat statistics explained. Structure of government debt.* Retrieved from http://ec.europa.eu/eurostat/statistics-explained/index.php?title=Structure_of_government_debt&stable=0&redirect=no

Harvey, D. (2010). *The enigma of capital and the crises of capitalism.* London: Profile Books Ltd.

Kennedy, G. (2016). Embedding neoliberalism in Greece: The transformation of collective bargaining and labour market policy in Greece during the Eurozone crisis. *Studies in Political Economy, 97*(3), 253–269.

Keynes, J. M. (1973). *The general theory of employment, interest and money.* Cambridge: Cambridge University Press.

Krugman, P. (2015). Europe's trap. *The New York Times,* January 5. Retrieved from http://krugman.blogs.nytimes.com/2015/01/05/europes-trap/?_r=0

Marx, K. (1990). *Capital* (Vol. 1). London: Penguin Classics.

Marx, K. (1991). *Capital* (Vol. 3). London: Penguin Classics.

Marx, K. (1992). *Capital* (Vol. 2). London: Penguin Classics.

Milios, J. (2016). Does social democracy hold up half the sky? The decline of PASOK and the rise of SYRIZA in Greece. In I. Schmidt (Ed.), *The three worlds of social democracy. A global view* (pp. 127–145). London: Pluto Press.

OECD. (2016). *Current account balance.* Retrieved from https://data.oecd.org/trade/current-account-balance.htm

Smithin, J. (1996). *Macroeconomic policy and the future of capitalism.* Northampton: Edward Elgar Publishing Ltd.

Sotiropoulos, D. P., Milios, J., & Lapatsioras, S. (2013). *A political economy of contemporary capitalism and its crisis: Demystifying finance.* London and New York: Routledge.

Sotiropoulos, D. P., Milios, J., & Lapatsioras, S. (2015). Addressing the rationality of 'irrational' European responses to the crisis. A political economy of the Euro area and the need for a progressive alternative. In A. Bitzenis, N. Karagiannis, & J. Marangos (Eds.), *Europe in crisis* (pp. 67–76). Basingstoke: Palgrave/Mcmillan.

Vallée, S. (2015). How the Eurozone exports deflation. Fiscal devaluation without wage growth will trigger bad side effects both at home and abroad. *The Wall Street Journal,* November 5. http://www.wsj.com/articles/how-the-eurozone-exports-deflation-1446757311

Wolff, R. D. (2008). Capitalist crisis, Marx's shadow. Retrieved from http://www.monthlyreview.org/mrzine/wolff260908.html

Troika's Economic Adjustment Programmes for Greece: Why Do They Systematically Fail?

Stavros Mavroudeas

INTRODUCTION

The Greek economic crisis is one of the major incidents of the crisis of the European Union (EU). The global capitalist crisis of 2007–2008 ended the period of the Great Moderation, the era that followed the previous global crisis of 1974 and was characterized by mediocre economic performance. Despite the latter, Mainstream economics (i.e. those that are dominant in Western governments and major international organizations like International Monetary Fund (IMF), World Bank, Organisation for Economic Co-operation and Development (OECD), etc.) portrayed this era as one of subdued volatility and even preached the end of the business cycles. The 2007–2008 global crisis ended abruptly this illusion and ushered a period of violent economic fluctuations. Mainstream economics' notoriously bad forecasting ability stems from their analytical perspective. Their current version, the New Macroeconomic Consensus, blends mild neoliberalism with conservative New Keynesianism (Arestis 2009) by coupling long-run New Classical rational expectations, general equilibrium

S. Mavroudeas (✉)
Department of Economics, University of Macedonia,
Thessaloniki, Greece

© The Author(s) 2017
J. Marangos (ed.), *The Internal Impact and External Influence of the Greek Financial Crisis*, DOI 10.1007/978-3-319-60201-1_3

and real business cycles with short-run New Keynesian disequilibria. This awkward mix downplays crisis tendencies and consequently fails systematically to predict and diagnose crises.

The Great Moderation is not the only illusion that Mainstream economics and systemic elites nurtured. Various scenarios of containment of the global crisis appeared in its aftermath around notions of decoupling of one block of economies from another ailing one; all to be disproved soon. At the beginning of the crisis, the EU toyed with the idea that the crisis was an American problem (as it erupted firstly in the US) and that the European economies have 'decoupled' from US and were immune to the latter's problems (e.g. Gross (2008), who maintained rather unwisely that Europe will not fall into recession). It was angrily rejected by US Mainstreamers (e.g. Krauss 2008). The same argument resurfaced later as the decoupling of the struggling US economy from the better-faring newly emerging markets (e.g. Economist 2008), soon to be disproved when the crisis hit the latter in 2015. The more recent version of this argument is that US is now decoupling from EU as the former enjoys some weak but positive post-crisis growth whereas the latter trails behind dismally (e.g. Economist 2010). The decoupling argument is a superficial Mainstream construct that neglects fundamental economic structures and particularly the role of profit and accumulation in capitalist economies and focuses on cursory analyses.

EU's wishful thinking about decoupling from the US was very soon shattered as the crisis erupted in the EU as well. Moreover, EU's resilience to the crisis proved to be far inferior than that of the US. Several years after the eruption of the crisis, the EU is faring considerably worse than the other major poles of the world economy. Literally, the EU has become the 'big sick man' of the international economy, and its ambitious European integration process is in severe trouble. EU's problems began with the crisis in its periphery (Greece followed by Portugal, Ireland and Cyprus) but soon expanded to the very core of the union. UK's decision of Brexit and the economic problems in Spain, Italy and France are obvious proofs of EU's crisis.

The Greek crisis was the first of the crises of the euro-periphery economies. It broke out formally in 2010 and initially the EU nurtured the illusion that it was an isolated 'Greek disease'. Mainstream analyses opted for a *conjunctural explanation of the Greek crisis*, that is as the product of erroneous political decisions by Greece rather than as the outcome of deep-seated capitalist structural problems (see Mavroudeas (2016) for a detailed critique). Therefore, the crisis was characterized as simply a debt crisis with concomitant liquidity problems.

This is a superficial understanding of the Greek crisis. In Mavroudeas (2015), three broad currents of competing explanations of the Greek crisis are discerned: Mainstream, Radical and Marxist. There are three versions of Mainstream explanations. The first, stemming mainly from the dominant EU circles, considers the Greek crisis as a national historical accident, a case of policy-driven economic imprudence. The second version, having more Anglo-Saxon origins, recognizes certain structural causes of this crisis, namely, the Eurozone being a non-optimal currency area. It argues that Economic and Monetary Union (EMU's) fundamental flaws cannot be rectified and its collapse is on the table. The third version is a 'middle-of-the-road' blend: While the Greek crisis has national origins, it abated existing flaws of the EMU. However, these flaws can be rectified. All these versions fail to account for the 2007–2008 global crisis and its effects on the EU. They are all based on the unverifiable in the case of Greece Twin Deficits Hypothesis (i.e. the argument that fiscal deficit [FD] causes current account deficit). On the other hand, Radical explanations revolve around the erroneous 'financialization thesis'. They vary from versions that attribute the crisis to the supposedly neo-mercantilist nature of the Eurozone to versions that focus upon the equally supposed 'indeterminacy of class struggle'. These explanations mimic the Mainstream ones by regarding the 2007–2008 crisis as simply a financial crisis, thus neglecting its origins in real accumulation. Concomitantly, they fail to explain satisfactorily the Greek crisis in both analytical and empirical terms. On the contrary, Marxist explanations focus on real accumulation, the structural and systemic dimensions of the Greek crisis and particularly on the contradictions of capitalist accumulation and the specificities of Greek capitalism. In this vein, Mavroudeas and Paitaridis (2014) show that the Greek crisis has two interlinked causes. Its 'internal' cause is the 2007–2008 economic crisis (a crisis à la Marx, stemming from falling profitability) that hit Greek capitalism contemporaneously with the Western economies. This crisis was initiated in the production sphere and then spread to the financial system. Its 'external' cause is the imperialist exploitation of euro-periphery economies from the euro-centre ones (through value transfers and qualitative changes) that worsen further the condition of Greek capitalism. In this way, Marxist explanations grasp better the deep structural and systemic causes of the Greek crisis.

Following from the erroneous Mainstream understanding of the Greek crisis and guided by the political and economic interests of EU's elites, the Economic Adjustment Programmes (EAPs) for Greece were hastily conceived and implemented as a remedy for the crisis. Their hurriedness emanated from two crucial factors. First, the EU—but also the IMF—did not expect this rapid expansion of the global crisis. Second, there was a widespread 'groupthink' in official circles that Eurozone economies were immune to debt problems and, hence, the EU lacked both the expertise and the mechanisms to confront such problems. For all these reasons, EU required IMF's long-standing technical expertise on these issues.

IMF's involvement in an EU crisis and the resulting curious troika formula (EU–ECB–IMF) had a precursor in the IMF–EU conditional lending operations to three EU, but non-euro, members during 2008–2009 (Hungary, Latvia and Romania). However, the EU continued to lack serious expertise in debt management, and thus its involvement was required for purely technical reasons. But they were also overwhelming political reasons behind its involvement. The EU, setting aside its initial hesitations, opted for making US co-responsible for the management of the Greek crisis. On the other hand, the US wanted to have a strong interventionary lever in this affair. For this reason, the US government in its contacts with European governments urged IMF involvement in Greece (Kincaid 2016, p. 11). Moreover, the resultant framework of dual conditionality (i.e. each institution proceeds independently with its own financial assistance according to its own standards) is a major instrument in the hands of the US because IMF despite being a junior finance partner (as it advances only a small part of the required loans) is an equal policy partner (Kincaid 2016, p. 47).

The Greek EAPs are the result of an uneasy agreement between asymmetric 'partners'. On the one side, there are successive Greek governments (encompassing at different stages almost all the parties of the socio-economic establishment and ranging from the right-wing to the centre-left) that are the 'junior' partner of the agreement in the sense that their ability to influence the structure and the implementation of the programme is lower and diminishing rapidly. These governments represent the collective interests of the Greek elite, although each one may put the footprint of a particular elite fraction. They all acquiesced to this unequal deal because of sheer inability to find another solution and at the same time remain within the EU. Greek elite's main priority is to avoid much of the 'pain' associated with the adjustment programme at the expense of the middle and working classes that bear till today its cost. It understands that the EAP's radical overhauling of Greek capitalism's post-war structure endangers its stability. But on the other hand, the Greek elite is inextricably linked to the European integration and does not dare even to envisage a solution to the crisis outside it (see Mavroudeas 2013). On the other side, there are the 'major' partners, the EU and the IMF, which represent different major poles of the world economy. The EU expresses the vested interests of the euro-centre economies (with Germany at the helm), whereas the IMF expresses mainly those of the US. These international poles share a lot but also have major differences in a wide range of areas. Moreover, the 2007–2008 global crisis aggravated their differences as each one jockeyed to pass part of the crisis burden to others.

The Greek EAPs provide financial assistance in the form of loans (to avoid a Greek default) conditional upon the implementation of a policy of extremely austere fiscal consolidation and structural reforms. The first one was inaugurated in 2010 and envisaged a 3-year shock programme that would achieve in a short time the return of Greece to loaning from the international markets (from which it has been blockaded). Very soon and before its formal end, it was obvious that the first EAP failed. Thus, it was superseded in mid-course by the second EAP in 2012. Its successor, despite numerous revisions, exhibited the same systematic failures with its predecessor. Consequently, in 2015 a third EAP was devised. However, problems and failures continue to mar the programme, and currently (in 2016) before its very end, there are widespread talks about a fourth programme.

This chapter addresses two crucial questions. The first one is why the Greek EAPs systematically fail to achieve their own goals. The second one is why despite their systematic failures the instigators of these programmes insist on this problematic course. The chapter is structured as follows. The next section presents the historical timeline of the Greek EAPs and pinpoints their failures. The third section analyses the background of these programmes (which lies in the neoconservative notions of pro-cyclicality and expansionary austerity and the blueprint of the IMF's Structural Adjustment Programmes (SAP) created in the end of 1990s) and explains the peculiarities of the Greek EAPs (especially the lack of a currency devaluation mechanism and the belated, half-baked and ineffective debt restructuring). Finally, the last section explains the political economic reasons of these systematic failures but also of the insistence of the EU elites in this systematically failing strategy. The main argument is that the neoconservative restructuring strategy of these programmes, despite its obvious problems and failings, is the only course available for the EU and its dominant euro-core countries. Thus, they are compelled to pursue this overambitious and simultaneously precarious strategy.

The Greek EAPs' Chronicle

The Greek crisis erupted in the end of 2009, in the aftermath of the global crisis. Previously, Greece had for quite lengthy periods high FDs and public debt but was able to finance them via either internal or/and external borrowing without serious problems. Greece's accession to the EMU placed FD and public debt under the constraints of the Maastricht treaty. However, these were violated not only by Greece but by almost every other EMU country since these constraints proved to be rather unsustainable. The Greek crisis erupted when the newly elected PASOK government revised upwardly the estimates of the Greek FD amid internal and external talks for 'Greek statistics' (i.e. manipulation of statistics by successive Greek governments). This ignited a crisis of confidence in international markets concerning Greece's ability to meet its debt obligations which resulted in the widening of bond yield spreads (particularly the one related to the German bund) and the increase of the cost of risk insurance on credit default swaps (again compared particularly to that of Germany). This led, in April 2010, to the downgrading of Greek government debt to junk bond status by the international credit rating agencies which signified that international private capital markets practically ceased financing Greece's sovereign debt.

The Greek government requested EU assistance which led to the first EAP, signed in March 2010: a medium-length bailout and structural transformation programme. It offered to Greece loans (to avoid default) accompanied by economic policy conditions formalized in a Memorandum of Understanding (MOU) on Specific Economic Policy Conditionality. The programme was designed as a shock treatment that has most of the 'pain' in the beginning (frontloaded) and during a very condensed time period and leads rapidly 'out of the woods' (that is to a return to borrowing from the markets). In its more long-term aspect, it was envisaged that after this 3-year period, the Greek economy would have harnessed its debt viability problem by returning to 'normal' debt-to-GDP ratios. The first EAP had two declared aims (EC 2010, p. 10):

1. Its short-term objectives are to restore confidence and maintain financial stability by (a) fiscal consolidation and (b) stabilizing the financial sector.
2. Its medium-term objective is to improve competitiveness and alter the economy's structure towards a more investment- and export-led growth model.

The first EAP entailed a €110bn bailout loan (€80bn by the EU and €30bn by the IMF) advanced during a 3-year period with a 5% interest rate. The 3-year period was designed on the utterly failed assumption that after that Greece would be able to return to borrowing from the market. According to Colasanti (2016), the amount of the loan was calculated according to a rough estimate of the country's financing needs for these 3 years. This exercise led to an estimate of €190 billion for the gross financing needs: €80bn considered to be feasibly sourced from capital markets, thus leaving a shortfall of €110bn. This amount was to be provided by the IMF (€30bn) and the euro-area countries (€80bn).

Since the EU had not at that time a bailout mechanism (as the European Financial Stability Fund [EFSF] and its successor European Stability Mechanism [ESM] did not exist yet), euro-area loans took the form of bilateral loans from each individual country, packaged by the European Commission (EC) into a single loan to Greece (dubbed the 'Greek Loan Facility'). Each country's contribution was proportional to its share in ECB's capital (itself determined on the basis of its economic and demographic weight) (Table 3.1).

Table 3.1 First EAP's EU loans

Countries	Share	Actual amounts (bn €)
Belgium	3.5	1.942
Germany	27.92	15.165
Ireland	1.64	0.347
Spain	12.24	6.650
France	20.97	11.388
Italy	18.42	10.008
Cyprus	0.20	0.110
Luxemburg	0.26	0.139
Malta	0.09	0.051
Netherlands	5.88	3.194
Austria	2.86	1.555
Portugal	2.58	1.102
Slovenia	0.48	0.244
Slovakia	1.02	0
Finland	1.85	1.004
Total	100.0	52.9

Source: EC (2012, p. 6)

Actually, only €52.9bn were actually disbursed during the lifetime of the first EAP as Slovakia decided to abstain, Ireland and Portugal did not contribute to further disbursements once they themselves entered into similar EAPs and the original programme was superseded by the second EAP half-way through its implementation.

The disbursements to Greece were foreseen according to the following indicative calendar: €34.8bn in 2010, €44.6bn in 2011, €28bn in 2012 and the last €8bn in the first half of 2013. These loans were supplemented by short-term notes issued by Greece and bought mainly by Greek banks (e.g. 2010 €4.5bn).

The first EAP aimed at cutting the FD from 13.6% of the GDP (2009) to below 3% by 2014. It was envisaged that after 5 years the Greek economy would be out of the tunnel and into a virtuous trajectory. In particular, it was projected that during the first 2 years of the EAP, there would be a cumulative contraction of the GDP by 6.6% which would be recovered, to a great extent, during the next 3 years by a cumulative 5.3% growth (Table 3.2).

Moreover, the whole programme was strongly frontloaded (EC 2010, p. 42), aiming at a speedy return to private markets for long-term funding in early 2012. Although the programme's aims mentioned apart from fiscal consolidation the improvement of competitiveness as well, most of its measures concerned the public sector leaving the private sector mainly unaffected, at least directly (see EC 2010, Table 1, p. 51). The first EAP underwent five reviews and respective recalibrations.

However, very soon it was obvious that the programme was not working and needed radical overhauling. The main reason for its failure was the deeper-than-expected recession caused by the programme itself. As will be explained later, the austerity policies and the structural reforms instigated

Table 3.2 First EAP's projections

	2009	2010	2011	2012	2013	2014
Real GDP growth (% change over the previous period)	−2	−4.0	−2.6	1.1	2.1	2.1
General government balance (% of GDP)	n.a.	−10.5	−14.2	−15.6	−15.9	−15.6
General government gross debt (% of GDP)	115.1	133.2	145.2	148.8	149.6	148.4

Source: EC (2010, pp. 12–13)

by the programme necessarily led to an increased recession. This is explicitly recognized by all the relevant EU and IMF studies. Nevertheless, the experiment got out of control. The inherently pro-cyclical character of the IMF programmes was augmented by its frontload character (at the request of the EU), the lack of ameliorating mechanisms (e.g. currency devaluation) and the deterioration of the world economy ('double dip'). The contraction of the GDP (Table 3.3) was 21.5% for the period 2009–2012 and 8% (instead of the projected 6%) for the period 2009–2010.

The uncontrolled recession derailed (a) the fiscal balance and (b) the debt-to-GDP ratio. The recession reduced the public income for taxation and required additional tax measures that in return diminished demand further. This led to the emergence of successive financing gaps (as the programme could easily calculate the debt servicing burden but not the future budget deficits). This spiralled the debt/GDP ratio (the strategic pivot of the programme) out of control and towards an uncontrollable increase that made Greece's return to borrowing from the markets unfeasible in the foreseeable future. On top of that, political instability crept in as there was a tremendous popular abhorrence and resistance to the EAP that led to pro-EAP parties losing rapidly their support.

In several studies (e.g. EC 2012, pp. 11–16), EU and IMF attributed the first EAP's failure to faults in its implementation that led to a greater-than-expected recession, fall of demand, increase of unemployment and stubbornness of inflation and a current account remaining unsustainable. These were supplemented with a weaker-than-expected export increase.

Thus, in February 2012, a second EAP was initiated and a respective MOU signed between the same covenanters. This second bailout package worth €130bn was accompanied by more harsh austerity measures and a voluntary debt restructuring agreement with the private holders of Greek government bonds (banks, insurers and investment funds) called Private Sector Initiative (PSI). The PSI organized a 53.5% voluntary nominal

Table 3.3 Actual GDP growth rates

	2009	2010	2011	2012
Real GDP growth (% change over the previous period)	−3.1	−4.9	−7.1	−6.4

Source: EUROSTAT http://epp.eurostat.ec.europa.eu/tgm/table.do?tab=table&plugin=1&language=en&pcode=tec00115

write-off and a bond swap with short-term EFSF notes and new Greek bonds with lower interest rates and longer maturity (their initial maturity was prolonged to 11–30 years). This is the biggest debt restructuring ever done, affecting €206bn of Greek government bonds and leading to a €107bn write-off. However, the net debt reduction was only €16bn since the write-off was supplemented with the new loan and also literally bankrupted the Greek pension system and the banking sector. A new feature of the second EAP was its emphasis not only on fiscal consolidation (as in the first versions of the first MOU) but also on wider changes in the Greek economy in order to improve competitiveness. Thus, the private sector was also affected by a series of austerity measures. This had only shyly been done by the first EAP. With the second EAP not only fiscal consolidation but also increasing competitiveness became the standards of the adjustment programme. On the other hand, building upon the measures dictated by the first EAP and its reviews, the new austerity package deepened even further the recession of the Greek economy, leading to a dismal −6.4% for 2012 amid growing social and political unrest. The new pro-EAP government difficultly elected in June 2012 asked for a 2-year prolongation of the adjustment programme (which would require an additional third bailout worth €32.6bn) which was denied by the troika. Thus, the new government legislated a new €18.8bn austerity programme including a vicious labour market deregulation. In return, the EU lowered interest rates, prolonged debt maturities and provided €10bn for a debt-buy-back programme.

However, even after the second EAP and its PSI, the programme continued to perform dismally. Growth rates continue to trail dismally behind their projections and this derails both the public debt-to-GDP and the FD-to-GDP ratios. Additionally, public revenues from taxes and privatizations also continued to disappoint. Tax revenues were hit hard not only from tax evasion but mainly by the recession. Privatizations—literally 'fire sales'—staggered as there was a meagre demand for them and also payments offered were negligible because few capitals ventured in the deteriorating Greek economy, either because of increasing risks or for expecting an even lower price. Therefore, the artificially devised target of a 120% public debt/GDP ratio by 2020 and a speedy return to private markets was unachievable.

These continuing failures brought to the open the conflicting interests of the programme's 'major' partners as the IMF and the EU began sparring. In this vein, IMF (2013)—in its wide-ranging Ex Post Evaluation of the Greek programme—recognized that 'public debt overshot program projections by a large margin'. Consequently, the programme's successive debt sustainability analyses (DSA) proved to be wide off the mark. For example, at the outset of the programme, debt was projected to peak at 154–156% of GDP in 2013 (depending on data revisions). However, by the fourth review in July 2011 (before the PSI), the end-2013 debt ratio was projected at 170% of GDP. As the programme unfolded, the underlying debt dynamics worsened significantly because output contractions and deflation were more pronounced than expected. Lower nominal growth raised the interest rate-growth differential and led to progressively higher expected debt paths. Data revisions affecting both public debt and GDP exacerbated these trends. On top of these, privatization outcomes were disappointing. Tellingly, IMF (2013), in a fleeting remark, recognized that 'PSI exerted opposite effects on debt sustainability', meaning in simple words that it worsened debt instead of ameliorating it. Consequently, GDP forecasts for the period May 2010–May 2013 had been revised downwards eight times. Similarly, the forecasts for the required fiscal austerity measures changed from €25bn initially to €66bn.

IMF (2013) attributed these blatant failures to two factors. First, its underestimation of the fiscal multipliers caused a deeper-than-expected recession. In the beginning of the programme, the IMF estimated them at around 0.5, whereas later it admitted that they were more than 1. But the second reason was even more interesting. The IMF points out that 'the deeper-than-expected contraction was not purely due to the fiscal shock. Part of the contraction in activity was not directly related to the fiscal adjustment, but rather reflected the absence of a pick-up in private sector growth'. This is an implicit recognition that despite fiscal consolidation the market forces cannot solve the crisis on their own. Of course, this was rapidly supplemented with the dictum that what prohibit them from performing their crisis-solving role are Greek institutions' entrepreneurial unfriendliness and the lack of adequate structural reforms.

Notwithstanding, the IMF (2013, p. 13) provided a telling picture of the grossly inaccurate projections of the EAP's designers (Fig. 3.1).

However, in the end, the IMF (2013) defended the EAPs' structure and aims. It even added a few Parthian shots (like 'Actions were not taken to adjust private sector wages' in the first EAP), although it had itself agreed to that (EC 2010).

On the other hand, studies reflecting the EU side offered scathing critiques of IMF's programmes. Pisani-Ferry et al. (2013, p. 55) argue that:

> [i]t is not unusual for IMF programmes to disappoint in comparison to initial forecasts, but orders of magnitude are usually much smaller. On the basis of an assessment of 159 programmes, the IMF Independent Evaluation Office found that growth disappointed in about 60 percent of programmes, and that the average output shortfall over a two-year period was 1.5 percent and −6.4 percent in cases of capital account crises (IEO 2016, Table 5.3). An output shortfall as large as Greece's could only be found in one percent of the programmes.

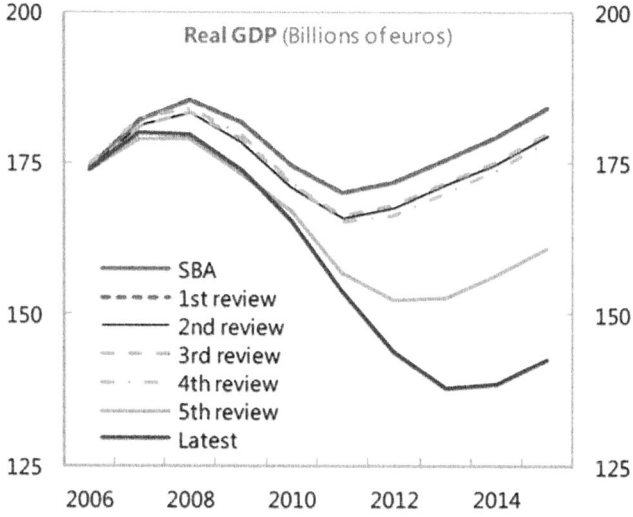

Fig. 3.1   GDP projections versus reality. Sources: IMF country reports and IMF staff calculations

They pointed out that the failure in the projections of performance indi-cators was remarkable. Greece under the programme experienced a true collapse in domestic demand and especially of fixed investment. In January 2013, unemployment in 2013 was expected to be more than 12% higher than foreseen at the outset of the initial programme. But the government deficit was expected to be 2% higher only and the current account was expected to be closer to balance (Table 3.4).

Yet, Pisani-Ferry et al. (2013)—after putting much of the blame on IMF's door—proceeded to attribute the obvious failure of the programme to Greece's internal political situation. Thus, although they recognize that 'weak equity market conditions undermined potential revenues', they put the blame for the failure of the privatization programme on the lack of enthusiasm, the political accusations that the Troika was 'pushing for the dismantling of state property' (an argument certainly on the mark) and the subsequent elections.

In these conditions, even before SYRIZA's election to government, there was widespread talk of a new EAP. After SYRIZA's ridiculous nego-tiations with the EU and the IMF and its subsequent unconditional capitu-lation to their prerogatives, this third EAP was hastily signed in July 2015. Essentially, it is a continuation of the previous failed EAPs. It envisages

Table 3.4 Greece in 2013: EAPs projections versus reality

	Initial programme (May 2010)	January 2013 (forecast)
Real GDP (2009 = 100)	96.5	79.6
Nominal GDP (base estimate for 2009 = 100)	99.2	77.8
Real domestic demand (2009 = 100)	89.7	72.5
Gross fixed capital formation (2009 = 100)	82.6	56.6
Unemployment rate (%)	14.3	26.6
Government deficit (% of GDP)	−4.8	−4.5
Government gross debt (% of GDP)	149	178.5
Exports of goods and services (billions of euros)	60.6	50.6
Imports of goods and services (billions of euros)	57.5	51.2
Current-account balance (% of GDP)	−4.0	−1.2

Source: IMF programme documents

that Greece will get a new loan of up to €86bn, disbursed gradually from 2015 until June 2018. This includes a buffer of up to €25bn for the banking sector who despite three previous recapitalizations remains in danger. The rest will go to meet debt servicing and fiscal needs. In return, Greece will have to undergo another round of severe austerity cuts. Currently, it is being negotiated a package of approximately €5.4bn austerity measures supplemented by another €3.6bn (in case the initial projections fail) for the period 2016–2018. The third EAP's aims are the same (with added emphasis on institutional change) with its predecessors: (1) fiscal sustainability; (2) safeguarding financial stability; (3) growth, competitiveness and investment; and (4) modern state and public administration structure.

Table 3.5 summarizes the total loan disbursements after the third EAP.

On the other hand, Table 3.6 describes the bleak conditions of the Greek economy after 6 years of EAPs.

Table 3.5 Gross disbursements to Greece from the euro-area and the IMF (€bn)

Date	EFSF	IMF	Total	Cumulative total
First Economic Adjustment Programme				
1. May 2010	14.5	5.5	20.0	20.0
2. September 2010	6.5	2.5	9.0	29.0
3. December 2010/January 2011	6.5	2.5	9.0	38.0
4. March 2011	10.9	4.1	15.0	53.0
5. July 2011	8.7	3.3	12.0	65.0
6. December 2011	5.8	2.2	8.0	73.0
Total first programme	*52.9*	*20.1*	*73.0*	
Second Economic Adjustment Programme				
1. March/June 2012	74.0	1.6	75.6	148.6
2. December 2012/May 2013	49.1	3.2	52.3	200.9
3. May/June 2013	7.5	1.8	9.3	210.1
4. July/December 2013	2.9	1.8	4.7	214.9
5. April/August 2014	8.3	3.6	11.9	226.8
February 2015	−10.9		−10.9	215.9
Total second programme	*130.9*	*12.0*	*142.9*	
Total of the two first programmes	183.8	32.1	215.9	
Third Economic Adjustment Programme				
1. August/December 2015	21.4		21.4	237.3
Overall total at end of December 2015	205.2	32.1	237.3	

Source: Colasanti (2016, p. 10)

Table 3.6 Greece's basic economic indicators

Indicator	2009	2015
GDP (€bn)	237	176
Debt (€bn)	299	321
Debt/GDP ratio	126%	183%
Deposits in banks (€bn)	240	120
Investment (€bn)	50	17
Imports (excluding oil products in €bn)	45	30
Exports (excluding oil products in €bn)	15	18
Unemployment rate	9.6%	24.4%

Source: EUROSTAT

Origins and Peculiarities of the Greek EAPs

The blueprint for the Greek programmes is the SAPs devised by the IMF in the 1990s. At that time capitalism suffered from the long-term stagnation generated by the 1974 global crisis. In order to surpass it, capital embarked in a series of systemic restructurings. After experimenting with *conservative Keynesianism* and *monetarist national neoliberalism*, with rather dismal results, the system employed *open economy neoliberalism* (or 'globalization'[1]). Its *differentiae specificae* are the deregulation of international capital movements and the dismantling of national barriers to capital accumulation. Its longevity is derived from its greater efficiency than national policies in increasing labour exploitation and also in subjugating imposing less developed capitalist economies to the more developed ones.

However, soon 'globalisation' showed its own limits and contradictions. While it bolstered capital profitability, it did not restore it to its pre-crisis levels (because of its inability to devalorize the overaccumulated capitals to the necessary extent). Simultaneously, it increased instability by linking closer national economies and their economic cycles and thus facilitating the faster transmission of a crisis from one economy to the other. Additionally, the increased use of fictitious capital operations (the so-called financialisation) on a global scale aggravated further systemic fragility. Several crises that erupted in the 1990s (Mexico, Thailand, etc.) gave notice of these problems. Therefore, the IMF revised its previous programmes and created its new SAPs. They were based on the *Washington Consensus*, that is the application of open economy neoliberalism in Development Policy (for an extensive critique, see Mavroudeas and Papadatos (2007)). Its gist was that fiscal austerity and market deregulation would produce higher growth, something disproved even by Mainstream economists. Nevertheless, IMF's SAPs have been systematically applied since then with usually dismal results. Their main prescription is austerity, export-led growth and shrinking the public sector. Their main guidelines for debt-ridden economies are as follows:

1. Fiscal consolidation (to reduce FD)
2. Labour market deregulation (to improve competitiveness)
3. Privatization (so as the private sector becomes the economy's locomotive)
4. Currency devaluation (to ensure a real exchange rate that would improve international competitiveness and restructure economic incentives to expand the production of exports)
5. Opening of the economy (to attract foreign capital): removal of import quotas, tariff reductions and improved export incentives
6. Debt restructuring (to alleviate the debt burden)
7. Tax reforms—aimed at neutrality and administrative simplification including a shift from trade taxes to other taxes, e.g. VAT

These are pro-cyclical programmes in the sense that their austerity measures consciously deepen the crisis believing that in this way it will 'bottom' sooner and the rebound will also be very strong (Weisbrot et al. 2009). The underlying theory of *expansionary austerity* was initially suggested by Giavazzi and Pagano (1990) and, with the advent of the 2007–2008 crisis, reiterated by Reinhart and Rogoff (2010). The latter was disproved both analytically (e.g. Botta 2015) and empirically (e.g. Herndon et al. 2013). Despite these failures, it continues to inform IMF's programmes.

The Greek EAPs are a peculiar and even more problematic hybrid of IMF's SAPs. Essentially, they are one and the same programme that undergoes continuous modifications. In technical terms, it is a medium-length bailout and structural transformation programme. Its aims, as declared in the first EAP and reiterated in the second (EC 2010, p. 10), are:

1. in the short term, to restore confidence and maintain financial stability by (a) fiscal consolidation and (b) stabilization of the financial sector.
2. in the medium term, to improve competitiveness and alter the economy's structure towards a more investment-friendly and export-led growth model.

The third EAP added the goal of creating a 'modern state and public administration structure'. This goal implicitly existed from the very previous EAPs. Its explicit incorporation has to do with the third EAP's emphasis on institutional factors and structural reforms.

The Greek EAPs follow the IMF SAPs' guidelines but with significant modifications. First, they are lengthier. The first EAP was designated as a typical IMF 3-year programme. However, because of its failure, it was supplemented with the second EAP which extended the programme by 1 year. Then, because also of the failure of this new augmented programme, a third EAP was concluded in 2016. Thus, the Greek programme is—at least at this moment—an 8-year programme (expected to conclude by 2018).

Second, there is no devaluation mechanism because Greece belongs to the Eurozone. This excludes a crucial tool in IMF's toolbox for increasing competitiveness. Consequently, the whole burden of increasing competitiveness is placed upon 'internal devaluation' (austerity on wages).

Third, the first EAP excluded another crucial IMF tool: debt restructuring. Despite current IMF criticisms against the EU, they both agreed on its exclusion at that time because they feared its impact on the international financial markets. Additionally, the EU feared that this would damage euro's international status. With the first EAP's failure, there was a clumsy and insufficient restructuring of the Greek debt held by private lenders (PSI). Despite PSI's nominally high debt haircut, the actual reduction of the Greek debt was negligible as it bankrupted Greek banks and welfare funds which had to be recapitalized by the state with new loans (this time provided by the EU and the IMF). Practically, PSI's only serious result was that it moved Greek debt from private to public hands.

Fourth, the Greek programme is extremely frontloaded (EC 2010, p. 15), contrary to IMF's advice, because the EU wanted to solve the problem rapidly and avoid contagion to the rest of the Eurozone.

All these modifications make the Greek programme a very dysfunctional one. The mechanics of the Greek EAPs depend crucially upon debt sustainability as this is their immediate and more pressing problem. Structural reforms play a supportive role in debt sustainability, and loans simply solve immediate liquidity problems. Austerity in the public and private sectors would bring the debt/GDP ratio to viable levels. This ratio depends on:

1. the existing debt/GDP ratio
2. government's primary balance (budget balance excluding debt servicing) as a share of GDP
3. government bonds' real interest rate
4. real GDP's growth rate

All of them, with the exception of the primary surplus, are outside government's direct control. The programme set a target for the debt/GDP ratio that had to be achieved. Then the other variables are set accordingly. Given that the real interest rate for troika's loans could not be negative (for both technical and political reasons) and given EU's rush to return Greece to solvency (in order to avoid contagion and minimize its own exposure to risks), then the main burden for achieving the target fell on the primary balance (making fiscal austerity very brutal). The second programme set the goal of a 120% debt/GDP ratio by 2020, assuming that then the private international financial markets would be willing to finance it again. The 120% ratio does not derive from any economic analysis (e.g. Reinhart and Rogoff proposed 90%) but from political expediency: Italy has such a debt ratio, and if the Greek goal was set at a lower point, then Italy should be put in an adjustment programme. In order to achieve this artificial but also overoptimistic goal, all the other parameters of debt sustainability were tweaked accordingly and equally overoptimistically. Thus, unrealistically high primary surpluses (approximately 3.5%), growth rates (approximately 5%) and privatization revenues were projected for equally unrealistic long periods. Additionally, the recessionary effects of fiscal austerity were grossly downplayed by underestimating the fiscal multiplier (as Blanchard and Leigh (2013) admitted).

Unsurprisingly, the programme did not work as a greater-than-expected recession happened. The EAP's expectation that the private sector would cover rapidly the gap created by the withdrawal of the public sector did not materialize. In an economy in deep recession, with collapsing internal demand private capitals and in a tumultuous politico-economic environment private capitals do not risk investing and do it only in a few completely scandalous cases. Moreover, the expectation of a growth boost from exports did not materialize. Despite the barbaric 'internal devaluation', exports did not increase significantly. The trade balance's improvement came from the reduction of imports as consumer demand collapsed. However, Greek exports did not increase significantly for obvious reasons: the majority of exported goods depend upon imported intermediate inputs. Hence, reducing nominal labour unit costs affects only slightly the price of exports as its greater part depends upon the cost of imported goods.

Consequently, the Greek EAP caused a much greater-than-expected recession, leading to a cumulative loss, from its beginning till the end of 2016, of approximately 25% of GDP. As a consequence, the whole mechanics of the programme fail systematically and the latter continuously underperforms. Nevertheless, after each major failure, the programme's main instigators 'kick the can down the road' by applying a temporary patch and playing for time.

SYSTEMIC CONTRADICTIONS AND DEAD ENDS

The Greek EAPs are marred by technical faults and inflexibilities. Their numerous reviews recalibrated their aims and adjusted their projections. Notwithstanding, they continue to fail systematically and yet their major instigators insist on the same course. The explanation lies in the broader political and economic processes underlying technical choices.

The 2007–2008 global crisis of capitalism ushered a period of weak economic performance and violent fluctuations. The immediate reaction of all the major capitalist economies was an abrupt abandonment of neo-liberal mantras (that free markets would solve problems on their own) and the embrace of conservative Keynesian policies (lax monetary and expansive fiscal policies coupled with drastic wage cuts) in order to sustain the falling capitalist profitability. These were financed through big increases in public debt. As Marxist Political Economy accurately pinpoints, in a crisis of overaccumulation (that is overaccumulated capitals that cannot be invested sufficiently profitably) such policies can defer the crisis impact at the cost of augmenting it. That is, they postpone the necessary destruction of capitals through bankruptcies, but they foment 'bubbles' that are destined to burst.

In this game of gaining time at the cost of increased peril, each major capitalist pole has different position, objectives, costs and benefits and timetables. Additionally, each one attempts to pass part at least of its costs to others. In this vein, the EU opted for a less lax policy (interest rate cuts were slower and smaller than the FED's, fiscal expansion considerably smaller than that of the US). This meant that the EU sought to exploit the 'bubbles' of its competitors (by selling in their markets), while house-keeping its own economy and of course not providing similar facilities to its competitors. Simultaneously, the EU initiated a process of 'internal thirdworld-ization' by pushing the euro-periphery into the debt trap and imposing appropriate adjustment programmes. It aims to create 'special economic zones' of cheap wages and assets and unregulated labour and product markets that would serve as export hubs for EU's multinationals. These European 'special economic zones' are destined to be lower parts of European value chains producing low technology and value-added goods. Through this 'sleigh of hands' the EU aspires to upgrade its global position and possibly challenge US' global supremacy. Euro's projection as a safe international reserve currency in contrast to an unsecure US dollar is an essential part of this strategy.

This explains why the EU cannot opt for a more lax programme (less frontloaded, less anti-cyclical) since this would prolong the Greek problem and undermine EU's house-keeping. It cannot employ a combination of 'internal' and external devaluation (that would reduce austerity and the collapse of internal demand) because of Greece's participation in the Eurozone. It did not want and only belatedly accepted a half-baked debt restructuring because this loosens discipline within the EU and therefore negates the essence of its 'sleigh of hands'. For all these reasons, the EU imposed the problematic modifications of the IMF's blueprint that characterize the Greek EAPs.

The US took part in this game, through the IMF, because it wanted to continue being an influential player in EU's affairs and did not want to antagonize directly Germany and the EU by not taking part in the bailout. Concurrently, it continuously subverts EU's 'sleigh of hands' through various means (e.g. ECB adopting a quantitative easing policy). Thus, IMF participates in the dysfunctional Greek programme but also—from time to time and depending on the evolution of the US–EU conflicts—puts its own demands and objections. Its main objective is not the Greek EAP's success (as IMF's loans are more secure than those of others) but its use as a means to curtail EU's ambitions.

Aside from its 'major' partners' aims and controversies, the Greek EAP has much broader problems. It dislocates Greek capitalism's entire postwar architecture causing critical political and economic fragility. First, it alters violently the structure of the Greek economy by increasing the role of foreign capital, changing its sectoral structure (reeling even more towards services and increasing deindustrialization), favouring exportables and so on. This aggravates intra-capitalist antagonisms as established corporate groups are endangered and new ones are trying to emerge. Second, small and medium enterprises (SMEs)—an abnormally large by Western criteria layer of Greek capitalism—are dwindling rapidly as the crisis and the EAPs foment the concentration and centralization of capital. This leads the small bourgeoisie to proletarianization and undermines one of capital's crucial class supports. Also, it destabilizes crucial economic processes that are not adequately replenished by new ones. Third, the programme imposes a drastic reduction of the living standards of the great majority of the Greek population because only through such rapid devaluation of the value of labour power and the corresponding increase in labour's exploitation can capitalist profitability recover. Thus, the programme disrupts critically Greek capitalism's political economic structure without offering a convincing and viable light at the end of his tunnel.

However, the EAPs' 'shock therapy' is the only way the EU can achieve its strategic goals. The US does not object in principle to this type of therapy, but they do not allow EU to achieve its strategy so they play a 'cat and mouse' game. The Greek bourgeoisie is at one of its worse historical points as it is terribly weakened, inexorably tied to the European integration and its ability to move autonomously almost non-existent. Therefore, all the major and junior partners of the programme—despite their conflicts and grievances—remain committed to it.

The heavy-handedness of the programme transforms the crisis from primarily economic to socio-political. At the same time, no viable solution is seen in the foreseeable future and none of the programme's main agents is able or willing to furnish it. The only uncontrollable 'variable' in this faulty system of political economic equations is the popular factor. It carries the great part of the programme's burden without sharing any of the interests of its instigators. It is only one that can probably offer a solution to the Greek conundrum by cutting its Gordian knot and plotting a course away from that of the Greek EAPs.

NOTE

1. 'Globalization' is named the post-1980s trend of rapid internationalization of capital. It involves the deregulation of international trade and capital flows and the subsequent removal of protectionist barriers. Similar eras existed before (e.g. the nineteenth-century 'first globalization' in the) and were later reversed. Contrary to the globalization theorists the eras of internationalisation of capital do not eliminate the role of the national economies but rather reshape them.

REFERENCES

Arestis, P. (2009). *New consensus macroeconomics: A critical appraisal* (Levy Institute Working Paper No. 564).

Blanchard, O., & Leigh, D. (2013). *Growth forecast errors and fiscal multipliers* (IMF Working Paper 13/1).

Botta, A. (2015). *The theoretical weaknesses of the expansionary austerity doctrine* (Post Keynesian Economics Study Group Working Paper 1511).

Colasanti, F. (2016). *Financial assistance to Greece: Three programmes*. European Policy Centre.

EC. (2010, May). *The economic adjustment programme for Greece* (Occasional Papers 61).

EC. (2012, March). *The second economic adjustment programme for Greece* (Occasional Papers 94).

Economist. (2008, March 6). The decoupling debate. *Economist*.

Economist. (2010, February 24). Decoupling: True or false? *Economist*.

Gross, D. (2008, January 23). Decoupling: Can Europe avoid a recession? *CEPS Commentary*.

Giavazzi, F., & Pagano, M. (1990). Can severe fiscal contractions be expansionary? Tales of two small European countries. In *NBER Macroeconomics Annual* 5, pp. 75–122, http://www.nber.org/chapters/c10973.pdf.

Herndon, T., Ash, M., & Pollin, R. (2013). Does high public debt consistently stifle economic growth? A critique of Reinhart and Rogoff. *Cambridge Journal of Economics, 38*(2), 257–279.

IMF. (2013). *Greece: Ex post evaluation of exceptional access under the 2010 stand-by arrangement* (Country Report No. 13/156).

Independent Evaluation Office of IMF. (2016). The IMF and the Crises in Greece, Ireland and Portugal, IMF, Washington, DC, 1–62. Retrieved from http://www.ieo-imf.org/ieo/pages/CompletedEvaluation267.aspx

Kincaid, R. (2016). *The IMF's role in the euro area crisis: What are the lessons from the IMF's participation in the Troika?* (IEO IMF Background Paper).

Krauss, M. (2008, Winter). Don't bet on decoupling. *International Economy*, pp. 22–23.

Mavroudeas, S. (2013). Development and crisis: The turbulent course of Greek capitalism. *International Critical. Thought, 3*(3), 217–314.

Mavroudeas, S. (2015). *The Greek saga: Competing explanations of the Greek crisis* (Kingston University London Economics Discussion Paper Series 20015-1).

Mavroudeas, S. (2016). The Greek crisis: A structural or a conjunctural crisis? In T. Subasat (Ed.), *The great financial meltdown: Systemic, conjunctural or policy-created? New directions in modern economics series*. Cheltenham: Edward Elgar.

Mavroudeas, S., & Paitaridis, D. (2014). The Greek crisis: A dual crisis of overaccumulation and imperialist exploitation. In S. Mavroudeas (Ed.), *Greek capitalism in crisis: Marxist analyses*. London: Routledge.

Mavroudeas, S., & Papadatos, D. (2007). Reform, reform the reforms or simply regression? The 'Washington consensus' and its critics. *Bulletin of Political Economy, 1*(1), 43–66.

Pisani-Ferry, J., Sapir, A., & Wolff, G. (2013). *EU-IMF assistance to euro-area countries: An early assessment, Bruegel blueprint series* (Vol. XIX). Brussels: Brussels Bruegel.

Reinhart, C. M., & Rogoff, K. S. (2010). Growth in a time of debt. *American Economic Review Papers and Proceedings, 100*(2), 573–578.

Weisbrot, M., Rebecca, R., Cordero, J., & Montesino, J. (2009). *IMF-supported macroeconomic policies and the world recession: A look at forty-one borrowing countries*. Washington, DC: CERP.

CHAPTER 4

The ECB's Non-standard Monetary Policy Measures and the Greek Financial Crisis

Marica Frangakis

INTRODUCTION

Twenty years ago, following the signing of the Maastricht Treaty, the following question was posed by a student of European integration and the European Monetary Union:

> What will happen if (one is tempted to say 'when') there is a serious episode of financial instability in the European economy and a large number of private agents are on the brink of failure? The doctrines which inspired Maastricht simply assume that this will not occur, that such financial distress can be identified and isolated at a stage when only a few agents are in distress and can be dealt with by measures of purely microeconomic significance.

I thank the book editor for his valuable comments. Of course, all errors remain mine.

Marica Frangakis is an independent researcher (frangaki@otenet.gr; http://academia.edu). She is a member of the Board of the Nicos Poulantzas Institute and a member of the Steering Committee of the EuroMemo Group (http://euromemo.eu).

M. Frangakis (✉)
Nicos Poulantzas Institute, Athens, Greece

J. Marangos (ed.), *The Internal Impact and External Influence of the Greek Financial Crisis*, DOI 10.1007/978-3-319-60201-1_4

> But the whole history of Western financial relations points, rather, to the inevitability of such disturbances, particularly in periods marked, like the present by major structural changes and uncertainties. (Grahl 1997, p. 150)

In the light of the global financial crisis of 2007–2008, which morphed into a sovereign debt and an economic crisis in the Eurozone, the above question appears especially pertinent today.

The same student went on to identify three possible answers: (1) changing the rules, (2) interpreting the rules with a certain amount of flexibility and/or (3) doing nothing or doing too little too late (Grahl 1997).

With hindsight, it may be argued that the monetary policy response of the European Central Bank (ECB) to the global financial crisis of 2007–2008 and the Eurozone crisis has been a combination of all three answers, albeit in reverse order. That is, the ECB started from a 'too little, too late' position building up to a more flexible interpretation of the rules as the crisis deepened, without changing its underlying premises.

The non-standard monetary policy measures taken by the ECB to deal with the sovereign debt crisis originated in the Greek financial crisis. The failure of these measures to stem the Eurozone crisis led to their revision and the next set of non-standard policies, from which however Greece has been excluded, even though it is the country with the greatest need for such measures (De Grauwe 2016).

In this chapter, we analyse the 'non-standard' monetary policy measures applied by the ECB in the context of the crisis, comparing them to its pro-crisis, 'standard' policy. We argue that the increased flexibility of the ECB monetary policy has not transformed it into a lender-of-last-resort (LOLR) vis-à-vis the governments of the Eurozone member states. On the contrary, the conceptual and ideological underpinnings of the ECB monetary policy remain consistent to the policy agenda embodied in the Maastricht rules. More specifically, the overarching concern with inflation and the fiscal discipline of the Eurozone member states continue to influence the ECB's monetary policy stand.

Overall, the Greek financial crisis has influenced the shaping of ECB policy in response to the sovereign debt crisis, while it has been negatively impacted by the inadequacies and underlying non-monetary considerations of this policy.

The rest of the chapter is organized as follows. The next section examines the historical embeddedness of central banking linking it to its present state. Section 'Pre and post crisis ECB monetary policy' analyses the monetary policy of the ECB prior to and following the crisis, identifying its weaknesses which largely account for its 'too late, too little' syndrome. Section 'The Greek Financial Crisis and the ECB' discusses the Greek financial crisis and its relation to the ECB. It is argued that the belated response of the ECB to the upheaval of the government bond market allowed the escalation of the crisis in Greece in 2009–2010. Further, the creditor status adopted by the ECB vis-à-vis Greece has deprived the latter of the benefits accruing to the other Eurozone member states as the monetary policy rules have been relaxed. The last Section summarizes and concludes.

THE HISTORICAL EMBEDDEDNESS OF CENTRAL BANKING

Historically, central banking has been through different phases. Goodhart (2010) distinguishes three eras: (1) the Victorian era from the 1840s to 1914; (2) the government control era, from the 1930s to the end of the 1960s; and (3) the 'triumph of the markets' from the 1980s to 2007. The periods intervening between the different eras and the change in paradigm each signals are considered to be transitory periods, or 'confused interregnums'.

In the Victorian era, it was assumed that government debt was not related to any economic activity. Therefore, its use as a policy instrument was to be avoided. Such a non-activist view limited the scope of both fiscal and monetary policies. It took the interwar years and a Great Depression for this view to be displaced. In the next era, especially after World War II, the scope of economic policy was broadened and central banking became an integral part of overall policy. At that time, the functions of a central bank consisted of (a) providing advice on policy, (b) administering the system of policy controls and (c) overseeing the management of financial markets, especially the gilt-edged market, the money market and the foreign exchange market. As the international financial system came under increasing pressure, the Bretton Woods Agreement collapsed (1972–1973), ushering in a new era in economic policy, in general and in central banking, in particular.

The central bank paradigm of the third era was characterized by two main features: (a) a near exclusive concern with price stability, over other areas of policy, and (b) institutional independence of the central bank from the political authorities and the assumed 'political business cycle'. Furthermore, indirect market-based instruments, such as the short-term interest rate, became the primary tool of monetary policy after the 1980s. The underlying assumption of this view is the Efficient Market Hypothesis (EMH) whereby agents are fully informed and rational. Therefore, they may be expected to respond to the market signals monitored by the central bank. So commonly accepted was the neoliberal model of central banking during this period that it came to be considered as 'somehow "modern", even optimal and therefore worthy of emulation throughout the globe' (Epstein 2006, p. 13).

However, this view took a severe blow in 2007 and 2008, as what appeared to be a liquidity crisis of the financial sector rapidly turned into an insolvency crisis of major proportions. This encompassed the advanced economies, whereas previous episodes in the 1980s and 1990s had taken place in the emerging economies. As noted by an official of the Bank for International Settlements, 'The near collapse of the financial system happened not only in the back yards, but in our front yards, too' (Cecchetti 2011, p. 1).

Ironically, central banks have emerged from the crisis more powerful than previously. This is due to the primacy of monetary over fiscal policy since the 1980s, as well as to the political economy of central banking (Bibow 2012). However, inflation targeting is being seriously questioned, which may indeed herald the start of a new era in central banking, a more interventionist, policy-integrated era.

Pre- and Post-crisis ECB Monetary Policy

The ECB was set up in the late 1990s (1/6/1998), at a time when 'the inflation-targeting/independence from government' model of central banking was at its height. Thus, it is an example of this model in extremis (Forder, 2006). As it has been pointed out, 'The ECB appears to be the ultimate "narrow" central bank; it literally has a mandate for price stability and a very small role in ensuring financial stability' (Schinasi 2003, p. 3). Further, the independence constitutionally granted to the ECB is the most explicit both in writing and in practice, by comparison to other central banks, such as the Federal Reserve and the Bank of England, as noted by Alexander Lamfalussy (2011).

ECB Institutional Features

In order to comprehend the narrow character of the ECB policy approach, it is necessary to look into the pertinent key provisions of the Treaty of the European Union (EU), as well as of the ECB Statute, namely, its mandate, tasks, independence and accountability.

- *Mandate*—Price stability constitutes the core of ECB monetary policy. This is mentioned as one of the goals of the EU itself in the Treaty for the Functioning of the EU, taking precedence over other goals, which may be pursued only 'without prejudice to price stability' (art. 3.2 and 119.2). Also it is the central objective of the ECB and of the national central banks, which together constitute the European System of Central Banks (ESCB) for EU member states and the Eurosystem for Eurozone ones (art. 127.1 and 282.2).

    The ECB's quantitative definition of price stability was set in 1998 by its Governing Council, as follows: 'Price stability shall be defined as a year-on-year increase in the Harmonised Index of Consumer Prices (HICP) for the euro area of below 2%. Price stability is to be maintained over the medium term' (ECB 2004, pp. 50–51). In 2003, it was further established that the ECB aims at maintaining inflation below but close to 2% over the medium term. Until that time, the ECB also employed a reference value for monetary growth (M3) set in 1998 at 4.5% p.a. However, in 2003, it was announced that the Bank would 'no longer review the reference value for M3 on an annual basis because experience has shown that the underlying medium-term trend assumptions cannot be expected to change frequently' (ECB 2004, p. 64). Thus, the M3 reference value was dropped.

- *Tasks*—According to article 127.2 of the Treaty and article 3 of the ECB Statute, 'The basic tasks to be carried out through the ESCB shall be to define and implement the monetary policy of the Union'. Furthermore, the ECB has the exclusive right to authorize the issue of euro banknotes (art. 128.1). However, there is a clear prohibition of the ECB and the central banks of the member states lending to any public authorities, be they European or national (art. 124.1 of the Treaty and art. 21.1 of the Statute). In this sense, the function of the ECB as an LOLR to governments is suppressed. This marks a significant shift away from the traditional origins of central banks historically constituted as agents of government debt.

- *Independence*—According to article 130 of the Treaty, 'When exercising the powers and carrying out the tasks and duties conferred upon them by the Treaties and the Statute of the ESCB and of the ECB, neither the European Central Bank, nor a national central bank, nor any member of their decision-making bodies shall seek or take instructions from Union institutions, bodies, offices or agencies, from any government of a Member State or from any other body'. Also 'The European Central Bank … shall be independent in the exercise of its powers and in the management of its finances' (art. 282.3 of the Treaty). Thus, the ECB has by design both functional and operational independence from the European and national public authorities.
- *Accountability*—The independence of a central bank from the public authorities is the corollary of a lack of democratic accountability. In the case of the ECB, this is further compounded by the fact that its relation with the European Parliament, the only EU representative body, is limited to the submission of annual reports and its participating in the EP committees 'at the request of the EP or on its own initiative' (art. 284.3 of the Treaty and art. 15.3 of the Statute).

Overall, ECB monetary policy is narrowly defined. Furthermore, it stands institutionally apart from the rest of the economy and economic policy. Both these elements have been important during the Eurozone crisis, as they have reinforced the narrative of fiscal profligacy while overlooking the implications of financial market upheavals.

ECB Monetary Policy Prior to the Crisis

The monetary transmission mechanism of the ECB relies on the interest rate channel, which is assumed to work its way through the economy both directly through the money market and the other financial markets and indirectly through the formulation of expectations. In addition, the Bank's credibility is considered to be crucial to its anchoring inflation expectations, where 'credibility' demands that the Bank does not easily change its course of action, even in the face of adversity, such as that experienced in 2007–2008.

Through its monetary operations, the ECB aims at providing (1) regular refinancing to credit institutions and (2) facilities that allow them to deal with end-of-day balances and to cushion transitory fluctuations. Of these two types of monetary policy tools, the most important one is open market operations (OMO), executed on the initiative of the Bank, usually in the money market, in which the maturity of transactions is generally less than 1 year. Until 2008, weekly OMO, that is, with a maturity of 1 week, known as main refinancing operations (MRO), constituted the key policy instrument. Accordingly, the ECB and the national central banks lend money to counterparties against collateral, on the basis of certain eligibility criteria.

In addition to OMO, the Eurosystem also offers two standing *facilities* to its counterparties. More specifically, the marginal lending facility provides overnight loans from the central bank against collateral at a predetermined interest rate, which is higher than the market rate. The deposit facility, by contrast, allows banks to make overnight deposits with the central bank at a predetermined interest rate, which is lower that the market rate. The interest rates on the two standing facilities form a 'corridor', within which lies the ECB MRO rate. The three rates are the ECB key interest rates.

In addition, the ECB requires credit institutions to hold compulsory deposits on accounts with the national central banks, known as 'minimum reserves' allowing the credit institutions to smooth out daily liquidity fluctuations. Until January 2012, banks had to hold a minimum of 2% of certain liabilities, mainly customers' deposits, at their national central bank. Since then, this ratio has been lowered to 1%.

Overall, the framework of the ECB monetary policy consists of one instrument (interest rate)—one market (unsecured overnight interbank market)—one target (price stability) (Gabor 2012). The crisis revealed the weaknesses of this system and the need for a paradigm shift.

ECB Non-standard Monetary Policy

In 2008, the ECB published a special issue of the Monthly Bulletin, celebrating 'The first ten years' since the introduction of the single currency. In its Concluding Remarks, the following statement is made:

> After the launch of the euro, the Eurosystem's achievements have been no less important. The monetary policy strategy of the ECB is now well understood and viewed as credible. During the past ten years it has provided a solid basis for responding to a number of challenges. Average annual HICP inflation has been slightly above 2% since the introduction of the euro, despite a series of exogenous shocks. (ECB 2008, p. 145)

Unfortunately, the events of the global financial crisis were to challenge the ECB's optimistic assertions and lead it to devise 'non-standard' monetary policy tools, which became the new normal in the Eurozone as well as in other advanced economies.

The rationale of these policies is twofold: (a) the economic shock is so powerful that the nominal interest rate needs to be brought down to zero; (b) the monetary policy transmission process is significantly impaired even if the policy interest rate is above zero. Under these conditions, central banks need to provide additional monetary stimulus by resorting to measures considered to be 'non-standard' by comparison to the prevailing practices of central banking. These include reducing the nominal interest rate, thus guiding medium- to long-interest rate expectations and/or acting directly on the transmission process by changing the composition and/or the size of the central bank's balance sheet (Bini Smaghi 2009).

The 2007–2008 global financial crisis mainly involved the wholesale markets, as financial firms ran on other such firms. In particular, sale and repurchase agreements (repo), commercial paper and prime broker balances were run on as large demands for cash from financial institutions in exchange for short-term debt obligations were not satisfied (Gorton 2012).

In August 2007, two hedge funds run by BNP Paribas and specializing in US mortgage-backed securities suspended withdrawals. The Federal Reserve reduced its target Federal Funds rate repeatedly and injected liquidity into credit markets. The ECB, on the other hand, undertook a variety of liquidity-providing operations at the prevailing main refinancing rate (4%). Further, in July 2008, the ECB increased its key interest rate by 25 basis points to 4.25%, believing that the tensions in the euro area interbank market had subsided and that inflationary pressures were imminent. This move is indicative of the slow start of the ECB in realizing the dynamics of the global financial crisis, as well as of its main preoccupation with inflation.

In September and October 2008, with the collapse of Lehman Brothers (15/9/2008), the global financial crisis deepened dramatically. The ECB responded by reducing its key interest rates, albeit erratically. Thus, the interest rate on the MRO, which provide the bulk of liquidity to the banking system, fell from 4.25% in July 2008 to 1% in May 2009, rising to 1.50% by July 2010 and declining thereafter, reaching 0% in March 2016. The interest rate on the marginal lending facility also declined from 5.25% in July 2008 to 0.25% in March 2016. Further, the interest rate on the deposit facility became negative in June 2014 (−0.10%) reaching −0.40% in December 2016.

Technically, the zero lower bound was reached, although the fluctuations in the intervening period are indicative of the ECB's 'too little, too late' syndrome, inherent in its institutional setup and culture. As pointed out by Dimand and Koehn (2012, p. 113),

> The ECB, like the Bundesbank, obsessively recalls the German price level rising to one trillion times its previous level, while the Reichsbank president promised that with 38 new high-speed printing presses the central bank would print enough currency to catch up with the soaring prices.

The so-called Enhanced Credit Programme, introduced by the ECB in 2009, was the first of a series of 'non-standard' policies designed to ease liquidity pressures on the banking sector. This included the following measures:

- Providing unlimited liquidity at a fixed rate in all refinancing operations against collateral;
- Lengthening the maximum maturity of refinancing operations;
- Extending the list of assets accepted as collateral;
- Outright purchasing of long-term debt securities issued by banks to refinance loans often in connection with real estate transactions ('covered bonds');
- Providing liquidity in foreign currencies and especially in US dollars.

From the start, the ECB stressed that its non-standard measures were of a temporary nature. Thus, in December 2009, it was announced that emergency liquidity measures were going to be phased out (Trichet 2010). However, by 2010, the public debt crisis in Greece and other peripheral Eurozone countries threatened the stability of the Eurozone. Accordingly, the ECB reintroduced and extended its non-standard measures in order to deal with the sovereign debt crisis, without however changing its fundamental policy precepts. In the next section, we examine the ECB's non-standard monetary policy measures originating in the Greek financial crisis, reflecting thus the latter's external influence. We also analyse the impact of the ECB on the management of the Eurozone debt crisis and its implications for the Greek crisis.

The Greek Financial Crisis and the ECB

Greece was the 12th EU member state to join the Eurozone in January 2001, 1 year after the launching of the single currency by the original 11 member states. After joining the Eurozone and prior to the crisis, Greece was a high-performing economy. As shown by Frangakis (2015), over the period 2002–2006, Greece had the fourth highest rate of growth in the Eurozone both in aggregate and in per capita terms, reflecting the dynamism of its economy. This was however largely spurred on by the public sector mainly through borrowing. For example, in 2006 public debt amounted to 103% of GDP in Greece by comparison to 53% in the Eurozone and 46% in the EU on average. Private debt also reached 93% of GDP in 2006, although it was considerably lower by comparison to the Eurozone and the EU averages (140% and 124%, respectively).

The prevailing low interest rate in the Eurozone and the financial deregulation of the EU in the 1990s and 2000s provided Greece with the means to finance its public debt and its current account deficit. This was based on the assumption by the financial markets that all Eurozone government bonds were subject to the same degree of risk. For example, the credit rating awarded to the Greek government bonds (GGBs) increased in the early 2000s. Indeed, in October 2003, Greece was upgraded from an emerging economy to an advanced one. Its rating remained high, declining somewhat in 2007–2008 and plunging thereafter, thus marking the start of the Greek financial crisis. In 2013, Greece was the first country to be downgraded to emerging-market status. Figure 4.1 displays the rise and fall of Greece's financial market status, as signalled by the Credit Rating Agencies.

The multiple downgrades of the Greek sovereign bonds were instrumental in the precipitation of the crisis in 2009–2010 as GGBs came under increasing pressure from the financial markets. Whereas 10-year GGBs were trading at a yield of 5% in 2009, this increased to over 12%

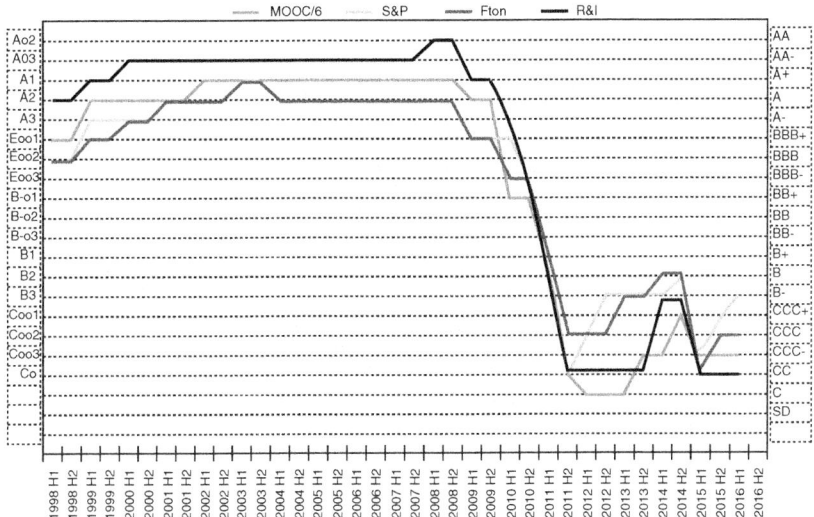

Fig. 4.1   Greece's rating by Moody's, Standard & Poor's, Fitch and Rating & Investment Agencies 1998–2016. Source: Public Debt Management Agency. Available from: http://www.pdma.gr/en/public-debt-strategy/public-debt/credit-rating

in 2010 and it went on climbing, signifying the reduction in the price of the bonds and the difficulty in refinancing the Greek public debt through the bond market. Figure 4.2 shows the highest yields and corresponding prices over the period 2009–2016.

The onset of the sovereign debt crisis which began in Greece in 2010, spreading to Portugal and Ireland by 2011, presented the ECB with a new set of problems, to which not only was it unaccustomed, but also unprepared. As Cour-Thimann and Winkler (2013, p. 6) have remarked, 'The concept of ensuring the financial stability of the euro area as a whole had to be "invented" in the crisis'.

Financial Bailouts and Austerity

The sharp rise in the yields of GGBs was a warning sign of the anomaly in the bond markets and of the risk of a sovereign debt crisis. The response of Greece's Eurozone partners was to provide financial assistance conditional on a range of austerity policies, including extensive fiscal consolidation,

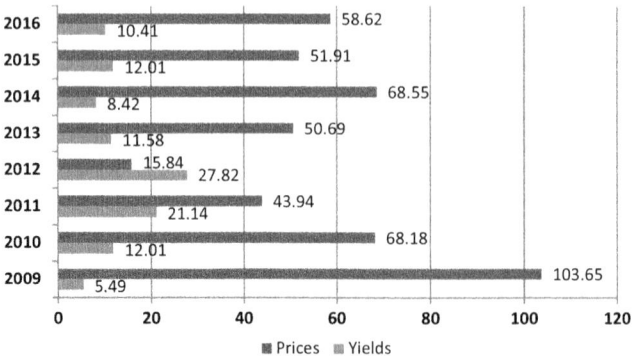

Fig. 4.2 Ten-year GGB highest yields (%) and corresponding prices (per Euro100 nominal) 2009–2016. Source: Bank of Greece Statistics. Available from: http://www.bankofgreece.gr/Pages/en/Statistics/rates_markets/titloieldimo-siou/default.aspx

the deregulation of the labour market and of other sectors of the economy, as well as a far-reaching privatization programme (Frangakis 2015).

The first bailout (2010–2012) was financed by the Greek Loan Facility, which was a pooling of bilateral loans by each member state of the Eurozone with the exception of Slovakia, as well as of Ireland and Portugal, when these received similar bailouts. The Loan Facility was on commercial terms; that is, it bore 5% interest rate and it was for a 3-year period.

The second bailout was financed by the European Financial Stability Fund (set up in late 2010), which borrowed the necessary funds in the bond market with the guarantee of the Eurozone member states. The second bailout (2012–2015) was also for 3 years, while the interest rate was equal to that at which the EFSF borrowed plus expenses, approximately 2% at the time.

The 2012 loan financed the restructuring of the public debt by way of (a) the exchange of old bonds for new ones, equal to half their nominal value (the so-called Private Sector Involvement) and (b) the bond buy-back by the government. The bond swap covered 57% of the debt (27% domestic investors and 30% foreign investors), while a small number of investors held out. The ECB did not participate in the exchange even though it held 16.3% of the GGBs at the time (February 2012).

Overall, the net benefit of the debt restructuring exercise was limited, in view of the fact that it came too late after the start of the crisis (2009–2010), it left out the bonds held by the ECB, and it relied on further borrowing (Frangakis 2014).

In 2012, the EFSF was succeeded by the European Stability Mechanism, which granted a new loan under the third bailout agreement signed in August 2015 for a further 3-year period (2015–2018). The new loan maturity was set at 32.5 years, while the interest rate, equal to the ESM funding cost plus fees (approximately 1%). The new agreement was also conditional on the implementation of further fiscal consolidation and structural/institutional reforms. In particular, the deficit/GDP targets were set at −0.25% for 2015, +0.5% for 2016, +1.75% for 2017 and +3.5% for 2018, while any primary surplus is to be transferred to a segregated account for debt service.

The total amount of funds agreed and actually disbursed to Greece is shown in Table 4.1.

It should be noted that only 4.5% of the funds under the first two bailout agreements covered the needs of the Greek economy. The remaining 95.5% covered the needs of Greece's creditors and of the recapitalization of Greek banks (Rocholl and Stahmer 2016). Similarly, 92% of the funds of the third bailout are destined for the European and Greek banks (EC 2015).

While the bailouts aimed at covering the needs of the financial sector both in the Eurozone and in Greece, the implications of the auster-

Table 4.1 Financial assistance: agreed/paid out funds (Euro billion; May 2010–October 2016)

	Eurozone	IMF	Total
First agreement (2010–2012)			
• Agreed sum	77	30	107
• Of which paid out	53	20	73
Second agreement (2012–2014)			
• Agreed sum	145	19	164
• Of which paid out	133	8	141
Third agreement (2015–2018)			
• Agreed sum	86	–	86
• Of which paid out	32	–	32
Total payments (10/2015)	218	28	246

Sources: European Commission; European Stability Mechanism. *Notes*—The difference between the agreed and paid out sums is the result of transfers from one agreement to the other

ity measures for the economy and for Greek society at large were quite unprecedented. Output declined by more than 25%, investment by more than 50%, wages by 30–40%, as did pensions, while unemployment rose from 7.8% of the labour force in 2008 to 27.5% in 2013 falling back to 23.5% in 2016, which was still more than double the average rate (10.2%) of the Eurozone (Frangakis 2015).

Not surprisingly, the collapse of the economy led to the heavy indebtedness of the private sector and the strangling of Greek banks, as political uncertainty led to a flight of deposits (15% decline between January and June 2015), while non-performing loans—defined as 90 days past due—soared from 3% of the total loan book in 2008 to 33% in 2015 (European Parliament 2016).

The radical fiscal consolidation undertaken did reduce the public deficit from 15.1% of GDP in 2009 to 2.5% in 2016, while excluding interest payments turned the deficit into a primary surplus equal to 0.8% of GDP in 2016. However, the shrinking of the economy in combination with the heavy borrowing of this period meant that the ratio of public debt to GDP steadily increased, reaching 181.6% in 2016 from 126.7% in 2009.

In March 2016, Greece's public debt was equal to Euro 321.65 billion, approximately 75% of which was due to the country's official creditors (EFSF, Eurozone, IMF, ECB), as shown in Fig. 4.3. As one of the country's official creditors, the ECB acts in the capacity of a creditor rather than of a central banker vis-à-vis Greece.

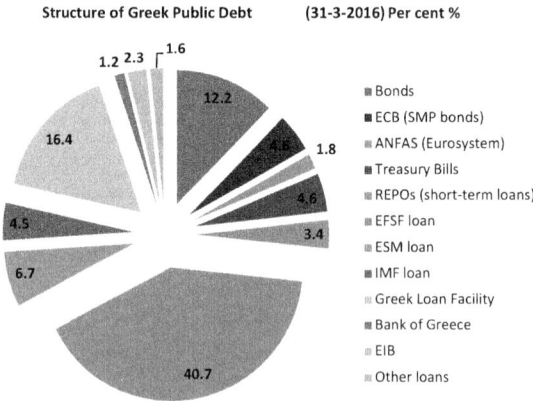

Fig. 4.3 Structure of Greek public debt (31/3/2016—%). Source: Hellenic Republic, Public Debt Management Agency (2016)

ECB Involvement in the Greek Financial Crisis

At the onset of the sovereign debt crisis in 2009, the role of a central bank would have been to intervene in the bond market on a large enough scale so as to prevent the explosion of bond yields and the widening of bond spreads in the Eurozone, thus dampening the speculative trends driving the market. Such action was however not undertaken by the ECB, even though the share of GGBs held by the European banks was small by comparison to those of other peripheral Eurozone countries, especially Spain and Italy. Instead the ECB, together with the European Commission and the IMF, became one of the official creditors, which undertook the management of the Greek financial crisis.

Securities Market Programme—More specifically, on 10/5/2010, the ECB announced the Securities Market Programme (SMP), the first of a number of non-standard measures devised to deal with the Eurozone sovereign crisis. This aimed at supporting the monetary policy transmission mechanism. Interventions were strictly limited to secondary bond markets while they were fully sterilized through liquidity-absorbing operations in order to avoid a rise in inflation. Further, the ECB claimed preferred creditor status for the bonds it acquired in the context of this Programme. The SMP was later extended to include more countries. It was terminated in 2012. Table 4.2 shows the outstanding Eurosystem's SMP holdings by issuer country over the period 2010–2015.

By 2015, the Eurosystem's SMP holdings had been reduced by 40% since the start of the Programme, while the bulk of the securities had been issued by Italy (50%) and Spain (21%). Thus, while the fear of contagion

Table 4.2 Outstanding amounts of Eurosystem SMP holdings (end year; Euro billion)

	May 2010–December 2011	*2012*	*2013*	*2014*	*2015*
Ireland	19.0	14.2	9.7	9.7	9.7
Greece	36.0	33.9	27.7	19.8	14.6
Spain	46.0	44.3	38.8	28.9	26.4
Italy	90.0	102.8	89.7	76.2	63.5
Portugal	20.0	22.8	19.8	14.9	12.4
Total	211.0	218.0	178.8	149.4	126.7

Source: ECB (various years). SMP data were first published in 2013 'in line with the envisaged transparency stance for the Outright Monetary Transactions (OMTs) as communicated on 6/9/2012'. (https://www.ecb.europa.eu/press/pr/date/2013/html/pr130221_1.en.html)

in the government bond market was real enough, Greece did not present a major risk, as its share was relatively small (11% in 2015, having declined from 17% in 2010–2011). In this sense, it may be argued that the main purpose of the SMP was to shield the European banks holding government bonds of Greece and other peripheral countries from the implications of the crisis, rather than to address the problems of the indebted countries.

This is especially true of the GGBs which are being repaid on maturity, constituting a form of 'reverse quantitative easing', since Greece is thus deprived of 'free borrowing'. In other words, when the ECB buys bonds from a Eurozone member state, the government pays interest to the Bank, which the latter rebates to the government of the member state in question. Therefore, when Greece repays the bonds held by the ECB, it loses the seigniorage gain it would enjoy in the form of the waiver on interest payments, if the bonds were kept on the ECB's balance sheet. Furthermore, the money base in the Eurozone shrinks by the same amount (De Grauwe and Ji 2015).

Greece has further been deprived of the net interest income realized by the Eurosystem on the GGBs, as shown in Table 4.3.

Although the ECB distributes the interest payments on bonds in its balance sheet to the Eurozone member states on the basis of their equity share in the Bank's capital, in the case of Greece these repayments are subject to the political agreement with the country's creditors. Thus, in November 2012, the Eurogroup agreed to transfer to Greece the gains of the Eurosystem on Greek bond holdings, conditional on 'a strong implementation of the agreed reform measures' (European Council 2012). However, such disbursements have only been made irregularly.

Overall, the SMP programme did not help address Greece's problems, while its limitations in terms of impact on the bond markets soon made

Table 4.3 Eurosystem net interest income from SMP holdings (Euro million; %)

	2011	2012	2013	2014	2015
Total	1003	1108	962	728	609
Of which from GGBs	654	555	437	298	224
Share of GGBs in total (%)	65	50	45	41	37

Source: Annual accounts of the ECB for 2013; Financial Statements of the ECB for 2014 and 2015

it redundant. The SMP temporarily bought time for the Eurozone, but it did not manage to halt the sovereign debt crisis. This was due to the flawed premise of the ECB that the monetary transmission mechanism had gone amiss, overlooking the fact that financial market speculation persisted. Thus, the crisis spread to the government bond markets of Spain and Italy in 2011, while the strain was felt also in other countries, such as France, Belgium and Austria. By that time, the main risk perceived by the markets was that of redenomination, that is, of the reversibility of the euro, giving new impetus to financial speculation. A new policy initiative was therefore introduced in September 2012, when the ECB president, Mario Draghi, announced that 'within our mandate, the ECB is ready to do whatever it takes to preserve the euro' (ECB 2012).

Outright Monetary Transactions—The SMP was succeeded by a new programme, known as 'Outright Monetary Transactions' (OMT), which differed from the SMP in a number of ways:

1. it was not time or volume constrained;
2. no sterilization commitment was made;
3. the ECB accepted the same (pari passu) treatment as private or other creditors.

Thus, on the one hand, it did away with the restrictions of the SMP. On the other hand, however, it was stipulated that a necessary condition for OMT is strict conditionality attached to an appropriate EFSF/ESM programme. OMT may be terminated if there is non-compliance with such a programme. It is on the basis of this condition that Greece was exempted from the benefits of OMT, as well as of its successor non-standard measure, the Asset Purchase Programme.

Asset Purchase Programme—The OMT programme was never invoked. It was however the precursor of the Asset Purchase Programme. In particular, in spite of the range of non-standard measures taken by the ECB, neither the financial nor the sovereign debt crises were brought under control. Instead, they combined in what has been called a 'diabolic loop', leading to a debt-deflation spiral of low or negative prices and growth rates and not only in Greece (Rodriguez and Carrasco 2014). This was the outcome of the ECB perception that such measures were a temporary deviation from its basic policy framework rather than a departure from it.

Thus, the range of non-standard monetary policy measures was extended to include an Asset Purchase Programme pertaining both to private and public sector securities. Accordingly, monthly purchases of public and private sector securities to the tune of 60 billion Euros were introduced in March 2015, raised to 80 billion Euros in March 2016. These are scheduled to continue until the end of March 2017, at which time they will revert to the sum of 60 billion Euros until December 2017 or beyond if necessary (ECB 2016).

The Eurosystem holdings and the monthly net purchases as at October 2016 are shown in Table 4.4.

Of the four programmes, the PSPP—also referred to as 'quantitative easing'—is the most important, accounting for nearly 82% of all holdings in October 2016. The PSPP is a form of debt relief. In particular, as long as the government bonds under the Programme remain on the balance sheet of the national central banks, the national governments do not effectively pay interest on these securities, as already discussed above.

With the exception of Greece, all 18 member states of the Eurozone participate in the PSPP. The main beneficiaries of the Programme are Germany (24% of cumulative monthly net purchases at end October 2016), followed by France (19%), Italy (16%) and Spain (12%). It is worth noting that the share of these countries in the PSPP exceeds their contribution to the ECB share capital, which is equal to 18% for Germany, 14% for France, 9% for Italy and 12% for Spain.

Table 4.4 Eurosystem holdings under Asset Purchase Programme (Euro million, month end)

Type of PP (starting date)	Asset-backed securities PP (November 2014)	3rd covered bond PP (October 2014)	Corporate sector PP (June 2016)	Public sector PP (March 2015)	Total Asset Purchase Programme
Holdings as at end September 2016	20,672	194,304	29,722	1,061,244	1,305,942
Monthly net purchases	589	3437	8422	72,974	85,422
Holdings as at end October 2016	21,261	197,741	38,144	1,134,218	1,391,364

Source: ECB (2016); holdings at amortized cost. Available from: https://www.ecb.europa.eu/mopo/implement/omt/html/index.en.html

Greece however is excluded from the most drastic, non-standard monetary policy measure taken by the ECB so far. The reason given by the ECB for the exclusion of Greece is that the GGBs do not meet the quality criteria required by the ECB in the framework of its PSP Programme. This is indeed paradoxical to the extent that countries that have issued 'quality' bonds enjoy debt relief (De Grauwe 2016).

On the whole, by the end of 2015, security purchases for monetary policy purposes made up 59% of the Eurosystem's monetary operations on the asset side of its financial statement, while the remaining 41% related to traditional refinancing operations (ECB 2015). However, the Eurozone crisis was not quelled, as the Eurozone finds itself mired in economic stagnation, while countries like Greece are in the grips of a debt/deflation spiral.

Capital Controls—In 2015, a number of events marked both the Greek financial crisis and the involvement of the ECB, leading to the introduction of capital controls by Greece, the second Eurozone country to do so after Cyprus.

These were triggered by the election to government of SYRIZA—acronym for 'Radical Left Alliance'—in the national elections of January 2015 and the formation of a SYRIZA-led government. As the 2012 bailout agreement had been extended until the end of February 2015, the new government entered into lengthy negotiations with the country's creditors, which led to the third bailout agreement.

During the 6-month period (January–June 2015), the policies pursued by the ECB vis-à-vis Greece increased the political pressure applied on the newly elected government in a number of ways, which were contrary not only to the OMT pledge of 'whatever it takes', but also to the concept of the Public Sector Purchase Programme, which had already been put into effect at that time.

More specifically, the ECB created conditions of asphyxiation for the Greek banks and the economy in a number of ways: (1) by lifting the waiver of minimum credit rating requirements for GGBs on 4th February, thus shifting banks to the Emergency Liquidity Assistance mechanism, which is an expensive way of bank refinancing while the risk lies with the national central bank; (2) by freezing the amount of funding (at Euro 89 billion) available to Greek banks in late June, after the government announced the holding of referendum to take place on 5th July; and (3) by imposing a haircut on GGBs used as collateral on 6th July.

In view of the fact that the Greek banking sector was already under severe pressure due to the flight of deposits and a steep increase in non-performing loans, capital controls were introduced on 28th June in order to avert the collapse of the banking system. The banks closed for 3 weeks, while the regime of capital controls, albeit relaxed, is still in place at the time of writing (December 2016).

Indeed, the ECB has been accused by various quarters for its handling of the Greek financial crisis. Sandbu (2015) of the *Financial Times* has pointed out that 'sectioning off the Greek banking system and blocking Greek residents' access to banking services flies in the face of the ECB's legal mandate'. Similarly, Jones (2015) also of the *Financial Times* attests to the fact that 'The central bank has stood accused of acting illegally over the decision to freeze the funding, with critics portraying it as complicit in what they view as Germany's blackmailing of Athens to a sign up to a humiliating bailout package'. Even more pointedly, Paul De Grauwe has been quoted as saying that '[t]he correct announcement of the ECB should be that it will provide all the necessary liquidity to the Greek banks. Such an announcement will pacify depositors. The ECB has other objectives than stabilising the Greek banking system. These objectives are political. The ECB continues to put pressure on the Greek government to behave well' (Quoted by Stewart et al. 2015).

SUMMARY AND CONCLUSIONS

Central banking is historically and institutionally embedded. Its main tenets reflect the prevailing dogmas and attitudes of the time. The present era of central banking has its origins in the 1980s and the process of financial deregulation, which spread across the advanced economies over the next quarter of a century.

Faith in the market as the arbiter of economic relations is a distinguishing mark of this era. Accordingly, the prevailing dogmas of central banking are (1) 'independence' from political authority and (2) operating through market signalling. The underlying assumption is that the market is rational. This is the so-called Efficient Market Hypothesis.

The 2007–2008 global financial crisis shattered the EMH. Deviations from the norm had to be made in order to avoid the collapse of the financial system. However, these did not reflect a paradigm shift. Instead, central banks adopted various 'non-standard' or 'non-conventional' measures signifying only a temporary departure from standard monetary policy.

The ECB is an extreme example of the latest era paradigm in terms of its founding principles and functioning. Further, the ECB's overarching concern with inflation and its functional and operational independence from the governments of the Eurozone have defined its approach to the sovereign debt crisis. This is especially true in relation to its handling of the Greek financial crisis.

The first 10 years of the ECB's existence (1998–2007) were incident-free. However, the outbreak of the global financial crisis called its mode of operation into question. In dealing with the crisis, the ECB introduced a variety of 'non-standard' measures. However, these reveal a 'learning-by-doing' process rather than a strategic shift. As a result, the ECB's non-standard measures suffer from a 'too little, too late' syndrome, which constrains the Bank's potential for crisis resolution (Bibow 2015).

Admittedly, the Eurozone's stringent fiscal policy, which became even more so during the crisis on the misguided belief that austerity is the answer to it, has been a major hindrance in the overcoming of the crisis. It has also been a significant constraint on ECB policy, especially as Germany, the dominant Eurozone partner, has doubted the legality of OMT, a non-standard policy measure which was never invoked, but it was the precursor of the Bank's public securities buying programme.

In particular, a group of more than 37,000 German academics, businessmen and politicians objected to the OMT scheme, arguing it violated German federal law through the illegal monetary financing of Eurozone governments. However, the European Court of Justice ruled in June 2015 that the OMT programme was in accordance with EU treaty law.

In spite of the fact that the sovereign debt crisis first made its appearance in Greece, the role of the ECB in dealing with the Greek financial crisis has been one of a creditor, rather than of a central banker. Initially, the ECB tried to insulate the government bond market from the implications of the Greek crisis. The Securities Market Programme was instituted for this purpose. It did not however prevent the spreading of the crisis to the Spanish and Italian bonds, as it was riddled with various constraints, rendering it ineffective in terms of influencing market developments.

As the Eurozone crisis escalated, so did the Greek financial crisis. The creditor status of the ECB vis-à-vis Greece was confirmed when the restructuring process of GGBs was put into effect in 2012. The ECB refused to participate, claiming a seniority status for its bond holdings.

The failings of the Securities Market Programme led to the necessity for further measures to deal with the Eurozone crisis. However, the ECB's renewed attempt to deal with the Eurozone crisis was directly linked to the austerity agenda imposed on indebted countries in return for financial assistance. Thus, the fiscal profligacy narrative, which has been adopted by the European elites by way of dealing with the crisis, has become an integral part of the ECB's non-standard monetary policy.

Not surprisingly, Greece has been excluded from the latest and most drastic ECB non-standard monetary policy measures, the Asset Purchase Programme, which was extended in 2015 to include public sector securities. Thus, Greece is not enjoying any of the advantages granted by the ECB to the other Eurozone member states.

Overall, the Greek financial crisis influenced ECB policy to the extent that the initial non-standard monetary policy measures were taken in its context. The limited impact of these measures on the Eurozone crisis led to their revision. However, Greece has been excluded from the renewed versions of the ECB's non-standard measures. The Greek experience in fact points to the inadequacies and the non-monetary aspects of ECB policy, which limit its role as an LOLR to governments. Indeed, the underlying principles of the European Monetary Union need to be re-examined, including a paradigm shift of monetary policy. The era of central banking which began in the 1980s has been challenged by the crisis. Dogmas and attitudes need to be adjusted accordingly.

References

Bibow, J. (2012). The euro and its guardian of stability: Fiction and reality of the 10th anniversary blast. In L.-P. Rochon & S. Y. Olawoye (Eds.), *Monetary policy and central banking, new directions in post-Keynesian theory*. Cheltenham, UK: Edward Elgar.

Bibow, J. (2015). *The euro's savior? Assessing the ECB's crisis management performance and potential for crisis resolution* (IMK Macroeconomic Policy Institute Study No. 42). Berlin.

Bini Smaghi, L. (2009). 'Keynote lecture', *Conventional and unconventional monetary policy*. International Centre for Monetary and Banking Studies (ICMB), Geneva. Retrieved from https://www.ecb.europa.eu/press/key/date/2009/html/sp090428.en.html

Cecchetti, S. G. (2011). 'Introductory Remarks', *The future of central banking under post-crisis mandates* (BIS Papers No. 55), pp. 1–5. Switzerland. Retrieved from http://www.bis.org/publ/bppdf/bispap55.pdf

Cour-Thimann, P., & Winkler, B. (2013). *The ECB's non-standard monetary policy measures* (ECB Working Paper No. 1528). Frankfurt.

De Grauwe, P. (2016, May 13). The ECB grants relief to all Eurozone nations except Greece. *VOX CEPR's Policy Portal.* Retrieved from http://voxeu.org/article/ecb-grants-debt-relief-all-eurozone-nations-except-greece

De Grauwe, P., & Ji, Y. (2015, July 16). Why the ECB should not insist on repayment of its Greek bonds. *VOX CEPR's Policy Portal.* Retrieved from http://voxeu.org/article/why-ecb-should-not-insist-repayment-its-greek-bonds

Dimand, R., & Koehn, R. (2012). Central bank responses to financial crises: Lenders of last resort in interesting times. In L.-P. Rochon & S. Y. Olawoye (Eds.), *Monetary policy and central banking, new directions in post-Keynesian theory.* Cheltenham, UK: Edward Elgar.

Epstein, G. (2006). *Central banks as agents of economic development* (UNU-WIDER, Research Paper No. 2006/54). Finland.

European Central Bank. (2004). The Monetary Policy of the ECB, Frankfurt. Retrieved from https://www.ecb.europa.eu/press/pr/date/2004/html/pr040130.en.html

European Central Bank. (2008). 10th anniversary of the ECB. *Monthly Bulletin,* Frankfurt.

European Central Bank. (2012). Press release. Retrieved from https://www.ecb.europa.eu/press/pressconf/2012/html/is120906.en.html

European Central Bank. (2015). *Consolidated balance sheet of the Eurosystem as at 31 December 2015* (ECB Annual Report 2015). Frankfurt.

European Central Bank. (2016). Press release. Retrieved from https://www.ecb.europa.eu/press/pr/date/2016/html/pr161208.en.html

European Commission. (2015, July 10). *Greece—Request for stability support in the form of an ESM loan* (Art. 13 ESM Treaty). Brussels.

European Council. (2012, November 27). *Eurogroup statement on Greece.* Brussels. Retrieved from www.consilium.europa.eu

European Parliament. (2016, March 18). *Non-performing loans in the banking union: Stocktaking and challenges.* Directory General for Internal Policies, Economic Governance Support Unit Brussels.

Forder, J. (2006). Monetary policy. In P. Arestis & M. Sawyer (Eds.), *A handbook of alternative monetary economics* (pp. 224–242). Cheltenham, UK: Edward Elgar.

Frangakis, M. (2014). The debt crisis and the adventure of the 'rescue. In S. Koskoletos & E. Papadopoulou (Eds.), *Crisis, debt and the development perspective.* Athens: Nissos Publications.

Frangakis, M. (2015). Public debt crisis, austerity and deflation—The case of Greece. *Review of Keynesian Economics, 3*(3), 295–313.

Gabor, D. (2012). *The ECB and the Eurozone debt crisis.* Retrieved from https://www.academia.edu/868218/The_ECB_and_the_European_Debt_Crisis

Goodhart, C. (2010). *The changing role of central banks* (BIS Working Papers No. 326). Switzerland.

Gorton, G. B. (2012). *Misunderstanding financial crises*. New York: Oxford University Press.

Grahl, J. (1997). *Alter Maastricht, A guide to European Monetary Union*. London: Lawrence & Wishart Ltd.

Jones, C. (2015, July 16). Mario Draghi casts himself as guardian of monetary union: ECB president pleases neither German hardliners not Greek sympathisers. *Financial Times*. Retrieved from www.ft.com

Lamfalussy, A. (2011). 'Keynote Speech', *The future of central banking under post-crisis mandates* (BIS Papers No. 55), pp. 6–12. Switzerland. Retrieved from http://www.bis.org/publ/bppdf/bispap55.pdf

Rocholl, J., & Stahmer, A. (2016). *Where did the Greek bail out money go?* (ESMT White Paper WP No. 16-02). Berlin: European School for Management and Technology.

Rodriguez, C., & Carrasco, C. A. (2014, September 14). *ECB policy response between 2007–2014* (FESSUD WP Series No. 65). Leeds, UK.

Sandbu, M. (2015, July 6). Free lunch: ECB, enemy of the euro? *Financial Times*. Retrieved from www.ft.com

Schinasi, G. J. (2003). *Responsibility of central banks for stability in financial markets* (IMF Working Paper, WP/03/121). Washington. Retrieved from https://www.imf.org/external/pubs/ft/wp/2003/wp03121.pdf

Stewart, H., Mason, R., & Inman, P. (2015, July 16). Greece debt crisis: New ECB cash lifeline could reopen Greek banks. *The Guardian*. Retrieved from https://www.theguardian.com

Trichet, J. C. (2010). State of the union: The financial crisis and the ECB's response between 2007 and 2009. *Journal of Common Market Studies, 48*, 7–19.

CHAPTER 5

Social Dialogue in Post-crisis Greece: A Sisyphus Syndrome for Greek Social Partners' Expectations

Theodore Koutroukis

INTRODUCTION

Before the unexpected financial crisis of 2008, industrial relations in Greece were rather centralized, and thus a high level of regulation in both the individual and the collective levels of employment relations prevailed (Ioannou 2011; Koukiadaki and Kretsos 2012). In May of 2010, an agreement was concluded between the Lenders' representatives (more specifically European Union [EU], European Central Bank [ECB] and International Monetary Fund [IMF]) and the Greek government. According to the terms of this agreement, Greece would apply a Memorandum of Mutual Understanding and would adopt a strict programme of austerity and fiscal adjustments (Kyriakoulias 2012). The implementation of those measures which were included in Memorandum 1 (6.5.2010), Memorandum 2 (13.2.2012) and Memorandum 3 (14.8.2015) has caused side effects in the social dialogue procedures.

T. Koutroukis (✉)
Department of Economics, Democritus University of Thrace,
Komotini, Greece

© The Author(s) 2017
J. Marangos (ed.), *The Internal Impact and External Influence of the Greek Financial Crisis*, DOI 10.1007/978-3-319-60201-1_5

The chapter examines a series of transformations that took part in the Greek industrial relations system and assesses the changes in the field of social partnership due to the implementation of the three Memoranda. Moreover, it analyses the consequences of the institutional amendments, which have been introduced in the last 7 years and 2016, towards more decentralized collective bargaining and more limited social dialogue regarding economic and social policy.

LABOUR MARKET POLICY WITHIN THE FRAMEWORK OF MEMORANDA

Memoranda included measures to improve public finance, regulation and supervision of financial and banking sector and implementation of State reforms that would increase competitiveness in Greece (Table 5.1). Moreover, measures of intervention in labour market, legal framework of employment relations and social partnership procedures in all levels were incorporated (Kyriakoulias 2012). Especially as far as social dialogue issues are concerned, the focus of the collective bargaining from the sectoral/craft level to the company level re-orientated radically the Greek collective bargaining system after 20 years (Kyriakoulias 2012). The main interventions of Government in the Greek labour market have promoted work flexibility through (a) the facilitation of dismissing and recruiting and the decrease of their cost, (b) the increase of flexible work patterns (temporary and part-time work, hiring-out of workers, employment under the form of "independent services provision", teleworking), (c) working time regulation (working time calculated on an annual basis, overtime restriction) and (d) wage flexibility (reduction of minimum wages, collective bargaining decentralization from the sectoral level to the company level and hindrance of recourse to arbitration procedure).

Memoranda have caused crucial changes in the institutional framework of the terms of wage and working conditions in the private sector: (a) possibility for differentiation of conditions between the collective agreements based on the favourability principle; (b) prohibition on increases beyond the EGSSE (National General Collective Labour Agreement); (c) changes in the procedure and content of Mediation and Arbitration, enhancement of Reconciliation procedure.

In that way, a decentralization of collective bargaining from the level of sector/craft to the company level has been promoted, and afterwards

Table 5.1   Memoranda measures on collective labour relations

Terms	Memorandum	Dates of implementation
Differentiation in collective agreement terms (Law 3845/10)	1	6.5.2010, 15.12.2010 29.6.2011,
(a) Employers' representation in the banking industry, (b) Electronic Database of Collective Regulation (Law 3846/2010)	1	20.10.2011
Prohibition on wages increases (Law 3871/2010)	1	
(a) Mediation and Arbitration, (b) Function of Organization for Mediation and Arbitration (OMED)	1	
Establishment of special company-level agreements	1	
(a) Abolition of special company-level agreements, (b) Collective Agreements with the "Unions of persons" associations, (c) Prevalence of company-level agreements, (d) Amendments in the provisions of Law 1876/1990, Law 4024/2011, Law 3996/2011—Conciliation (Law 3996/2011)	1	
Prevalence of legislative provisions against collective agreements in the public sector	1	
(a) Decrease in minimum wages of EGSSE; (b) Duration, extension of after-effect of collective agreements; (c) Freezing wage increases; (d) Abolishment of permanent employment in Public Enterprises and Utilities; (e) Waiver of the right for unilateral action to the Arbitration (Law 4046/12, Ministerial Council Act 6/29.02.2012)	2	10–12.2.2012
Wage cuts	3	(14.8.2016; expected
Draft Law on employment relations	3	adoption date)
Draft Law on collective bargaining	3	

Source: Based on Kyriakoulias (2012), Kouzis (2015), OMED (2012a)

to the individual bargaining between the employee and the employer (Kyriakoulias 2012; Ioannou 2011).

The specific measures of the Memoranda concerning collective labour relations have been described in Table 5.1.

The Dynamics of Social Dialogue Before Memoranda

According to the Greek Economic and Social Committee (OKE), social dialogue can be defined as attempts that aim to touch differing opinions and interests in order to solve common problems or efforts to explore and to appoint common targets regarding related issues or simply procedures that help distinct social groups to exchange ideas (OKE 1999). It is generally accepted that social dialogue procedures have been an essential prerequisite that promotes successful economic and social policies (Koutroukis and Kretsos 2004, 2008). A similar social dialogue procedure has begun in Greece during the 1990s when the government had accepted to consult with social partners before any of its initiatives concerning economic and social policy (OKE 2002).

Thus, social partners' role has been changed and a new model of coordination was adopted that promoted a limited intervention of the state in industrial relations. Furthermore, several developments towards a system of free collective bargaining and voluntary labour disputes settlement have been promoted (Lavdas 2007). In the early twenty-first century, Greece was one of the EU countries where the international trend to decentralize wage bargaining was hindered by the central regulation of wages (Lavdas 2007). That centralized bargaining played a key role in setting wages at sectoral, company and local levels (Ioannou 2011; Lavdas 2007).

Especially in Greece, OKE had a rather successful operation before the financial crisis of 2008. OKE, for example, has concluded 18 opinions in 2006, 26 in 2007 and 19 in 2008, and those opinions have partly incorporated in several laws (OKE 2009). However, the objective preconditions for efficient functioning of the social dialogue have not been fairly completed, resulting thus in moderate effectiveness of most social dialogue institutions (Vogiatzoglou 2014; Kouzis 2015; Zambarloukou 2014; Koutroukis 2004).

Developments in Social Dialogue After the Implementation of Memoranda

Social Dialogue at the Macroeconomic Level

Crisis has been a starting point for adaptation of employee relations to firm-specific circumstances. After the year of implementation of Memorandum 1 (2010), Government attempted to promote a social dialogue process on issues of economic, social and labour policy, but the Greek Worker Confederation refused to participate (Patra 2012). Although the provision for social partners' consultations before the implementation of labour policy measures was included in the Memorandum, trade unions avoided to participate, because they believed that the consultations would be fruitless.

The international and European institutions (EU, ECB and IMF) involved and the Greek government as well shaped the agenda of reforms without a minimum procedure of social dialogue. Furthermore, the Memoranda have affected long standard practices of social dialogue, that is, levels of bargaining and coverage rates of collective agreement, and contributed to the emergence of several new "negotiated" responses to the crisis.

The most important social dialogue forum, that is, the OKE, hardly ever has participated in those procedures, since most legislative initiatives regarding the labour market were introduced by urgent procedure (Lanara-Tzotze 2013). Nevertheless, most formal or informal social partners' proposals were rejected by the Lenders (Patra 2012). In ad hoc bipartite negotiations of employer's organizations and trade unions (General Confederation of Workers, Confederation of Greek Industries, Hellenic Confederation of Professionals, Craftsmen & Merchants, and Greek Confederation of Commerce and Entrepreneurship) revealed no results that would be accepted by the Ministry of Labour (Patra 2012). However, on 15.7.2010, the employer and employee organizations concluded the National General Collective Labour Agreement (EGSSE) for the years 2010–2012 after pertinent consultations.

On 14.5.2013, the EGSSE was concluded for the year 2013, the main points of which provided that the wages would be stable and the marriage benefit as well as the institutional terms of previous contracts of EGSSE would remain in force. A similar EGSSE was signed for years 2014 and 2015 at a social partners' roundtable.

Even in the summer 2015, an emergency procedure was followed in order to complete the adoption of the terms stipulated by the Third Memorandum. However, there were significant constraints in order to carry out some kind of social consultations with social partners (Zambarloukou 2014).

Six years after the beginning of joint EC-ECB-IMF Programmes, the implications of those developments, which have affected the bargaining process, could be summarized as follows:

(a) Decrease of sectoral collective agreements or arbitration decisions from 142 in 2008 to 17 in 2015 (Table 5.2).
(b) Increase of company-level agreements from 215 in 2008 to 975 in 2012 and 263 in 2015 (Table 5.2).
(c) Lower coverage of the workforce by collective agreements from 65% before Crisis to approximately 10% in 2014 (Cutcher-Gershenfeld et al. 2015).
(d) Adoption of a new model of collective agreement within the union-free companies between the management and controversial worker groups, called "*association of persons*" (Cutcher-Gershenfeld et al. 2015).

The New Background of Collective Bargaining: Some Data

Memoranda caused enormous changes in the Greek collective bargaining system. In their study, Ioannou and Papadimitriou (2013) have reflected a significant decline in sectoral collective agreements (Fig. 5.1) and arbitration decisions (Fig. 5.2) and, furthermore, an increase of the company-level ones (Table 5.2 and Fig. 5.3).

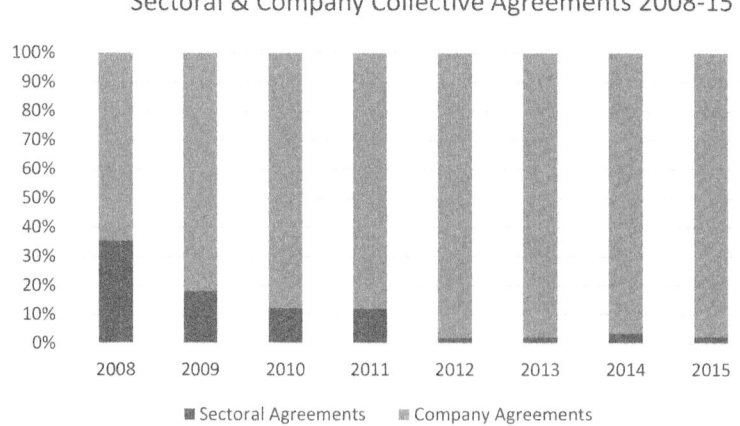

Fig. 5.1 Collective agreements, 2008–2015. Source: Based on OMED (2012b, 2013, 2014, 2015, 2016)

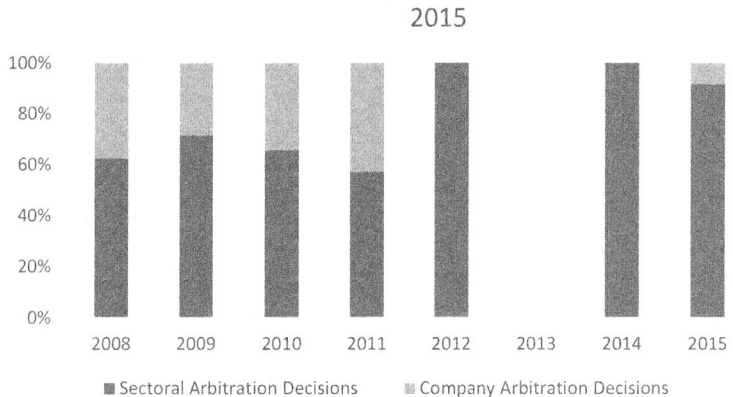

Fig. 5.2 Arbitration decisions during 2008–2015. Source: Based on OMED (2012b, 2013, 2014, 2015, 2016)

Table 5.2 Collective bargaining in Greece by sort and output 2008–2015

Year	Craft				Sectoral		Company		Total			Rate %	
	National		Local										
	CA	AD	CA	AD	CA	AD	CA	AD	CA	AD	CA+AD	CA	AD
2008	43	17	27	2	117	25	215	15	403	59	462	87.2	12.8
2009	15	11	12	5	47	30	215	12	289	58	347	83.3	16.7
2010	33	8	14	6	31	21	227	11	306	46	352	86.9	13.1
2011	15	5	7	1	23	12	170	9	215	27	242	88.9	11.1
2012	4	1	6	4	19	7	975	–	1004	8	1012	99.2	0.8
2013	4	–	10	–	9	–	409	–	433	–	433	100	0.0
2014	3	–	5	–	10	2	286	–	305	2	307	99.3	0.7
2015	5	–	7	–	6	11	263	1	282	12	294	95.9	4.1

Source: Based on OMED (2012b, 2013, 2014, 2015, 2016) (*CA* collective agreements, *AD* arbitration decisions)

The trend towards decentralization of collective bargaining is noticeable, while from 2012 to 2014, just ten arbitrator decisions were issued (Fig. 5.2). During the period of 2011–2014, the number of sectoral agreements was decreased mainly due to the temporary waiver of the right to unilateral action arbitration and the large increase of company-level

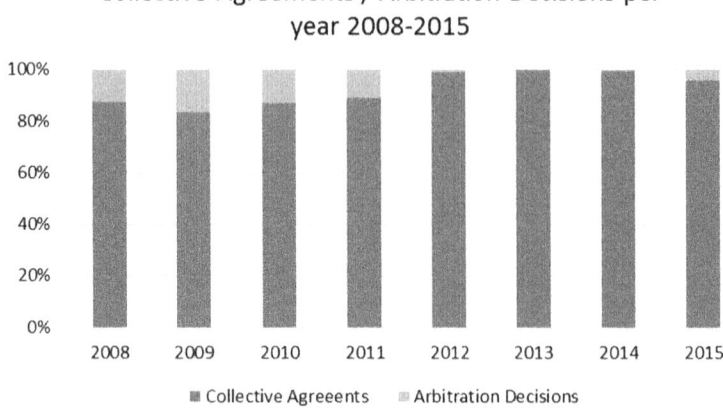

Fig. 5.3 Collective regulation by sort, 2008–2015. Source: Based on OMED (2012b, 2013, 2014, 2015, 2016)

agreements (Fig. 5.1). At the same period, the coverage of labour market by collective agreements was strictly limited, that is, the average of 190 agreements, which regulated the wages and working conditions in large sectors of production (Ioannou 2015).

At the end of 2015, not even 10% of the regulations provided by Collective Labour Agreement (CLA) were in force or the existing agreements did have significant impact on employee relations. Moreover, the company-level agreements were increased in comparison with the past years (Ioannou 2015). However, that decentralizing trend of company-level agreements slowed down after a certain period of time (during the years of 2012–2015 earnings, reduction of 15% in wages was completed).

"*Association of persons*" was the mechanism that was used to avoid the sectoral agreements. In 2012, 976 company-level agreements were concluded (83.4% with "*Association of Persons*", 5.1% with company unions and 11% with primary local branch unions). Finally, with the company-level agreements, the national collective bargaining system has been decentralized, while the initiative to terminate the company-level agreements has been undertaken by the employers (Ioannou and Papadimitriou 2013). In autumn of 2014, the legal framework for arbitration in collective labour disputes was updated, and the competent arbitrating mechanisms of the Organization for Mediation and Arbitration (OMED) (Arbitrators, three-member and five-member Arbitration Committees) have begun to issue arbitrator decisions (Ioannou 2015).

The failure in providing sectoral collective agreements is connected with (Ioannou 2015): (a) social partners' disagreements during the negotiations on wages and benefits, (b) institutional amendments during the years 2012–2014 (waiver of the right of unilateral action to arbitration) and (c) structural reasons linked with the collapse of Greek economy (large fall in employment and the number of enterprises due to Crisis).

In Fig. 5.1, the evolution of the CA during the period 2010–2015 is reflected, and in Fig. 5.2, the evolution of AD during the same period has been shown. In Fig. 5.3, the sort of collective regulation (collective agreement or arbitrator decision) is reflected too.

Memoranda and Their Impact on Greek Industrial Relations: An Assessment

Over the last 20 years, our country has experienced an uncompleted but significant venture of social partnership (Vogiatzoglou 2014). Mainly in issues of economic and social policies, a certain culture of social partner dialogue has been embedded and institutions, such as OKE and OMED, have developed a remarkable activity. That situation changed radically in recent years due the effect of Memoranda.

In 2010, the Greek government, facing a huge public debt, had requested for financial aid from the EU and IMF (Tsarouhas 2012) and was obliged to adopt measures of austerity, reforms in the markets and fiscal discipline. Therefore, those measures are claimed to have violated the Constitution and several International Labour Conventions (Venieris 2011; Kouzis 2015).

Attempting to justify its measures, government claimed—and this was partly inaccurate—that strong pressures raised by the market did not provide adequate time to discuss those agreements with our Lenders in social dialogue fora (Kyriakoulias 2012). Greek collective bargaining system provided by Law 1876–1890 that was used to function effectively in years of prosperity was unprepared to discuss profoundly the competitiveness and internal devaluation issues highlighted by the financial crisis and the country's agreement for the activation of the support mechanism (Ioannou 2011; Zambarloukou 2014).

In the new era, the tripartite social partners' cooperation was set aside and Troika—later on as a Quartet—co-decided with the government a series of measures to adapt labour market in the new conditions. The apparent domination of the usual approach of the IMF in shaping economic and social policies has abandoned the culture of tripartism of EU and International Labour Organization (ILO) and contributed to the collapse of any social partnership elements (Koutroukis and Roukanas 2016).

Those reforms in the labour market and collective bargaining system were pursuit without reliable social dialogue, confirming thus Hyman (2010, p. 7), who claimed that "…in countries with little previous tradition of such concentration, the crisis of 2008–2009 does not seem to have had the same effect. This may be in part a reflection of the speed and enormity of the crisis: where the necessary institutions were not already well established, the urgency of the situation provided little scope for their creation".

The new legislation and austerity measures have created a new social environment that has strongly affected the re-distribution of power and the role of actors of Greek industrial relations system.

After Memoranda having been implemented, the procedures of social partnership and wage bargaining were replaced by Lenders' monologue (Lanara-Tzotze 2013). Government's strategy and policies on the issues of economy obeyed more Lenders' directions than social partners' will, though employers' organizations and trade unions had limited impact and low bargaining power thus far (Voskeritsian and Kornelakis 2011).

The uncertain future of social dialogue will be dramatically affected by the weakening of trade unions (due to the rapid decline of unionization and workforce employment in more unionized sectors, such as banks) and the loss of their economic independence (Koutroukis and Roukanas 2016).

Furthermore, the high unemployment rate and consequences of growing work flexibility have in any case undermined trade unions' effort to recruit new members in the private sector. In those circumstances, it seems that the trade unions' willingness to make concessions to the employers, by hoping to save jobs, has significantly increased (Glassner and Keune 2010). Anyhow, globalization has already increased the imbalance of power between capital and labour and in combination with the crisis has minimized the possibility to conclude win–win agreements (Hyman 2010).

In the new labour market background, employers side is not sufficiently motivated to adopt the social partnership culture, while they may avoid the sectoral collective agreements and to regulate de facto (unilaterally) the terms of remuneration and working environment status (Koukiadaki and Kretsos 2012; Patra 2012). Consequently, the market itself—and not the government or the social partners at collective level—will rule the remuneration and working conditions (Zambarloukou 2014). Moreover, a pertinent study has found that certain social, equity-related and redistributive aspects of collective bargaining and its subsidiary role concerning social and employment security had been weakened (Eurofound 2015, p. 53).

The activation of an arbitration procedure on wages and working conditions has been more difficult (Fig. 5.3); it seems that the future terms of the labour contract will be mainly determined with company-level agreements and individual contracts in a labour market with a high degree of flexibility. The alternative tripartite approach to economic and social crisis was considered to be a "*waste of time*" that would delay the implementation of the measures and was abandoned when some interesting outputs could be delivered (Zambarloukou 2014; Lanara-Tzotze 2013).

CONCLUSIONS

To sum up, bipartite or tripartite partnership in pertinent reforms has become meaningless. If the directions of Memoranda are fully implemented in the Greek labour market, neither will there be any room for social dialogue nor for sectoral collective bargaining. Lender representatives and the market, with governments to obey to their directions, seem to remain the powerful partners in the unsuccessful Greek project of social partnership. Although this is considered to be a temporary and necessary practice, it may prove to be permanent within the next years. That development will be affected by the industrial relations climate, the durability of social dialogue institutions, the social partners' willingness to participate in such procedures and the influence of the European social partnership model.

In the long term and given the current balance between capital and labour, a realistic response to the crisis would be the adoption of an "*organized decentralization*" of social dialogue, that is to say a process by which the agreements at the higher level would establish a framework of principles and regulations, in which the collective bargaining at decentralized level will be conducted (i.e. local employment pacts, company-level agreements). Consequently, social partners could determine certain minimum wages and working conditions at decentralized level via a dialogue procedure. Thus, beyond any national and/or sectoral regulations, flexibility and individualized determination of terms of the labour contract will be partially limited, if it so wished.

REFERENCES

Cutcher-Gershenfeld, J., Brooks, D., Cowell, N., Ioannou, C., Mulloy, M., Roberts, D., Saunders, T., & Viemose, S. (2015). Financialization, collective bargaining, and the public interest. In C. Weller (Ed.), *Inequality, uncertainty and opportunity: The varied and growing role of finance in labor relations* (pp. 31–56). Champaign, IL: LERA Series.

Eurofound. (2015). *Collective bargaining in Europe in the 21st century.* Luxemburg: Publication Office of the European Union.

Glassner, V., & Keune, M. (2010). *Negotiating the crisis? Collective bargaining in Europe during the economic downturn* (Working Paper 10). Geneva: International Labour Office.

Hyman, R. (2010). *Social dialogue and industrial relations during the economic crisis: Innovative practices or business as usual?* (Working Paper 10). Geneva: International Labour Office.

Ioannou, C. (2011). Tectonic changes in the wage formation system in Greece. *Greek Review of Social Research, 134–135*(A–B), 133–164. (in Greek).

Ioannou, C. (2015). Collective bargaining, collective agreements and wages in Greek economic crisis. *Labour Law Review, 74*(11), 1373–1401.

Ioannou, C., & Papadimitriou, K. (2013). *Collective bargaining in Greece in 2011 and 2012: Trends and perspectives.* Athens: OMED, No 2. (in Greek).

Koukiadaki, A., & Kretsos, L. (2012). Opening Pandora's box: The sovereign debt crisis and labour market regulation in Greece. *Industrial Law Journal, 41*(3), 276–304.

Koutroukis, T. (2004). Social dialogue at the local level: The case of Imathia. *Social Science Tribune, 40*, 149–169. (in Greek).

Koutroukis, T., & Kretsos, L. (2004). *Social dialogue in Greece: The national and the local dimension, in Labour.* Athens: Institute for Urban Environment and Human Resources. (in Greek).

Koutroukis, T., & Kretsos, L. (2008). Social dialogue in areas and times of depression: Evidence from social Greece. *African Journal of Business Management, 2*(4), 077–084.

Koutroukis, T., & Roukanas, S. (2016). Social dialogue in the era of Memoranda: The consequences of austerity and deregulation measures on the Greek social partnership process. In A. Karassavoglou, Z. Aranelović, S. Marinković, & P. Polychronidou (Eds.), *The first decade of living with the global crisis, economic and social developments in the Balkans, and Eastern Europe* (pp. 73–82). Cham: Springer.

Kouzis, G. (2015). Labour at the gunpoint during the period of crisis and Memoranda. *Social Policy, 3*, 7–18. (in Greek).

Kyriakoulias, P. (2012). *Labour relations after the memorandum: Overview of labour legislation reform 2010–12.* National Institute of Labour and Human Resources, 2/2012, February. (in Greek).

Lanara-Tzotze, Z. (2013). *The impact of anti-crisis measures and the social and employment situation: Greece.* European Economic and Social Committee.

Lavdas, K. (2007). Interest groups in disjointed corporatism: Social dialogue in Greece and European 'competitive corporatism'. *West European Politics, 28*(2), 297–316.

OKE. (1999). *Social dialogue in Southeastern Europe* (Opinion No. 29). Athens. (in Greek).

OKE. (2002). *Social dialogue in Greece: Assessment-trends-prospects* (Opinion). Athens. (in Greek).

OKE. (2009). *Report of activities 2008.* Athnes: OKE.

OMED. (2012a). *Legal framework of collective bargaining, mediation and arbitration* (updated legislation). Athens: OMED. (in Greek).

OMED. (2012b). *Annual report 2011.* Athens: OMED. (in Greek).

OMED. (2013). *Annual report 2012.* Athens: OMED. (in Greek).

OMED. (2014). *Annual report 2013.* Athens: OMED. (in Greek).

OMED. (2015). *Annual report 2014.* Athens: OMED. (in Greek).

OMED. (2016). *Annual Report 2015.* Athens: OMED. (in Greek).

Patra, E. (2012). *Social dialogue and collective bargaining in the time of crisis: The case of Greece* (Working paper No 38). Geneva: ILO.

Tsarouhas, D. (2012). The political origins of the Greek crisis domestic failures and the EU factor. *Insight Turkey, 14*(2), 83–98.

Venieris, D. (2011). Economic crisis and social policy deregulation: The new "Greece minor disaster" 2010–2011. *Greek Review of Social Research, 134–135*(A'–B'), 101–131. (in Greek).

Vogiatzoglou, M. (2014). Die griechische Gewerkschaftbewegung: Protest und Sozialbewegungen im Kontext der austeritatspolitiki. *WSI Mitteilungen,* 5.

Voskeritsian H., & Kornelakis, A. (2011). *Institutional change in Greek industrial relations in an era of fiscal crisis* (Working paper No 52). Hellenic Observatory, London: LSE.

Zambarloukou, S. (2014). Social dialogue and collective agreements before and after crisis. In S. Zambarloukou & M. Kousi (Eds.), *Social views of crisis in Greece* (pp. 247–272). Athens: Pedio. (in Greek).

CHAPTER 6

Unregistered Economic Activities During the Greek Multidimensional Crisis

Aristidis Bitzenis and Vasileios Vlachos

The political, economic and social dimensions of the Greek economic, banking, social and sovereign debt crisis have turned attention to the size and impact of the unofficial economy. The relation between corruption and the unofficial economy in Greece and their role in the Greek crisis have stimulated discussion at an international level about the potential of unregistered economic activities to provide economic succor in times of crisis. The particular discussion has evolved into two core themes, one about whether the unofficial is a substitute for the official economy in economic downturns and another that concerns the means through which there can be a transfer of a part of the unofficial to the official economy (i.e. to register unregistered economic activities). The latter theme has also gained attention from supranational institutions, as, for example, there was a discussion in the European Parliament on the subject (EESC 2014).

This chapter mentions the roots of the multidimensional Greek crisis as far as their relation with the levels of corruption and the size of the unofficial economy in Greece are concerned. Moreover, based on the European Union (EU) institutions' definition and interest in unregistered economic

A. Bitzenis (✉) • V. Vlachos
University of Macedonia, Thessaloniki, Greece

© The Author(s) 2017
J. Marangos (ed.), *The Internal Impact and External Influence of the Greek Financial Crisis*, DOI 10.1007/978-3-319-60201-1_6

85

activities, it explores what part and under what circumstances can these activities be transferred to the official economy in Greece. The aim is to discuss these issues and to focus on the least explored aspect of tax compliance in Greece, namely tax morale, through unique primary data collected in the auspices of an EU THALES project[1] on the Greek shadow economy.

With the shortcomings of Greek tax authorities on the one hand, either with regard to tax collection or with reference to auditing and enforcement, and the large size of the country's shadow economy on the other hand, the chapter aims to answer the question whether someone may evade taxes in Greece because he/she wants or can (or both). The findings from primary data collected in the auspices of the EU THALES project on the Greek shadow economy contribute to the ongoing international debate on enforced versus voluntary tax compliance (slippery slope framework) and highlight the factors favoring the transfer of unregistered economic activities to the official economy in Greece.

The chapter is organized as follows. The next section discusses the increasing attention that unregistered economic activities have drawn as the Greek economic crisis deepened. The third section discusses factors associated with the Greek crisis and the country's shadow economy. The fourth section presents estimates of tax morale and participation in unregistered economic activities in Greece. The fifth and final section discusses these estimates and makes some conclusions.

The Transfer of Activities from the Shadow to the Official Economy After the Economic Crisis in the EU

Although the global financial and economic crisis (henceforth crisis) which was triggered in 2007 (subprime and energy crises) has admittedly ended in the first half of the 2010s, full recovery is still in question.[2] The disastrous peripheral impact of the crisis is evident in the financial assistance received by eight members of the EU from European financial assistance mechanisms (DG ECFIN 2014). Four of them were members of the euro area at the time of receiving assistance and the assistance programs to these states but Greece, namely Cyprus, Hungary, Ireland, Latvia, Portugal, Romania and Spain have expired (the latest being Cyprus who completed its three-year Economic Adjustment Program in March 2016). Greece receives its third assistance program, which was launched under the European Stability Mechanism framework in August 2015.

Although the crisis ended, the picture is very different with regard to recovery progress in terms of income, investment and unemployment. The impact of the crisis is still visible across the euro area as several members have not yet fully recovered in terms of Gross Domestic Product (GDP), fixed capital formation and employment. Eurostat (2016) data reveal that by the end of 2015, 10 out of 19 euro area members (only France and Malta from the Mediterranean) recovered (i.e. surpassing the amount reported before they were hit by the crisis) in terms of GDP, four members (Belgium, Germany, Malta and Finland) in terms of gross fixed capital formation and merely two members (Germany and Malta) in terms of employment. The worst recovery performance belongs to the periphery and the south in particular, Greece being the tip of the iceberg. Eurostat (2016) data reveal that by the end of 2015, Greece lost more than a quarter of the GDP and approximately two thirds of the gross fixed capital formation reported in 2007 (in 2008, both indicators started to decrease). With the exemption of 2014 where GDP marginally increased, GDP in Greece decreased from 2008 onward, indicating thus the country's experience of economic depression. In addition, unemployment almost quadrupled from 2008 (last year with decreasing unemployment rates) and remains the highest in the euro area.

The requirement for a broader-based and more sustained recovery has led EU institutions to undertake initiatives such as the European Commission's (EC) Investment Plan for Europe (known as the Juncker Plan) which led to the development of the European Fund for Strategic Investments. The particular investment plan aims to substitute for public investment expenditure, since the latter has been contracted under the requirements of debt sustainability and the generation of balanced government budgets (if not surpluses). Before the fruition of this initiative, EU institutions have considered alternate options to enhance government revenue and assist economic recovery.

Following the request by the European Parliament's Committee on the Internal Market and Consumer Protection, a report was prepared by the Directorate-General for Internal Policies about transferring activities from the unofficial to the official economy (Muller et al. 2013). It is stated in the particular report that illegal activities of the unofficial economy, involving the supply of legal goods and services (and not illegal activities), constitute the shadow economy (Muller et al. 2013). The reason for preferring the particular definition (among others) of unregistered economic activities is due to the prospect of transferring activities from the shadow to the official economy. After the European Parliament discussion on the shadow economy, which was based on the Muller et al. (2013) report mentioned above, several initiatives have developed toward transferring activities from the shadow to the official economy (indicating thus the importance of this matter on an EU (supranational) level).[3]

The preference to focus on the shadow economy (as defined above) was also revealed by EC Notes on the shadow economy as part of the Europe 2020 strategy. This preference was again due to the prospect of transferring activities from the shadow to the official economy. For example, according to an EC Note on undeclared work: *"the transformation of undeclared work into formal work is an important issue for the current employment policy … and represents an important step towards job creation and the fulfillment of the employment targets of the Europe 2020 strategy"* (EC 2013, p. 3). Although co-operation between the European Parliament and the EC regarding this matter is evident in official EU documents published at a later date (see EESC 2014), it is clear from the earlier documents that the transfer of activities from the shadow to the official economy is *an important step toward job creation and the fulfillment of the employment targets of the Europe 2020 strategy* (EC 2015, p. 4). Moreover, it is stated in the EC Note on undeclared work (EC 2013, p. 4) that the EC will provide support and technical assistance to Member States for transferring activities from the shadow to the official economy and a reference is made to Greece.

Outside the attention and focus of EU institutions discussed above, several European States have considered tackling the shadow economy for economic recovery. It was 2013 when the abovementioned reports and notes were published and the topic was gaining attention from international organizations, such as VISA and A.T. Kearney. The difference between the EU focus and the perspective of these organizations is in the treatment of the shadow economy for achieving economic recovery, since the latter (i.e. VISA) propose to restrain unregistered economic activities through electronic payments.

Academic research and opinions on tackling the shadow economy for economic recovery have also preceded the abovementioned attention and focus of EU institutions. Again, although these studies shared the same goal, only a few discussed why it is crucial to transfer activities from the shadow to the official economy for economic recovery (e.g. see Bitzenis et al. 2013).

The efforts to restrain unregistered economic activities do not account for factors, such as tax morale, which enable the transfer of these activities to the official economy. On the contrary, these factors have been accounted for, in the support and technical assistance of the EC to Member States. For example, in a report on undeclared work in Greece (ILO 2016), prepared in the process of the support and technical assistance that the country receives during the economic adjustment programs, tax morale is explored as a driver and is related to the (possible) measures (to be) adopted. The contrasting perspectives regarding the measures to combat the shadow economy indicate that the Greek experience may actually be the first attempt toward the formation of policies aiming to transfer activities from the shadow to the official economy rather than to simply reduce the size of the shadow economy.

THE MULTIDIMENSIONALITY OF THE GREEK CRISIS AND THE GREEK SHADOW ECONOMY

By the end of 2009 and in the beginning of 2010, as a result of the global crisis and uncontrolled government spending, economic scandals, large tax evasion rates, high corruption and large numbers of bureaucratic procedures, the Greek economy faced its most severe crisis since 1974 as the Greek government revised its deficit from an estimated 6 percent to 15.4 percent of GDP in 2009 (Vlachos 2013, p. 137). Since then, the country faces three interlocked (banking, sovereign debt and growth) crises, which fuel a deflationary spiral that has entrapped the economy into depression (henceforth Greek economic crisis).

The factors contributing to the escalation of the Greek economic downturn are not unrelated to each other and reflect an institutional setting that needs to be altered for Greece to exit from the economic crisis. Within this context, corruption, bureaucracy and official (and unofficial) economic activity in Greece are interlinked and constitute a dangerous mixture which is responsible for the country's low productivity rates and the unfriendly business setting.[4] Literature surveys on the Greek economic crisis and the country's shadow economy (e.g. see respectively Vlachos 2013; Bitzenis et al. 2016a) indicate that clientelism and rent-seeking behavior are the main phenomena inflating systemic corruption. The relationship between corruption and institutional ineffectiveness is the primary indicator for the existence of a complementary relationship between the size of the shadow economy and corruption. Bitzenis et al. (2016a) discuss the relation between the size of corruption and the size of the shadow economy in Greece, and find that their relationship is complementary. Moreover, the authors refer to the rapid decline of Greece's Corruption Perception Index scores in 2009 and relate this decline with the events starting in the summer of 2009 (Greek elections following the announcements of austerity measures, the issue of falsified Greek statistics, the continuously revised deficit and the rise of Greek sovereign bond spreads), which led to the eruption of the Greek sovereign debt crisis and the disclosure of several political scandals. The increase in perceived corruption did not reflect an increase in actual corruption but rather the realization that the economic benefits from systemic corruption would decrease sharply.

In relation to the abovementioned, very interesting findings are derived from Cooray et al. (2017) about the complementary relationship between corruption, shadow economy and public debt. Since large shadow economies reduce tax revenues and increase public debt levels, a reduction in the levels of corruption leads to a fall in the size of the shadow economy and thus public debt.

Greece's Corruption Perception Index scores are among the worst in the EU. Macroeconomic estimates indicate that the average size of the Greek shadow economy (2003–2014) was 25.4 percent of GDP and is among the largest in the euro area. The same estimates indicate that the size of the Greek shadow economy has been declining since 2011 (Schneider et al. 2015; Bitzenis et al. 2016a). This trend contradicts all expectations, since the effect of the policies adopted after the eruption of the crisis on three of the main drivers of the shadow economy (tax and social security burden and unemployment are record high and tax morale has worsen) should have led to a different outcome. Possible explanations may be statistical errors, miscalculations (e.g. these methods do not account for the effect of migration), the decrease of self-employment (Eurostat data indicate that self-employment in Greece decreased from 1.33 million in 2008 to approximately 1.1 million in 2015), the relocation of Greek enterprises to neighboring EU countries with lower corporate tax rates (under the assumption that it is more efficient to be taxed at a lower rate than to evade higher taxes) and the increase of credit/debit card payments (not only due to the capital restrictions imposed in 2015 but mainly as a result of the rising use of credit as disposable income decreases).

The effect of the crisis on the determinants of the shadow economy suggests that the contraction in Greek shadow economy may well be the outcome of ceasing unregistered economic activities and not that of transferring them to the official economy. The act of ceasing unregistered economic activities contrasts with the discussion in the preceding section about the importance of transferring part of the shadow to the official economy. Bitzenis et al. (2016a) highlight this issue and argue that since the economic adjustment programs do not allow for a reduction of the tax and social security burden and for policies that would drastically decrease the levels of unemployment, all efforts should turn into the improvement of citizens' tax morale.

Indeed, the importance of tax morale is also discussed in the report of International Labour Organization (2016, pp. 9–10) on fighting undeclared work in Greece. The report stresses that a major difference between formal institutions that prescribe "state morality" about what is socially acceptable (i.e. laws and regulations) and informal institutions that prescribe "citizen morality" (i.e. socially shared rules) persists in Greece. The failings of formal institutions are responsible for the levels of undeclared work in Greece, where state morality is different from citizens' morality. The formal institutional failings considered in the report are institutional voids (e.g. weak welfare "safety net" which forces citizens into undeclared work to survive), institutional inefficiencies or resource misallocations, institutional uncertainty and institutional weaknesses and instability. The particular failings result in citizens viewing as socially acceptable what is deemed illegal by the state and undeclared work arises by the misalignment between their moralities with formal institutions (state morality). The report highlights their importance and states that unless these failings are addressed, then the asymmetry between state and civic morality will persist, and so will the prevalence of undeclared work.

The emphasis of the report on the difference between formal and informal institutions is clearly related with the context of tax morale (Luttmer and Singhal 2014): intrinsic motivation, reciprocity, peer effects and social influences, cultural factors and information imperfections. An exploration of these dimensions would provide policy orientations for the successful transfer of unregistered economic activities to the official economy.

Greek Tax Morale and Participation in Unregistered Economic Activities Amid the Crisis

Although the terms unregistered/informal/unofficial and registered/formal/official economy are used interchangeably in the literature, we prefer to use the term shadow and official economy. These terms are found in the initiatives of European institutions regarding the transfer of unregistered economic activities to the official economy. More specifically, (unregistered) activities of the shadow economy may be transferred to or absorbed by the official economy. The EU THALES research project on the shadow economy discussed in this section aimed to determine the causes behind these activities and to develop proposals that would enable their transfer to the official economy.

Although much has been written on the Greek shadow economy, the dimensions of Greek tax morale remain the least explored. For example, Vlachos and Bitzenis (2016) who investigate the issue within the context of firm tax compliance base their findings on data before the crisis emerged. Kaplanoglou and Rapanos (2015) base their findings on questionnaires filled by undergraduate university students. Bitzenis et al. (2016a) use macroeconomic estimates, and the International Labour Organization (ILO) report on undeclared work in Greece explores the concept through data from the 2013 Eurobarometer survey data (2016, pp. 114–115). Unfortunately, either all five dimensions of tax morale are not explored by these studies and/or their data are not sufficient (i.e. before the crisis or the sample does not reflect the population).

The data presented in this section are the outcome of a questionnaire survey on tax compliance[5] conducted for the EU THALES project titled "The Shadow (Black Economy) in Greece: Size, Reasons and Impact". The purpose of the project was to research and measure all the aspects of the shadow economy in Greece (i.e. tax and social contribution evasion and avoidance, undeclared work, self-consumption, tax morale and tax compliance) including corruption illegal and criminal and acts (i.e. black or underground economy, money-laundering, human and drug trafficking and briberies). Data were gathered from all economic agents in Greece, both citizens and corporations. The research was performed across all sectors/areas of economic activity and aimed the measurement of the Greek shadow economy and the selection and analysis of primary data about its determinants and impact on the official economy. Approximately 15,000 companies and individuals have contributed to the 6 questionnaires of the project.[6]

The following tables present data on Greek citizens' morale (total responses of 4373). Specific questions from the aforementioned questionnaire aimed to reveal the five dimensions of tax morale. Table 6.1 presents the frequencies of responses to the following questions:

(a) Given the economic difficulties that we currently face in Greece, is it expected for someone not to declare part of his/her economic activities?

(b) Do you feel that your tax contribution is rewarding?
(c) If not, is it due to unequal allocation of the tax burden?
(d) If not, is it due to low quantity and quality of public goods and services?
(e) Do you believe that you should pay your tax burden even if other citizens believe otherwise and/or do not pay?
(f) Does morality discourage citizens to evade taxes?
(g) Do high fines discourage citizens to evade taxes?

The responses to all questions except (b) and (e) follow a seven Likert-type scale form, where 1 denotes no, 4 means indifferent and 7 means yes. The data are further analyzed with regard to employment status. Responses to questions (b) and (e) follow a yes or no (and maybe for question (b)) format. The frequencies of the responses in Table 6.1 regard scales 5–7 (positive reaction) for all questions except (b) and (e). Frequencies to responses of questions (b) and (e) are about "no" concerning (b) and "yes" for (e).

The frequencies presented in Table 6.1 reflect the levels of tax morale in Greece amid the crisis. The first column refers to question (a) and indicates that 40 percent of respondents justifies unregistered economic activity due to economic impact of the crisis. The approval rate is much greater for self-employed and entrepreneurs (the latter being employers, while not the former) and much lesser for pensioners and public sector employees. The rest of the columns in Table 6.1 concern the dimensions of tax morale.

With regard to reciprocity, four out of five respondents believe that the tax burden is not rewarding. All employment status categories except entrepreneurs and public sector employees believe that the unfair allocation of the tax burden and the low quantity and quality of public services received are equally important. Entrepreneurs and public sector employees believe that the unfair allocation of the tax burden is more important. Approximately half of the respondents consider peers' actions and will, before deciding whether or not to pay their tax burden. Peers' actions become slightly more important to entrepreneurs than the rest of the employment status categories. Approximately 4 out of 10 respondents have moral restraints (cultural factor) toward tax evasion. Morality becomes slightly more important to pensioners and slightly less important to entrepreneurs. Finally, three out of four respondents regard the imposition of fines as deterrents to unregistered economic activities. Fines are slightly less important to entrepreneurs, self-employed and private sector employees.

Table 6.1 Tax morale in Greece by employment status (frequencies in percentages)

Employment status/ tax morale indicators	Activity in the shadow economy is justified	High tax burden and no reciprocity	No reciprocity due to unfair allocation of the tax burden	No reciprocity due to low quantity and quality of public services received	Considering peers' actions and will, before paying the tax burden	Morality discourages tax evasion	High fines discourage tax evasion
Total[a]	39.9	82.8	77.1	72.0	46.6	41.9	73.9
Unemployed	46.7	80.6	73.8	71.6	49.2	40.8	75.7
Employed (public sector)	32.4	86.9	81.1	67.0	46.6	39.6	71.1
Self-employed (not an employer)	50.4	86.8	82.2	81.1	43.8	41.5	67.9
Entrepreneurs (employers)	52.4	78.7	72.8	61.2	54.4	33.0	67.0
Pensioners	30.7	85.3	78.0	74.7	48.7	47.3	73.3
Employed (private sector)	42.5	87.9	79.5	77.7	47.6	44.0	68.3

[a]Total includes more status categories than those presented here

Table 6.2 Unregistered economic activity by employment status (frequencies in percentages)

Employment status/shadow economy indicator	Participation in unregistered economic activities
Unemployed	71.6
Employed (public sector)	51.8
Self-employed (not an employer)	60.7
Entrepreneurs (employers)	57.3
Pensioners	61.3
Employed (private sector)	64.4

Table 6.2 presents unregistered economic activity (unreported income) by employment status. Unreported income is estimated by the difference in expenses covered by income received and expenses not covered by income received. If the latter is greater than the former, missing income would have to be covered either by credit or by unreported income. Although the provision of loans has been extremely difficult in Greece after the crisis emerged (since Greek banks have been recapitalized three times), credit is still provided to individuals with a steady level of income and is used primarily for installment payments of goods and services purchased and confirmed tax payments. Under the consideration that these purchases do not concern nondurable consumer goods (i.e. daily needs) and that approximately one third of the population lives in a situation at risk of poverty and/or social exclusion (see OECD 2016, p. 17), it is not likely that the expenses not covered by income received (if they are nondurable consumer goods) would be paid through credit. Therefore, the excess of expenses not covered by income received is more likely to indicate the presence of unreported income corresponding to these expenses.

Table 6.2 indicates the percentage of each employment status category that has to cover excess expenses. For the reasons discussed above, the indicator becomes more accurate by concerning (probable) participation in unregistered economic activities and not the size of unreported income. Moreover, the indicator of the unemployed reflects participation with more certainty than the respective indicators of the other employment status categories, since the unemployed have very limited (if no) access to credit. Approximately two out of three unemployed citizens generate their income through unregistered economic activities. Except from public sector employees, the rest of employment status categories have a maximum participation rate in unregistered economic activities a little less or above 60 percent of the sample. Finally, 5 out of 10 of those employed in the public sector participate in the unregistered economic activities.

The participation rates presented in Table 6.2 are well over the percentage of the population justifying unregistered economic activities due to economic depression in Table 6.1, across all employment status categories. This may well be the outcome of respondents' reluctance to discuss such delicate matters (for a discussion about the problems of questionnaire surveys on the shadow economy, see Bitzenis et al. 2016a).

DISCUSSION AND CONCLUSIONS

Recent macroeconomic estimates of the Greek shadow economy indicate a contraction after 2010. The official economy follows a similar trend and continues to shrink as economic depression deepens. Unavoidably, the impact of the economic adjustment programs on the size of the Greek shadow and official economies has brought attention to the possibility of transferring activities from the shadow to the official economy. This possibility has been discussed from a broader perspective by EU institutions and has become an official target of the Europe 2020 strategy. Since there is no particular "recipe" for achieving such a transfer, the discussion in the literature of shadow economy and tax compliance has been about formulating policies according to the importance of the factors determining the size of the shadow economy or tax compliance behavior. More specifically, about whether enforced or voluntary tax compliance (i.e. the slippery slope framework) is more appropriate for fighting the shadow economy. It seems that the lack of a specific process for transferring activities from the shadow to the official economy is due to the bold supposition that all efforts for fighting the shadow economy would end up in achieving this transfer. In other words, it is somehow assumed that any reduction of the shadow economy is an automatic increase (through its transfer) of the official economy. However, this is not the case and we cannot simply assume that by seizing unregistered economic activities, economic agents would continue these activities in the official economy.

The complementarity relationship between the size of the shadow economy and the level of corruption highlights the critical role of institutional efficiency. Institutional efficiency offers an explanation why countries with similar tax burdens (and in the same phase of the economic cycle) have different shadow economy sizes. In the case of Greece, there have been official declarations (e.g. from the ILO) about formal institutional failings which are responsible for the difference between state and citizens' morality (i.e. what should be and what is acceptable). These failings signify the importance of tax morale. Along with the country's experience of economic depression, tax morale indicates whether citizens participate in the shadow economy because they want to or because they can. Greek citizens would want to participate in the shadow economy due to the rising tax burden and the worsening economic conditions and moreover, due to the absence of reciprocity. Moreover, by considering the country's large shadow economy preceding the crisis (i.e. before the tax hikes and the decline in official economic activity), it becomes obvious that Greek citizens would participate in the shadow economy simply because they could (e.g. due to absence of audits or ways to circumvent them). Unveiling the preferences of Greek citizens for unregistered economic activities is critical to the formulation of policies (i.e. enforced or voluntary tax compliance) that would reduce the size of the shadow economy by transferring part of the shadow to the official economy. Policies which seize unregistered economic activities would be extremely harmful for the economy, if they seize the unregistered economic activities of those who do not and cannot have other (or have very limited) sources of income in the official economy due to economic depression. Therefore, policies should altogether aim to find ways to succeed in transferring unregistered economic activities in the official economy.

Tables 6.1 and 6.2 indicate the inclination of Greek citizens for unregistered economic activities. Table 6.1 indicates that approximately 40 percent of Greek citizens approve the participation in unregistered economic activities due to the devastating consequences of economic depression. Table 6.2 indicates that depending on the employment status category, participation in unregistered economic activities may be up to 70 percent. These figures indicate the devastating consequences of adopting policies that do not succeed in transferring unregistered economic activities in the official economy. Alas, this is already taking place since the reduction of the shadow economy from 2011 onward is the outcome of neither economic growth nor institutional adjustment contributing to tax morale improvement or reducing corruption.

The exploration of the dimensions of Greek citizens' tax morale is also presented in Table 6.1. The approval of the participation in unregistered economic activities and the participation rate itself (Table 6.2) indicate that intrinsic motivation is high because of economic depression on disposable income levels. Low reciprocity is a major issue of concern and is attributed to low quantity and quality of public services, the extremely high tax burden and its unfair allocation. The size of the tax burden is the most important of all three indicating the effect of the tax hikes that have taken place amid economic depression. Peer effects and cultural factors (morality) are also present in the shaping of Greek citizens tax morale, with peer effects being more important. Finally, the negative impact of high fines on tax evasion indicates that either the probability to be audited is low, or taxpayers in Greece believe that this may be the case (due to lack of audits in the past). The latter is a sign of information imperfections about the probability to be audited.

The findings on the level of tax morale amid the crisis contribute to the ongoing international debate on enforced versus voluntary tax compliance (slippery slope framework) and highlight the factors favoring the transfer of unregistered economic activities to the official economy in Greece. The low levels of tax morale signify the ethical dimensions of Greek citizens' preference for unregistered economic activities, which in combination with the effect of economic depression on the level of official economic activity indicate the requirement for policies toward institutional adjustment (i.e. boosting the level of tax morale). Similarly to the contribution of the Greek crisis (i.e. economic depression and large activity in the shadow economy) to EU economic growth and social inclusion target setting about the transformation of unofficial into official economic activity, the differential impact of measures on the level of tax morale will inevitably contribute to the formation of policy orientations at a supranational level for achieving this transformation.

Notes

1. The THALES programme was about "Reinforcement of the interdisciplinary and/or inter-institutional research and innovation with the possibility of attracting high standard researchers from abroad through the implementation of basic and applied excellence research". The programme has been co-financed by the European Union (European Social Fund—ESF) and Greek national funds.
2. For a brief overview, see Bitzenis and Marangos (2015).
3. For a discussion of EU initiatives with regard to tax transparency, tax evasion and undeclared work, see Bitzenis et al. (2016b).
4. For a full discussion on unfriendly business environment and difficulties in attracting investment, see Bitzenis and Marangos (2008).

5. Tax compliance questionnaire for citizens available at http://www.paraoikonomia.gr/quest2/?page_id=119 (accessed on 18 Oct. 2016).
6. Information about the project in English is available at http://excellence.minedu.gov.gr/thales/en/thalesprojects/380420 (accessed on 18 Oct. 2016). Further information (publications, questionnaires, etc.) is available at http://www.paraoikonomia.gr (accessed on 18 Oct. 2016).

REFERENCES

Bitzenis, A., & Marangos, J. (2008). The role of risk as an FDI barrier to entry during transition: The case of Bulgaria. *Journal of Economic Issues, 42*(2), 499–508.

Bitzenis, A., & Marangos, J. (2015). Preface. In A. Bitzenis, N. Karagiannis, & J. Marangos (Eds.), *Europe in crisis: Problems, challenges, and alternative perspectives.* New York: Palgrave Macmillan.

Bitzenis, A., Papadopoulos, I., & Vlachos, V. (2013). The euro-area sovereign debt crisis and the neglected factor of the shadow economy. In A. Bitzenis, I. Papadopoulos, & V. Vlachos (Eds.), *Reflections on the Greek sovereign debt crisis.* Newcastle upon Tyne: Cambridge Scholars Publishing.

Bitzenis, A., Vlachos, A., & Schneider, F. (2016a). An exploration of the Greek shadow economy: Can its transfer into the official economy provide economic relief amid the crisis? *Journal of Economic Issues, 50*(1), 165–196.

Bitzenis, A., Vlachos, V. A., & Skiadas, D. (2016b). The legal framework for the shadow economy in the European Union. *International Journal of Diplomacy and Economy, 3*(2), 131–143.

Cooray, A., Dzhumashev, R., & Schneider, F. (2017). How does corruption affect public debt? An empirical analysis. *World Development, 90*, 115–127.

Directorate General for Economic and Financial Affairs (DG ECFIN) of the European Commission. (2014). *Financial assistance in EU member states* [online]. European Commission. Retrieved October 7, 2016, from http://ec.europa.eu/economy_finance/assistance_eu_ms/index_en.htm

European Commission [EC]. (2013). *Europe 2020 thematic fiche "shadow economy and undeclared work"* [online]. European Commission. Retrieved October 17, 2016, from http://ec.europa.eu/europe2020/pdf/themes/07_shadow_economy.pdf

European Commission [EC]. (2015). *Europe 2020 thematic fiche "undeclared work"* [online]. European Commission. Retrieved January 4, 2017, from http://ec.europa.eu/europe2020/pdf/themes/2015/undeclared_work.pdf

Eurostat. (2016). *Eurostat database* [online]. Retrieved September 2016, from http://ec.europa.eu/eurostat/data/database

International Labour Organization [ILO]. (2016). *Diagnostic report on undeclared work in Greece.* Geneva: International Labour Office.

Kaplanoglou, G., & Rapanos, V. T. (2015). Why do people evade taxes? New experimental evidence from Greece. *Journal of Behavioral and Experimental Economics, 56,* 21–32.

Luttmer, E. F. P., & Singhal, M. (2014). Tax morale. *Journal of Economic Perspectives, 28*(4), 149–168.

Muller, P., Conlon, G., Lewis, M., & Mantovani, I. (2013). From shadow to formal economy: Levelling the playing field in the single market. Brussels: European Parliament, Directorate General for Internal Policies. Retrieved October 3, 2016, from http://www.europarl.europa.eu/RegData/etudes/etudes/join/2013/507454/IPOL-IMCO_ET(2013)507454_EN.pdf

OECD. (2016). *OECD economic surveys: Greece 2016.* Paris: OECD Publishing.

Palmieri, S. [rapporteur] (2014). European economic and social committee (EESC), opinion on "A strategy against the shadow economy and undeclared work". *OJ C 177,* pp. 9–14. Retrieved January 4, 2017, from http://eur-lex.europa.eu/legal-content/EN/TXT/?uri=CELEX%3A52013IE2138

Schneider, F., Raczkowski, K., & Mróz, B. (2015). Shadow economy and tax evasion in the EU. *Journal of Money Laundering Control, 18*(1), 34–51.

Vlachos, V. (2013). Not business as usual. In A. Bitzenis, I. Papadopoulos, & V. Vlachos (Eds.), *Reflections on the Greek sovereign debt crisis.* Newcastle upon Tyne: Cambridge Scholars Publishing.

Vlachos, V., & Bitzenis, A. (2016). Tax compliance of small enterprises in Greece. *International Journal of Entrepreneurship and Small Business, 28*(2/3), 380–389.

CHAPTER 7

The Impact of the Financial Crisis on Greece's Defense Diplomacy

Fotini Bellou

The Greek reticence of the early 1990s toward peacetime military engagements was to be replaced in the decade that followed by a growing understanding of the benefits of military and/or defense diplomacy. The post-cold war environment was encouraging forms of cooperative activities among militaries or former adversaries. In addition, the acceleration of peace support operations (PSOs) in response to regional military conflicts leading to humanitarian catastrophes also prompted governments to fashion their involvement through their militaries in operations with humanitarian purposes. The multiple strategic benefits that could be gained from such a state posture were not always visible to national governments. Greece has been such a case. Only in the mid-2000s and after having experienced a learning process through an increasing military engagement especially in PSOs in the Balkans, Greece started to appreciate the strategic benefits of military diplomacy. Yet, the financial crisis which started to have practical implications in 2010 made Greece withdraw from a number of operations and to become reticent to be actively involved in major PSOs or other cooperative military initiatives.

F. Bellou (✉)
University of Macedonia, Thessaloniki, Greece

© The Author(s) 2017
J. Marangos (ed.), *The Internal Impact and External Influence of the Greek Financial Crisis*, DOI 10.1007/978-3-319-60201-1_7

101

This chapter examines the implications of the financial crisis for the defense expenditure and upon reflection for the country's defense priorities, especially those related to its military diplomacy. It would be argued that severe defense budgetary cuts were detrimental to Greece, thus inflicting a strong reconsideration in evaluating its participation in cooperative multilateral activities. A strict rationalization process commenced based on cost–benefit analysis, which fashioned a posture emphasizing military-to-military cooperative initiatives rather than a stance of more diplomatic nature. The evolving difficult geopolitical environment surrounding Greece, especially in the 2010s, also highlighted that contemporary security challenges would require cooperation with allies and neighbors and thus military defense diplomacy could also contribute in practice to this line of thinking. However, the immense budgetary cuts during the last 6 years have prevented Greece from playing a more active role in military defense diplomacy. As this chapter argues, this was not always the case. Greece experienced a learning process through its progressive participation in multinational PSOs since the mid-1990s that seemed to have moderated its previous reticence in defense diplomacy commitments. Athens started to ascertain the multiple benefits of its emerging military defense diplomacy during the 2000s. However, the financial crisis inflicted a strong filtering process to its decisions related to initiatives and programs connected to defense diplomacy. Greece started to prioritize only those initiatives or practices having multiple benefits mainly in the context of its commitments within NATO and the EU and those involving countries of key strategic importance to Athens.

The chapter will first examine the discussion around the concept of military or defense diplomacy and its relevance to a state's national security strategy. It will then analyze the trajectory of reductions in Greece's defense budgeting as compared to the defense cuts of its NATO allies and EU partners. It will be shown that despite its severe cuts following the fiscal crisis starting in 2009, today Greek defense budgeting remains at the level of 2.38% of the country's GDP. Although it appears to slightly exceeding the threshold of 2% of GDP as pledged at the NATO Summit in Wales in 2014, such a percentage in defense spending is related to the progressively shrunk GDP of recent years. Analysis will follow with a discussion on the effects of these budgetary reductions upon the different facets of Greece's military and defense diplomacy. Two key assumptions have emerged. The first is that budgetary reductions in defense have dramatically affected the number of Greek military personnel serving at PSOs abroad. It occurred at time when Athens had started to appreciate the diplomatic, operational as well as strategic value of its military engagement in cooperative or humanitarian multinational peace support initiatives. It was reflecting a belated understanding that such a posture was after all projecting the country's self-image as a regional *status quo* stabilizer. For this reason, a rationalization process has occurred, wherein Greece's military cooperative engagements are considered on a strict cost–benefit analysis for the country's interests.

The second assumption to be made is related to an emerging oxymoron. At a time of severe budgetary reductions, the Greek military is called, as it is the case with rest of its NATO allies and EU partners, to engage in an adaptation process in order to meet the emerging security challenges in the context of European security. This particular development has increased Greece's military engagement in multinational efforts of operational or training cooperative nature. Moreover, the Hellenic Armed Forces have undertaken an unanticipated assignment following the refugee-migration crisis of 2015. Since early February 2016, they have started to coordinate and manage the refugee/migration issue by also involving national agencies. In effect, the military has been inevitably involved in supporting the largely unprepared local authorities, initially in a number of islands in the Aegean and soon in other places in mainland Greece to manage the migration crisis. Its role involved not only assisting in search and rescue operations but also establishing and managing the majority of hosting structures in an effort to provide shelter, and other humanitarian assistance in the face of the mass waves of refugees and migrants smuggled from the Turkish shores.

At first sight, managing the refugee-migration crisis has been an effort that can hardly be considered as serving the country's military and defense diplomacy. After all, the military is assisting in the management of a national humanitarian emergency, as it is usually the case at the international level in similar occasions. However, the international cooperative modes of action that this management has generated, especially with the respective NATO and EU ongoing operations in the region as well as with other EU internal security agencies and Non-Governmental Organizations (NGOs), have arguably rendered the entire endeavor utterly consistent with the logic of defense diplomacy. It has engaged the Hellenic Armed Forces to an unprecedented mode of action during peacetime that involves international and national cooperative activities having a positive humanitarian effect as well as key security and strategic implications.

The Concept of Military/Defense Diplomacy

The idea of employing military capabilities and assets during peacetime to promote an activity, mainly abroad, in order to serve a country's diplomatic and foreign policy objectives is centuries old. In the past, military diplomacy was known with its intimidating face which was known as *gunboat diplomacy* (Cable 1994). It implied the overt use of (naval) power, 'in kinetic or non-kinetic operations designed to intimidate militarily to further a political goal, often unstated, of deterring or coercing an opponent' (Le Miere 2011, p. 57). Although such a practice is often visible today, its non-intimidating counterpart, known as military or defense diplomacy, has gained prominence in recent decades. Conceptually, it refers to 'the use of (peaceful) military in diplomacy, as a tool of national foreign policy' (Muthanna 2011, p. 2). Although the terms military diplomacy and defense diplomacy are used rather interchangeably, a number of scholars prefer to use the term defense diplomacy to denote (du Plessis 2008, cited in Muthanna 2011, p. 2) all those activities 'other than war' performed by the military personnel, including military attachès, whose skills are employed to serve their countries national and international strategic objectives abroad. Muthanna (2011, p. 2) makes a distinction between military and defense diplomacy to argue that the former denotes all those activities performed primarily by a country's military personnel, whereas the latter denotes the entanglement of the entire (non-uniformed) military establishment including the Ministry of Defense (MoD), and perhaps its respective training and educational institutions. In this chapter, the two concepts are treated as synonyms while the term defense diplomacy is preferred and is consistent with the respective academic literature (New Challenges to Defense Diplomacy 1999; Baldino and Carr 2016).

The practices involved in defense diplomacy include military-to-military cooperational activities that facilitate interoperability among friendly countries and at times foster mutual trust among rather inimical countries. During the Cold War, defense diplomacy was extensively performed by the United States and the Soviet Union toward their allies to which they usually provided military equipment, training and certain defense cooperational schemes. With the end of the Cold War, defense diplomacy concentrated mainly on supporting states in transition from Central and Eastern Europe. It involved what Cottey and Forster (2004, p. 6) describe as 'peacetime co-operative engagement with other countries' giving emphasis, on providing military and technical assistance including training to those states experiencing transitional periods toward democratization and post-conflict peacebuilding. Thus, defense diplomacy not only involved the traditional realist understanding of supporting and empowering allies through exchanges, mutual training and transfer of equipment to counterbalance adversaries. It also started to be fashioned as a mode of action that was bound to facilitate 'co-operative relationships with former or potential enemies' (Cottey and Forster 2004, p. 7). For example, '*the Partnership for Peace*' (PfP) program launched by NATO in 1994, fostering military cooperation and assistance to countries of Central and Eastern Europe, is regarded as one of the most successful multilateral programs in the history of defense diplomacy. Moreover, the terms *military assistance* and *training* have also been treated as elements of defense diplomacy (Sachar 2003). Today, these notions are embraced under the understanding of *military capacity building*, which is a term increasingly favored by Western developed democracies as the preferred mode of action toward countries in transition wherein civil–military relations are not always determined by the democratic civilian control of the armed forces.

In addition to the aforementioned activities, defense diplomacy entails two more practices. The first regards the practice of defense attachés that governments exchange primarily on the basis of promoting their defense and other security interests. The second activity that is embedded in defense diplomacy regards the support of and participation in multinational PSOs led by the United Nations (UN) or other regional organizations or state coalitions. It also includes a country's contribution to humanitarian assistance, relief programs or other joint humanitarian initiatives. For this reason, there is a growing conviction among scholars and practitioners that defense diplomacy is essentially contributing to conflict prevention and to crisis management (Singh 2011; Taylor et al. 2014). Its proponents advocate that 'defense diplomacy is the most efficient and cost-effective policy for preventing conflicts today, and for helping to prevent countries from becoming adversaries tomorrow' (New Challenges to Defense Diplomacy 1999, p. 40). This is an understanding shared by several governments (National Framework for Strategic Communication 2012; Tan 2016).

For this reason, defense diplomacy is included as an increasing number of national security and defense strategies describing a number of cooperative military commitments to which governments should be committed to advance their strategic interests and image (New Challenges to Defense Diplomacy 1999, p. 39; Defense Diplomacy Plan 2012; Baldino and Carr 2016, p. 143). Defense diplomacy has also been considered as an instrument of states' strategic communication policy aiming at empowering their peaceful influence abroad (Cheyre 2013, p. 371). Not surprisingly, therefore, the notion has gained a new dynamic in Asia and is extensively practised either on a bilateral basis or on a multilateral basis by regional governments (Storey 2012; Laksmana 2012; Cai 2016). After all, in recent years, it has become evident that military activities having a cooperational character and/or a humanitarian purpose can have at times a stronger leverage in the pursuit of a country's national objectives than aggressive military postures.

THE GREEK MILITARY/DEFENSE DIPLOMACY

Defense diplomacy had been an idea not particularly favored in Greece in the past. Greece started to appreciate the salience of defense diplomacy primarily through its military engagement in the post-conflict Balkans. The country's 'difficult' geographical location as well as its traditional foreign policy stance as a *status quo* state have established for decades a certain conviction in Greece favoring a strong defense posture. This has been a position visible since the 1960s when the Cyprus issue started to dominate Greek–Turkish relations and was to be compounded by Turkey's invasion and consequent occupation of the northern part of Cyprus in 1974. In effect, during the last three decades of the Cold War, defense spending in Greece had been the highest in Europe, with an average of 5.5% of GDP (Kollias 1995, p. 306). The peculiarity of Greece's defense spending was commensurate with its stance adopted in 1985 to declare Turkey, a NATO ally, as the 'main long term strategic threat to Greek national interests' (Kollias 1995, p. 306). Constant challenges in the Aegean, compounded by a conviction of an ineffective reliance on NATO to deter Turkey's increasing revisionism, turned Greece into fashioning an internal balancing through strengthening its armed forces (Dokos and Kollias 2013, p. 2). Indeed, during the last two decades of the Cold War, Greek defense spending as a percentage to GDP ranged between 7.1% and 5.6%, while it 'averaged 15.5% of total government expenditure' (Chletsos and Kollias 1995, p. 884). The Greek average of 6.4% of GDP in defense spending was well above the NATO average of 3.4% (Chletsos and Kollias 1995, p. 884). Defense spending remained high in Greece even after the end of the Cold War.

During the 1990s, the logic of defending its territorial integrity and sustaining high military readiness remained prevalent in Greek considerations despite the emerging popularity of military and defense diplomacy at the time in its wider vicinity. Although Greece was never absent from multilateral initiatives of defense diplomacy, especially those promoted by NATO, the Organization for Security and Cooperation in Europe (OSCE) or the UN, it certainly did not optimize its great number of forces to empower its self-declared image as a regional stabilizer. By sustaining military forces at a level well above 200,000 personnel throughout the period between 1990 and 2003, Greece's posture was indicating that the Cold War had not ended in that part of the world (NATO 2003).

Despite its substantial number of military forces, Greece remained particularly hesitant to play any active role in UN-led operations. Greece had a marginal presence in UN-led operations with the exception of those conducted in its immediate neighborhood. Greece had contributed only to the collective security operation in the first Gulf War in 1991 against Iraq and its ensuing UN observation operations as well as in the operations in Somalia (UNITAF). In other multinational operations, Athens had only a marginal presence, including monitoring elections in South Africa, Palestine and Georgia (Hellenic National Defense General Staff 2016a).

As regards the Balkans, Greece had no presence in the UN-led operation that was launched in 1992 known as UNPROFOR and had a rather marginal presence in the context of the two small operations which were conducted at the time by NATO in cooperation with the Western European Union (WEU) in order to enforce two UN Security Council Resolutions, regarding the enforcement of a no fly zone over the airspace of the former Yugoslavia and the arms embargo applied to the respective territory. Following the Dayton peace agreement in 1995 in Bosnia and Hercegovina and NATO's consequent involvement in implementing its military provisions, Athens started to play a more visible role in PSOs. Through a gradual involvement in all operations that followed in the region; in Bosnia and Hercegovina (since 1995), in Kosovo (since 1999), in FYROM (mainly since 2001) and in Albania, following the crisis of 1997, Greece started to evaluate in practice the multiple advantages of participating in PSOs.

In NATO's operations in Bosnia and Hercegovina, Implementation Force (IFOR) and Stabilization Force (SFOR), Greece contributed with one Special Transport Company of 250 military personnel and 117 vehicles, while one frigate and two Mine Sweepers were supporting operation 'Sharp

Guard', the aforementioned operation enforcing the military embargo over the Adriatic Sea. In addition, 1 C-130 and 17 military personnel were offered to assist the transportation of personnel and material for IFOR/SFOR as well as 15 officers in support of the HQS (HNDGS 2016b). In SFOR operation that followed IFOR in 1996, Greece participated with a Company of 280 military personnel to be included in a Multinational Transportation Battalion led by Belgium which after its withdrawal in April 1997 transferred its authority to the Hellenic Contingent which remained on the ground until early 2003. As officially noted, 'the Hellenic Contingent was transformed into a Transportation Company with one Medical Platoon and one National Support Element', the total strength of which amounted 100 members, while 6 additional officers were assigned to SFOR Headquarters (HNDGS Bosnia-Hercegovina 2016b, p. 3). Greece participated as leading nation from February 2003, with one Military Police Company of 45–50 men, to the SFOR International Military Police, stationed at BUTMIR Camp in Sarajevo.

In the Kosovo operation as authorized by UNSCR 1244/1999, Greece participated in KFOR with a mechanized brigade of 1162 military personnel and 1 C-130 a/c with 10 crew members, and 30 officers and soldiers were to contribute to Allied staffs, HQs and commands. In addition, 157 officers and soldiers were offered to provide host nation support, whereas 1 additional infantry company with engineer elements, consisting of 60 officers and soldiers, as well as 1 support detachment and 1 facilities detachment with a total force of 10, was stationed at Communication Zone South, in Thessaloniki (HNDGS 2016c).

By the time the peacebuilding operation was launched in Kosovo in summer 1999, Greece had already participated in an operation in Albania in 1997 (operation ALBA), formed by a coalition of neighboring nations to help stabilize the country after a financial scandal had forced the government to resign, thus generating a chaotic situation threatening a wider regional destabilization. Athens participated in the stabilization operation with more than 1025 officers and soldiers (HNDGS 2017a). It had already launched an additional large evacuation operation during the days of the crisis with a number of naval vessels in order to safely evacuate nationals from friendly and partner countries (HNDGS 2017b). Greece also participated with a small number of officers and soldiers and some visible supporting medical facilities in all NATO and EU operations taking place in the Former Yugoslav Republic of Macedonia following the 2001 internal crisis which led to the Ohrid Peace Agreement in August 2001.

Greece has also a small presence in the NATO operation in Afghanistan of about 175 officers and soldiers and 2 a/c C-130. Between 22 August 2005 and 2 April 2007, it participated 'with a Field Surgery Hospital which was a medical-treatment unit of 30 beds capacity and 47 cadres, with operational function' (HNDGS 2010). From 2011 onward, Greece's contribution to PSOs has been waning.

The growing interest to bolster its defense diplomacy was reflected in Greece's efforts to empower its position as a mainstream country within the framework of the Euro-Atlantic structures. Thus, Greece welcomed the decision by NATO and later by the EU to establish their regional Headquarters in Greece. The NATO sustains in Thessaloniki one of its nine Graduated Readiness Forces Land Headquarters of the NATO Force Structure known as NATO Rapid Deployable Corps—Greece (NRDC-Gr). By the same token, after Greece's declared availability, the EU Operational Headquarters (OHQ) in Larissa was formed in 2003 which was accredited in 2009 as one the five OHQs of the EU, following a successful exercise (MILEX 09). In 2014, Greece expressed its intention to make available the EU OHQ in Larissa for the deployment of EUFOR CAR in the Central African Republic in February 2014 which was effectively concluded in March 2015.

Greece is also participating in one Battlegroup in the context of force availability to EU operations. It participates in the *HELBROC* Battlegroup which was established in 2005 by the Ministers of Defense of Greece, Bulgaria, Romania and Cyprus and to which Ukraine joined in 2011 (White Paper 2014, p. 75). In addition, a regional initiative to which Greek participates was launched in 2001 known as *South-Eastern Europe Brigade (SEEBRIG)*. It is currently a brigade-size formation which in 2006 was mobilized by Greece to participate with 28 officers (from February to August) in Afghanistan assuming command of the KABUL Multinational Brigade. *SEEBRIG* is one of the practical products of an earlier important defense diplomacy initiative since 1996 involving six Balkan countries (Albania, Bulgaria, Greece, FYROM, Romania and Turkey) which cooperate militarily in order to promote interoperability and to generate trust. Given the current security challenges in the region, Greece considers today this initiative as a particularly important instrument in reinforcing mutual interests with neighboring countries.

Another aspect in Greece's defense diplomacy regards its commitment to various training structures located in different areas of Greece for national and international military personnel. It includes the NATO

Maritime Interdiction Operational Training Centre (NMIOTC) in Souda, Crete, which has evolved into one of the most important military training structures in Greece. It enhances the ability of trainees to perform surface, air and underwater surveillance missions as well as other special operations related to Maritime Interdiction tasks (NMIOTC 2016). Another International Training structure accredited by the UN and other organizations involves the Multinational Peace Support Operations Training Centre (MPSOTC) in Kilkis, in Northern Greece. An additional multinational training facility regards the NATO Missile Firing Installation (NAMFI) in Chania Crete, used by a number of NATO allies such as Germany, the Netherlands, Greece and Belgium on a permanent basis. The Athens Multinational Sealift Coordination Centre (AMSCC)—is another facility offered by Greece aiming to facilitate countries or international organizations to generate assets related to strategic sealift (White Paper 2014, pp. 83–89).

As already indicated, Greece gradually developed a defense diplomacy that not only improved its influence in its region and within its allies, but importantly made clear domestically, especially to the military and political leadership, that the country's national role conception as a regional *status quo* stabilizer required respective practices in order to be convincing abroad. By mid-2000s, it was becoming evident within Greece that the country's participation in PSOs, in multinational military exercises and respective training programs were offering an invaluable learning process that made visible the inevitability of combining international commitments with national defense responsibilities.

Greece, as a member of NATO and the EU, was not a stranger to military and defense diplomacy. Yet, its respective commitments were never commensurate with its hitherto strong defense resources. The substantive transformation of both organizations per se to which Greece has been fully committed promoted extensive cooperational defense modes of action. Training programs, exchanges of military personnel, military exercises and official military and high-level defense visits have been all part of an emerging understanding that diplomatic practices optimizing military components have a multiplying positive effect upon the country's strategic priorities. Such an assumption was further augmented following Greece's effective role as commanding country of operation EUNAVFOR ATALANTA in Somalia, between 2008 and 2009. However, at the time when defense diplomacy started to gain some ground and be appreciated within the Greek military and political thinking, budgetary restrictions posed by the financial crisis visible since 2010 led to a strong reconsideration of the elements through which Athens would pursue its defense diplomacy.

GREEK DEFENSE BUDGET REDUCTIONS: IMPLICATIONS TO DEFENSE DIPLOMACY

Defense spending in Greece remains among the highest within the Alliance, amounting to 2.38% of its GDP, rendering the country one of the four countries whose defense spending exceed the 2% threshold of the Alliance. The others are the United States (3.61%), United Kingdom (2.2%), Estonia (2.16%) and Poland (2%) (NATO 2016b). However, as Fig. 7.1 shows, although Greece's defense expenditures per capita in 2010 US dollars remain above average among its European NATO allies, Athens has experienced a dramatic level of reduction in the last 6 years. In budgetary terms, defense reduction regards a level from 7.31 billion euros in 2009 to 4.15 billion 2016 (Nedos 2016).

By implication, budgetary reductions have also affected the number of military personnel which in turn has been reduced from 135,000 in 2009 to 106,000 in 2016 (NATO Press Release 2016b, p. 8). Yet, Greece remains 'the country with the largest share of military person-

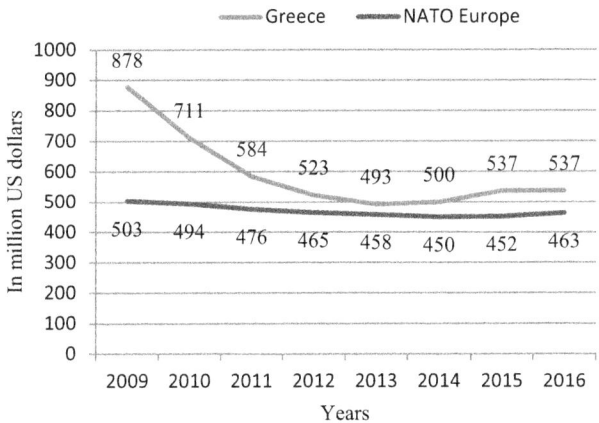

Fig. 7.1   Defense expenditures per capita in 2010 US dollars of European NATO allies. Source: NATO Press Release (2016b)

nel to population in the EU' (Spiegel 2015). Strong criticisms have been observed regarding Greece's large number of military personnel and its high defense budget, despite its financial crisis (Grebe and Sommer 2010; Dempsey 2012; Hooper 2015). Although such criticisms may sound reasonable, one can hardly challenge the argument related to Greece's threat perceptions. The latter are prevalent among Greek public thinking, giving emphasis on Greece's ability to address the challenges as observed in its 'difficult' neighborhood, especially in light of a largely revisionist Turkey (Kouskouvelis 2013; Waszkiewicz 2016; Dokos and Kollias 2013). At a time when different challenges are mounting within and around Europe prompting European governments to reconsider their previous stances on defense spending (Bellou 2016), Greece continues to experience an additional strategic challenge from its eastern neighbor.

Indeed, Turkey appears unhelpful through its constant violations of Greece's sovereign air space and waters, as seen in Figs. 7.2 and 7.3 (HNDGS 2016g). Such an aggressive behavior inevitably initiates a number of military engagements by the Hellenic Armed Forces as long as a number of Turkish violations are conducted by armed aircrafts. No doubt this is a totally undesired waste of resources within the Alliance which pose an inevitable yet unhelpful burden to Greece's budget. Turkey has also publicly expressed its intention, as voiced by President Erdogan, to alter the entire legal framework defining its external borders, including those with Greece as long as they are regarded as outdated and unfair (Danforth 2016).

Such an aggressive stance by Turkey has only compounded an already ambiguous behavior that has raised serious questions about the prospects

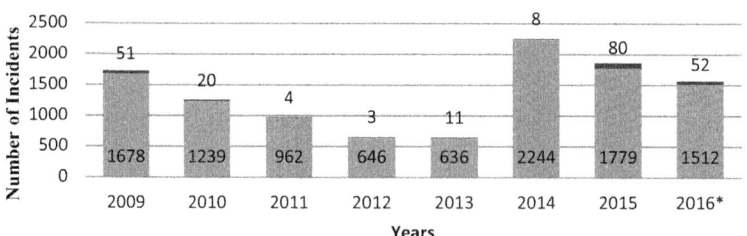

■ Violations of Hellenic Sovereign Airspace ■ Engagement with HAF interception fighters

Fig. 7.2   Turkish violations of Hellenic sovereign airspace including engagement incidents with Hellenic Air Force interception fighters. *Until November 2016. Source: Hellenic National Defense General Staff (2017c)

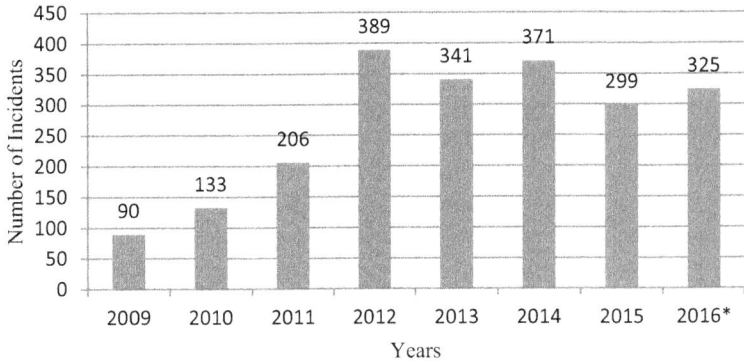

Fig. 7.3 Turkish violations of Hellenic territorial waters. *Until November 2016. Source: Hellenic National Defense General Staff (2017d)

Table 7.1 Annual trajectory of Greek GDP shrinking

Years	2008	2009	2010	2011	2012	2013	2014	2015
Real GDP growth (%)	−0.3	−4.3	−5.5	−9.1	−7.3	−3.2	0.4	−0.2

Source: Eurostat (2016)

of good neighborly relations and has aggravated Greece's security concerns. These are not without reason. For example, as Dokos and Kollias (2013, p. 4) indicate, revelations in the Turkish press some years ago about the infamous trials of few Turkish military officers because of their efforts to plot a staged conflict with Greece, including occupation of its territory, in order to overthrow the Erdogan government (Balyoz plan), or the accusations as voiced by the former Turkish prime minister Mesut Yilmaz 'about Turkish agents being responsible for forest fires in Greek Islands in the 1990s', are only few practical examples of a rather uncertain neighbor. In this light, strong security concerns among Greek public opinion and its political leadership can hardly be entertained.

Against such a background, the substantial reductions in defense expenditures as percentage of the country's progressively shrinking GDP (as shown in Table 7.1) have prompted a serious review process regarding defense priorities, including those related to defense diplomacy.

Although a discussion of the wider changes in Greece's defense policy escapes from the scope of this analysis, it is important to note that the MoD has adopted a New Force Structure for the period 2013–2027 aiming at reorganizing the Hellenic Army in a fashion conducive to the country's responsibilities within the Alliance and its international commitments. Pointing to an important shift toward a greater emphasis on Greece's international commitments, the latest White Paper (2014, p. 58) highlights the country's predilection '*to adapt its structures to those of NATO, in order to respond to the whole range of missions of the Alliance and of international organizations in which the country participates. The changes in its structure aim at the reinforcement of the military capabilities, in order to meet national priorities, in the context of NATO*'. Accordingly, and given its strong budgetary restrictions, the Hellenic MoD is undergoing a multiple reorganization based on a rationalization of its procurement programs, capabilities and character of its forces. Yet, the evolution of such as commitment is yet to be seen in practice.

The financial crisis has caused a strong revision of Greece's previous posture. The key assumption shared among the military leadership is that nowadays all actions are filtered through a strict decision-making process in which the *optimization* of resources and capabilities is *rationalized* on a cost–benefit analysis that certainly reveals a strong sense of *prioritization*, perhaps not always visible before. This very understanding has been diffused in decision making also as regards the country's defense diplomacy. For instance, the number of defense attachés located in various countries has been substantially rationalized. As an EU member, Greece currently prioritizes the capitals to which it shall send its defense attaché strictly on the basis of its strong defense relations. The same logic applies to third countries of vital strategic importance.

A similar cost–benefit analysis has started to be applied to other aspects of Greece's defense diplomacy. A greater emphasis is given on military exchanges and training in the context of Greece's responsibilities within the Alliance and the EU by empowering, for example, its personnel in NRDC-GR in Thessaloniki or in the EU OHQ in Larissa. Given the general reduced interest in PSOs, Greece has strictly prioritized its presence only to operations of key strategic importance. Thus, according to the Hellenic MoD (HNDGS 2017e), Greece sustains a visible presence in the NATO operation Active Endeavour in the Mediterranean with 10 officers and 43 soldiers, 1 torpedo boat or cannon gunboat and 1 underwater demolition team while offering the naval base in Crete for logistic support.

It also participates in operation UNIFIL in Lebanon with 164 officers, 1 torpedo boat or cannon gunboat and 1 landing ship. It also participates in KFOR in Kosovo with no more than 25 officers and 194 soldiers, including an a/c C-130. Almost symbolic is currently Greece's presence in other ongoing operations. It contributes with one officer in operation ENDURING FREEDOM (coalition of the willing), four officers in EUTM Mali (EU-led), eight officers and one a/c C-130 in operation RESOLUTE SUPPORT in Afghanistan (NATO-led) and four officers in operation EUFOR Althea in Bosnia and Hercegovina. It also sustains two Liaison Officers in Belgrade and Skopje. Greece also participates in the Standing NATO Mine Counter Measures Group-2 (SNMCMG-2) to which it had the command for the last semester of 2016 (HNDGS 2016d).

Since February 2016, the Hellenic Armed Forces also participate in the NATO mission launched in the Aegean in order to support the country's efforts along with Turkey and the EU border agency FRONTEX to manage the refugee and migration crisis (NATO Fact Sheet 2016a). Greece's contribution includes one frigate, two naval units, one Super Puma (two sorties/week, one a/c for Intelligence Surveillance), and Reconnaissance-ISR (three sorties/week), three cannon gunboats and six coast guards destroyers in an Associated Support role (HNDGS 2017e). The nature of Greece's participation varies according to the time period discussed. Moreover, Greece had also contributed to the EU NAVFOR operation Sophia with one Erieye (EMB-145H AEW&C), an airborne Command and Control Platform and is currently offering its Forward Logistic Sites as well as its Forward Operation Base, both in Souda, Crete, involving also a small number of officers (HNDGS 2017f). EU Operation Sophia is another naval and information operation against refugee-migration smuggling to Europe coming from offshore of the Middle East and North Africa (MENA) region (EEAS, 2016).

In line of the above, and given the nature of security threats and challenges in the region surrounding Greece, it might appear rather ironic that Athens is substantially decreasing its defense budget, a considerable segment of which (69.93%) covering personnel expenditures including pensions (NATO 2016a, b, p. 8). In reality, Greece is facing a rather compound set of security concerns in its own neighborhood (Litsas and Tziampiris 2015). These security challenges include a number of failed or failing states easy to export certain aspects of destabilizing factors including networks of organized crime, Islamic fundamentalism and terrorism.

This security context is further compounded by the implications of the war in Syria and the military conflicts in the MENA region leading to the acceleration of the migration and refuge waves that culminated since 2015 into the current major refugee and migration crisis facing Greece and Europe in general. Moreover, developments in Eastern Europe, especially after the annexation of Crimea by Russia as well as the latter's involvement in the conflict in Ukraine, have also changed priorities within the Alliance, forcing NATO as well as its members to upgrade as well as to improve their defense and security capabilities and level of readiness.

Against such a compound strategic environment and given its immense budgetary limitations, Greece appears to fashion only those military diplomacy activities that can underpin the strong defense cooperation and security collaboration that is currently officially contemplated between NATO and the EU (Wosolsobe 2016). In effect, one can hardly escape the assumption, widely shared among the military leadership, that budgetary restrictions, to a large extent, almost compelled the Hellenic MoD to allocate efforts and resources to strictly rational actions optimized to offer multiple gains to targeted objectives. For this reason, the promotion of multinational training, targeted military exchanges and an emphasis on conducting common military exercises with allies and friends can be considered the current triptych arguably defining Greece's approach to defense diplomacy. Another aspect affecting the country's defense diplomacy as long as it currently involves some thousands of military personnel regards the role of the Hellenic military forces in managing the refugee and migration crisis in Greece.

THE ROLE OF THE HELLENIC MILITARY IN MANAGING THE MIGRATION CRISIS

In democratic states, it is usual to see the constructive role of the military in support to civil protection services or other internal agencies in major national emergencies of great magnitude. Indeed, the Hellenic Armed Forces had been at times used in national emergencies especially at times of big fire incidents during hot weather conditions or in extended floods during winter in certain regions of the country. More rarely, during harsh weather conditions, the military may provide transportation assistance to medical cases from the Aegean islands. Such activities are legally underpinned by a number of documents such as L2292/95 as well two Ministerial Decisions (1299/2003 (FEK 423 B′/10-4-2003) and 3384/2006 (FEK 776/28-6-06)). As the migration and refugee crisis evolved in 2015, the military forces offered humanitarian assistance as well as search and rescue services to assist the efforts by the Hellenic Coast Guards since it was becoming impossible for the Hellenic coast guards to manage the daily migrant flows entering Greek islands by the thousands. The migration/refugee crisis escalated in Autumn 2015 following the closing of Greece's northern borders, while the immense waves of refugees and migrants continued to cross the Aegean toward mainly the islands of Lesvos, Samos, Chios, Leros and Kos.

In light of the immediate need to provide food and accommodation to a substantial number of people that was increasing on a daily basis by the thousands, and given that civil protection services were meager, and in some places almost nonexistent, a humanitarian catastrophe was imminent. Against this background, the Hellenic Armed Forces commenced to perform their supportive role to the local civil protection agencies and to the police in order to provide humanitarian assistance but also to establish temporary camps for the refugees and migrants before they manage to register and then seek transportation means toward the Greek mainland.

In addition, as reportedly advocated by the regional military leadership at the time, all local military structures were already monitoring the situation providing surveillance and situation awareness at all times (Blaveris 2015). They had no orders to get activated but only to provide rescue or first aid services when necessary and perhaps make available the local military installations in the small islands as a temporary shelter to the most devastated cases until the police or the coast guards assume responsibility. The situation in the islands as regards the magnitude of incoming refugees and migrants, as Table 7.2 shows (HNDGS 2016e), was particularly difficult since local public order could be easily put in question as long as the numbers of the incoming population were by far exceeding local population. As shown in Table 7.2, the percentages of incoming population as compared to the local population were considerable.

Until May 2016, the Hellenic Armed Forces had inter alia assisted in the construction, function and management of 5 first reception-identification centers in the islands of Eastern Aegean and of 23 accommodation centers in other locations in mainland Greece. These were ultimately funded by the Internal Security Fund (ISF) and the Asylum, Migration and Integration Fund (AMIF) of the EU (HNDGS 2016e).

Table 7.2   Numbers of incoming migrants and refugees in Greek islands from 2015 to February 2016

Greek islands	Population approx.	Jan 2016–Feb 2016	2015	Total	Comparative % of incoming migrants
Lesvos	86,000	71,793	500,728	572,521	57.4
Chios	51,000	26,732	117,152	143,884	14.4
Samos	33,000	9085	104,126	113,211	11.3
Kos	33,000	3313	58,135	61,448	6.2
Leros	8000	7660	35,690	43,350	4.3
Total (5)	178,000	118,583	815,831	934,414	93.6
Total (all areas)	–	120,966	876,232	997,198	100

Source: National Coordination Border Control Center Immigration and Asylum, Hellenic Ministry of Defense (2017)

On 2 February 2016 and according to L.4368/16 (FEK 21 t.A'), the MoD was assigned the responsibility to assist other public services and authorities including social structures in managing issues occurred by the refugee-migration crisis. In practice, the Ministry of National Defense undertook the responsibility

> to manage and coordinate other public services and authorities, social organizations and NGOs assisting in the operation of the Hot spots and Relocation Centers, regarding exclusively the transport, accommodation, feeding and health care of refugees and migrants, for as long as required. For this reason a Central Coordinating Body for the Management of Refugee Crisis and Local Coordinating Centers were established in the Hellenic National Defense General Staff. (HNDGS 2016f)

This was an unprecedented assignment for the Hellenic military forces. During peacetime, it started to manage an internal emergency by optimizing its expertise, its command discipline and certainly the experience gained from previous humanitarian operations abroad. There should be no doubt that the skills and experience previously gained from their participation in PSOs abroad that had familiarized the military forces to cooperating with civilian agencies and NGOs almost by default encouraged effective civil military coordination. One could hardly escape the assumption that a detailed examination of the interaction of the Hellenic Armed

Forces with all local, regional and international civilian and military agencies in the context of managing the refugee-migration crisis is constituting a case study of unprecedented civil–military cooperation among local authorities, governments and international organizations at the service of a humanitarian crisis having wider security implications. Perhaps one key development emerging from the role of the Greek military in managing the migration crisis is that Greek public opinion came closer to the understanding regarding the important role military forces can play in international and national humanitarian crises.

Yet, one key shortcoming stemming from budgetary defense restrictions and be compounded by the immediacy of managing the refugee-migration crisis is that both developments have deprived the political leadership from contemplating the defense budgeting in the context of long-term military planning. It is not surprising that a segment within the military leadership is concerned about the reality that the current emergency, along with the financial deadlock, may negatively affect the nature of the Hellenic military forces and capabilities of the next decade, at best, including the country's defense diplomacy.

Conclusion

Certain aspects pertaining the notion of contemporary military or defense diplomacy have been elevated in recent years into important elements in states' strategy by empowering their defense credentials and primarily their security position in both their immediate and wider security contexts. The refugee-migration crisis is currently consuming a large segment of the Greece's military human resources, thus further discouraging an already marginal participation of military forces in peace operations abroad. Until a peacebuilding operation is launched in the Middle East following the wars in Syria to which Greece is more than likely to contribute, no further major Greek commitments abroad should be expected apart from those related to the management of migration crisis. For, in Greek military thinking, and given the severe budgetary restrictions on defense expenditures, it looks far more preferable for Athens to optimize its military forces and financial resources in training programs that are taking place within the Alliance or the EU. After all, such a rationale was often a driving force behind Athens' defense diplomacy initiatives.

To sum up, although rationalization, optimization and prioritization could be considered as the inevitable positive effects of the financial crisis upon Greece's defense diplomacy, defense reductions have reached a level at which it threatens to question the country's preparedness to meet, along with its allies, the emerging regional security environment. Such a development points also to the need for involving public audiences through effective public diplomacy to the understanding that defense diplomacy serves the country's contemporary strategic priorities and multiplies the efficiency of existing capabilities.

References

Baldino, D., & Carr, A. (2016). Defense diplomacy and the Australian defense force: Smokescreen or strategy? *Australian Journal of International Affairs, 70*(2), 139–158.

Bellou, F. (2016). Calibrating Fortress Europe at a time of austerity? In A. Bitzenis & P. Kontakos (Eds.), *International Conference on International Business 2015 & 2016 Proceedings*. Laboratory of International Relations and European Integration, University of Macedonia.

Blaveris, L. (2015, September 2). The invisible hero, the military [ΟΑφανήςΉρωαςοΣτρατός]. *Parapolitika Newspaper*. Retrieved September 8, 2016, from http://www.parapolitika.gr/article/afanis-iroas-o-stratos

Cable, J. (1994). *Gunboat diplomacy 1919–1991*. London: Macmillan, International Institute for Security Studies.

Cai, P. (2016). ASEAN's defense diplomacy and China's military diplomacy. *Asia Policy, 22*, 89–95.

Cheyre, J. E. (2013). Defense diplomacy. In A. Cooper, J. Heine, & R. Thakur (Eds.), *The Oxford handbook of modern diplomacy* (pp. 369–382). Oxford: Oxford University Press.

Chletsos, M., & Kollias, C. (1995). Defense spending and growth in Greece 1974–90: Some preliminary econometric results. *Applied Economics, 27*, 883–890.

Cottey, A., & Forster, A. (2004). Reshaping defense diplomacy: New roles for military cooperation and assistance. *Adelphi Papers, 44*(365), 1–84.

Danforth, N. (2016, October 23). Turkey's new maps are reclaiming the Ottoman Empire. *Foreign Policy*. Retrieved November 22, 2016, http://foreignpolicy.com/2016/10/23/turkeys-religious-nationalists-want-ottoman-borders-iraq-erdogan/

Defense Diplomacy Plan. (2012). *Ministerio de Defensa*. Retrieved November 22, 2016, from http://www.defensa.gob.es/Galerias/defensadocs/defense-diplomacy-plan.pdf

Dempsey, J. (2012). *EU and NATO look on at Greece's pampered armed forces*. Judy Dempsey's Strategic Europe. Retrieved March 18, 2017, from http://carnegieeurope.eu/strategiceurope/49185

Dokos, T., & Kollias, C. (2013). *Greek defense spending in times of crisis: The urgent need for defense reform.* ELIAMEP Thesis, March 2013, 1/2013, 1–11.

EEAS. (2016). *European Union Naval Force—Mediterranean Operation Sophia.* Retrieved November 22, 2016, from https://eeas.europa.eu/sites/eeas/files/factsheet_eunavfor_med_en_0.pdf

Eurostat. (2016). *European Commission, Eurostat, National Accounts, Real GDP Growth Rate Volume.* Retrieved March 18, 2017, from http://ec.europa.eu/eurostat/web/national-accounts/statistics-illustrated

Grebe, J., & Sommer, J. (2010). *Greece: High military expenditures despite the financial crisis.* BICC Focus 9, Bonn International Centre for Conversion.

Hellenic National Defense General Staff [HNDGS]. (2010). *Hellenic Contribution to the Reconstruction of Afghanistan, Public Affairs Office.* Hellenic National Defense General Staff. Retrieved December 20, 2016, from http://www.geetha.mil.gr/media/pdf-arxeia/afganistan/afganistan-en.pdf

Hellenic National Defense General Staff [HNDGS]. (2016a). *Concluded activities.* Somalia, Georgia. Retrieved December 20, 2016, from http://www.geetha.mil.gr/en/component/content/article.html?id=3968&Itemid=993

Hellenic National Defense General Staff [HNDGS]. (2016b). *Concluded activities, Bosnia-Hercegovina, IFOR-SFOR.* Hellenic National Defense General Staff. Retrieved December 20, 2016, from http://www.geetha.mil.gr/en/component/content/article.html?id=3968&Itemid=993

Hellenic National Defense General Staff [HNDGS]. (2016c). *The participation of the Hellenic Armed Forces in KFOR.* Hellenic National Defense General Staff. Retrieved December 20, 2016, from http://www.geetha.mil.gr/en/component/content/article.html?id=3985&Itemid=997

Hellenic National Defense General Staff [HNDGS]. (2016d). *Hellenic National Defense General Staff.* Retrieved December 20, 2016, from http://www.geetha.mil.gr/media/pdf-arxeia/2016/english/other-info/Tacking_the_refugee_crisis.pdf

Hellenic National Defense General Staff [HNDGS]. (2016e, May 27). *Hellenic National Defense General Staff.* Press release. Retrieved December 20, 2016, from http://www.geetha.mil.gr/media/pdf-arxeia/2016/greek/prosfigiko/20160527.pdf

Hellenic National Defense General Staff [HNDGS]. (2016f, March). *Tackling the refugee crisis, ministry of national defense.* Retrieved December 20, 2016, from http://www.geetha.mil.gr/media/pdf-arxeia/2016/english/other-info/Tacking_the_refugee_crisis.pdf

Hellenic National Defense General Staff [HNDGS]. (2016g). *Hellenic National Defense General Staff.* Retrieved December 20, 2016, from http://www.geetha.mil.gr/en/violations-en.html

Hellenic National Defense General Staff [HNDGS]. (2017a). *Concluded activities.* Somalia, Georgia. Retrieved January 20, 2017, from http://www.geetha.mil.gr/en/component/content/article.html?id=3968&Itemid=993

Hellenic National Defense General Staff [HNDGS]. (2017b). *Concluded activities*. Albania. Operation Kosmas. Retrieved January 20, 2017, from http://www.geetha.mil.gr/en/component/content/article.html?id=3968&Itemid=993

Hellenic National Defense General Staff [HNDGS]. (2017c). *2016 aggregate incidents' data*. Retrieved January 20, 2017, from http://www.geetha.mil.gr/en/violations-en/2015-01-27-12-57-42/5230-2016-aggregate-incidents-data.html

Hellenic National Defense General Staff [HNDGS]. (2017d). *2016 violations of territorial waters*. Retrieved January 20, 2017, from http://www.geetha.mil.gr/en/violations-en/2015-01-26-13-18-10.html

Hellenic National Defense General Staff [HNDGS]. (2017e). *Table of Hellenic participation in peace support operations*. Retrieved January 20, 2017, from http://www.geetha.mil.gr/en/component/content/article.html?id=3969&Itemid=994

Hellenic National Defense General Staff [HNDGS]. (2017f). *Table of peace support operations* [in Greek]. Retrieved January 20, 2017, from http://www.geetha.mil.gr/media/EIRINEYTIKES_DRASTIRIOTITES/pdf/pinakas/eirhneutikes-apostoles.pdf

Hooper, J. (2015, June 23). Why has Greece only now included defense cuts in its Brussels proposals? *The Guardian*. Retrieved November 3, 2016, https://www.theguardian.com/world/2015/jun/23/why-has-greece-only-now-included-defence-cuts-in-its-brussels-proposals

Kollias, C. (1995). Country survey VII: Military spending in Greece. *Defense and Peace Economics, 6*, 305–319.

Kouskouvelis, I. (2013). The problem with Turkey's 'zero problems' Turkey, past and future. *The Middle East Quarterly, 20*(1), 47–56.

Laksmana, E. (2012). Regional order by other means? Examining the rise of defense diplomacy in Southeast Asia. *Asian Security, 8*(3), 251–270.

Le Miere, C. (2011). The return of gunboat diplomacy. *Survival, 53*(5), 53–68.

Litsas, S., & Tziampiris, A. (2015). *The Eastern Mediterranean in transition. Multipolarity, politics and power*. London: Routledge.

Muthanna, K. A. (2011). Military diplomacy. Perspectives. *Journal of Defense Studies, 5*(1), 1–15.

National Coordination Border Control Center Immigration and Asylum. (2017). Hellenic Ministry of Defense. Retrieved May 17, 2017, from http://www.geetha.mil.gr/media/pdf-arxeia/2016/greek/prosfigiko/Presentation_March_2016.pdf

National Framework for Strategic Communication. (2012). *The White House*. Retrieved from https://fas.org/man/eprint/pubdip.pdf

NATO. (2003). Retrieved from www.nato.int/nato-static_fl2014/assests/pdf/pdf_200312/20100611p03-146e.pdf

NATO. (2016a). *Fact sheet, NATOs deployment in the Aegean Sea*. Retrieved December 20, 2016, from http://www.nato.int/nato_static_fl2014/assets/pdf/pdf_2016_10/20161025_1610-factsheet-aegean-sea-eng.pdf

NATO. (2016b, July 4). Press release PR/CP, 116, defense expenditures of NATO countries (2009–2016). NATO Press Release, Public Diplomacy Division.

Nedos, V. (2016, July 5). Greece Second in Defense Spending [Δεύτερη σε Αμυντικές Δαπάνες η Ελλάδα]. *Kathimerini*.

New Challenges to Defense Diplomacy. (1999). *Strategic Survey, 100*(1), 38–53. doi:10.1080/04597239908461108.

NMIOTC. (2016). *NATO maritime interdiction operational centre*. Retrieved December 20, 2016, from http://www.nmiotc.nato.int/#general/mission_roles_en.htm

Sachar, B. S. (2003). Cooperation in military training as a tool of peacetime military diplomacy. *Strategic Analysis, 27*(3), 404–421.

Singh, P. K. (2011). China's 'military diplomacy': Investigating PLA's participation in UN peacekeeping operations. *Strategic Analysis, 35*(5), 793–818.

Spiegel, P. (2015). *Leaked paper: Should Greece cut defense spending?* ft.com. Retrieved December 20, 2016, from http://www.ft.com/content/3a5d091e-24e7-32f4-b6d6-e8cfc288476c

Storey, I. (2012). China's bilateral defense diplomacy in Southeastern Asia. *Asia Security, 8*(3), 287–310.

Tan, S. S. (2016). Military diplomacy. In P. Kerr, C. M. Constantinou, & P. Sharp (Eds.), *The Sage handbook of diplomacy*. London: Sage.

Taylor, B., Bisley, N., White, H., Blaxland, J., Leahy, P., & Tan, S. S. (2014). Defense diplomacy: The possibilities and limits of defense diplomacy. In C. Andrew (Ed.), *Centre of gravity* (pp. 1–22). Canberra: Australian National University.

Waszkiewicz, G. (2016). Drivers of Greek and Turkish defense spending. *International Journal of Management and Economics, 51*, 33–46.

White Paper. (2014). Hellenic Republic Ministry of National Defense.

Wosolsobe, W. (2016, July 22). After the EUGS: Specifying the military tasks. European Union Institute for Security Studies, *Alert*, No. 35.

CHAPTER 8

Hierarchies, Civilization, and the Eurozone Crisis: The Greek Financial Crisis

Kyriakos Mikelis and Dimitrios Stroikos

INTRODUCTION

It is not controversial to suggest that the Greek Financial Crisis (GRFC) has been one of the most noteworthy challenges faced by the European Union (EU) over the last years. But while much attention has been paid to the economic and political causes of the crisis, less attention has been paid to the ways in which the management of the GRFC was engrained in the construction of Greece as a Eurozone/EU outsider. Building on the concept of the 'Standard of Civilization' (SoC) and themes from postcolonial studies, the aim of the chapter is to examine the transformation of Greece into a negative signifier and to illustrate the relevance of civilizational practices and narratives to the GRFC.

K. Mikelis (✉)
University of Macedonia, Thessaloniki, Greece

D. Stroikos
London School of Economics, London, UK

© The Author(s) 2017   125
J. Marangos (ed.), *The Internal Impact and External Influence of the Greek Financial Crisis*, DOI 10.1007/978-3-319-60201-1_8

The argument of the chapter is twofold. First, we argue that one of the most important, albeit neglected, features of the management of the GRFC has been the power politics of conditionality, which can be seen as a contemporary SoC. Briefly stated, the eventual reposition of Greece from a Eurozone member to Eurozone's 'Other' points to the enduring influence of civilizational narratives and hierarchical practices on the EU's crisis response, which has been reflected in the blame game and the pressure of Grexit. Second, although certain aspects of the EU's policies toward non-member countries have been usually underpinned by colonial impulses and hierarchical practices, we suggest that the response to the GRFC marks a significant departure from previous EU policies. This is because a member country is presented as a negative signifier. This has important implications not only for the future of Greece and its people, but also for the prospects of the EU project in general.

The chapter is organized in the following way. The first section revisits the SoC as a key characteristic of the expansion of the European international society of states to the non-European world during the nineteenth century. It also provides a brief overview of the literature that deals with the relevance of the SoC to contemporary practices in international society. The second section moves on to consider the ways in which EU practices and discourses have been reflective of the logic of the SoC. Consequently, the third section focuses on the construction of Greece as a negative signifier from the outset of the crisis and provides a discussion of the relevance of the SoC to assess EU's response to the GRFC. A key point that emerges from this discussion is that, in many ways, the EU's management of the GRFC indicates the enduring influence of colonial legacies echoing the importance of civilizational narratives and hierarchical practices. Crucially, however, what is novel and noteworthy is that this process has occurred within the EU. The chapter thus not only provides a reflective critique to exclusionary practices engrained in economic governance, but also offers a new lens through which to understand the complex dynamics of the GRFC in a historical and comparative perspective, highlighting the importance of hierarchy and civilization within the Eurozone. Finally, in doing so, new avenues are opened for an interdisciplinary research agenda on the GRFC, EU Studies, and the politics of the Eurozone.

The Standard of Civilization in International Society: A Relic of the Nineteenth Century or a Contemporary Practice in Global Politics?

The SoC has been one of the most important features of the expansion of the European international society of states into the non-European world in the nineteenth century (Bull and Watson 1984; Buzan and Little 2014), based largely on colonialism, racism, and coercion. Bull and Watson (1984, p. 1) define international society as 'a group of states (or more generally, a group of independent political communities) which form a system, in the sense that the behaviour of each is a necessary factor in the calculations of the others, but also have established by dialogue and consent common rules and institutions for the conduct of their relations, and recognize their common interest in maintaining these arrangements'. This violent process of the European civilizing mission gradually culminated in the establishment of a universal society of sovereign states in the twentieth century. It was against this historical backdrop that the SoC emerged as a set of administrative, socio-political, and legal practices formulated by the Europeans to assess and differentiate between members and non-members of the expanding international society of states (Gong 1984; Keene 2002; Bowden 2009; Stroikos 2014; Linklater 2016).

A key assumption of the SoC was that there was a society of 'civilized' European members that met these criteria and an outer tier of 'uncivilized' non-European political entities that did not. Therefore, during the nineteenth century and early twentieth century, entering the society of civilized states required the fulfillment of the society's SoC as a criterion for state recognition. According to Gong (1984, pp. 14–15), these standards included basic rights of life and property, the existence of an organized political bureaucracy, the adherence to international law, the operation of diplomatic interchange and communication, and the abstract notion that a 'civilized' state follows the norms and practices the 'civilized' international society. Notably, by the end of the nineteenth century, international law was a key part of the SoC, manifested in the unequal treaties and extraterritoriality (Koskenniemi 2001; Simpson 2004; Anghie 2004). In other words, the key issue was conforming to a set of organizing and normative standards of conduct regulating the interaction among states in order to be recognized as a full sovereign member in international society.

In principle, the aftermath of the Second World War and the subsequent process of decolonization marked the end of the operation of the SoC (Bowden 2009, p. 126). Yet, there is a burgeoning literature that examines the extent to which the logic of the SoC remains enmeshed in the normative structure of contemporary international society (Stroikos 2014). Significantly, like the old SoC, the new 'SoC' is not value-free, but it is interwoven with liberal values, ideas, and practices that demarcate insiders and outsiders in the liberal international order (Fidler 2001; Bowden 2009). These include: economic and financial standards (Gong 2002, pp. 84–92; Mozaffari 2001, pp. 77–96; Bowden and Seabrooke 2007), human rights (Donelly 1998), democratic government (Hobson 2008; Clark 2009; Navari 2013), the status of women (Towns 2009), development and environmental stewardship (Gong 2002, p. 84; Buzan 2014, pp. 590–592), peacebuilding and statebuilding (Paris 2002), and trusteeship (Bain 2003). What should be emphasized for the purposes of this discussion is that the logic of the new SoC also underpins the EU's membership conditionality (Behr 2007; Stivachtis 2008). The next section considers this aspect of EU policies and discourses.

THE NEW SOC AND THE EU

In the context of discussing the enduring relevance of the logic of the SoC, Behr (2007) argues that the dynamics of EU accession politics, especially the 2004 enlargement, echo the legacies of the nineteenth-century imperial rule and the SoC. Employing a historical comparative perspective, Behr identifies three common features between the nineteenth-century SoC and EU regulations on accession and membership: (a) the existence of regulations designed by European nations that demarcate between themselves as insiders and those who are outside the EU; (b) different modes of recognition and cooperation between those who are brought inside the EU and those perceived as the 'outside'; (c) the importance of a geopolitical imagination that projects a hierarchical world order, which distinguishes European states at the center from peripheries of perceived less politically developed states (Behr 2007). Likewise, according to Stivachtis (2008), the EU policy of 'membership conditionality', including monitoring the fulfillment of the so-called Copenhagen criteria, can be understood as a contemporary SoC.

More recently, in examining a number of EU policies and discourses, Nicolaidis et al. (2014) identify two patterns underpinning the operation of what they describe as a 'new standards typology'. The first is 'agency denial', given that it is still Europeans that unilaterally set standards and impose them on others. The second is 'hierarchy', considering how the standards set by the Europeans promote the institutionalization of conferring unequal status upon others. In this respect, the tendency to project the EU as a model that needs to be replicated by others is part of an influential narrative that echoes assumptions about Europe's civilizational superiority. Thus, the EU has only been partially successful in shaping its identity as a postcolonial global actor that leaves behind its colonial impulses and Eurocentrism.

Part of this debate is also the question of what kind of international actor is the EU (Stavridis and Sola 2011). In his influential introduction of the concept of 'Normative Power Europe' (NPE), Manners (2002, p. 239) suggests that the EU can be seen as a normative power with an ability to shape conceptions of 'normal' in international affairs. This involves the pursuit of normative aims, juxtaposed to self-interest material benefits, mainly through normative means, instead of using military and/ or economic means (Manners 2002). Since the publication of Manners' piece, there has been a great deal of debate about the merits and pitfalls of conceptualizing the EU as a normative power (Whitman 2011; Nicolaïdis and Whitman 2013). So, there is no need to rehearse the discussions, but what is noteworthy for the purposes of this chapter is the conceptualization of Europe as an empire, which can be related to the relevance of the logic of the SoC. More specifically, in response to the concept of NPE, it is maintained that, if we want to understand the politics and foreign policy of the EU, it makes more sense to treat it as an empire. In this regard, for example, it has been suggested that the EU bears the characteristics of a 'neo-medieval empire', centered on multilevel governance and the interpenetration of multiple political units (Zielonka 2006). In particular, the emerging system lacks a definite power center and it consists of concentric circles, fuzzy borders, soft power projection, and a shared/spread authority. Consequently, this contrasts with the notion of a neo-Westphalian empire, whereby the principal features are centralized governance, power relations of a 'metropolis/periphery' hierarchy and control through political and military means.

Conceptualizing Europe as empire is also related to the ways in which the EU expands and consolidates through the construction of the distinction between 'Civilized' and 'Other', which is reflected on certain EU policies, practices, and geopolitical projections (Foster 2013; Behr and

Stivachtis 2016). Essentially, this process rests upon the construction of third parties as EU's 'Others', including Turkey and Russia (Neumann and Welsh 1991; Zarakol 2011; Neumann 2011). In this vein, in addition to describing the process of European integration as empire in general (Gravier 2015), there is a growing literature that employs the analytical utility of the concept of empire in order to highlight key aspects of EU's external relations that reflect the legacies of Europe's imperial past and civilizational narratives. Examples include the 'eastern enlargement' of the EU, as noted earlier (Böröcz 2001; Behr 2007; Stivachtis 2008), the EU's external relations with the African, Caribbean, and Pacific (APC) countries (Sepos 2013), the geopolitical projection of what is known as *Eurafrica* (Hansen and Jonsson 2014), the European Neighborhood Policy (Pänke 2015), and its behavior toward North Africa and the Middle East (Del Sarto 2016). In fact, rather than seeing EU's policies toward African countries as an expression of its normative power, some authors (Schmidt 2012; Langan 2015) have suggested that the EU should be seen as a neo-colonial power. The key question then is whether the EU's response to the GRFC shares commonalities with how the EU deals with its external relations in its periphery on the basis of an 'empire' approach that echoes the logic of the SoC. This is the focus of discussion of the next section.

THE ENDURING RELEVANCE OF THE SoC AND THE GREEK FINANCIAL CRISIS

The Eurozone crisis has had an important impact on the legitimacy of the process of European integration. This has been manifested in a shift of public opinion away from favoring European integration (Vilpišauskas 2013). While it is too early to say what the long-term implications of the GRFC will be, it is clear that the crisis has revealed the inherent structural problems and limits regarding European fiscal rules, such as the dominance of financialization and impediments to political integration (Della Posta and Talani 2011; Patomäki 2013; Bitzenis et al. 2015; Constantopoulou 2016). However, it remains plausible that the crisis might spearhead the advancement of integration rather than its impediment, at least as far as the integration of the Economic Monetary Union (EMU) is concerned (Tosun et al. 2014; Ioannou et al. 2015).

Nevertheless, the GRFC has triggered an extensive set of explanatory/analytical frameworks and research questions. A multitude of causes contributing to the crisis have been identified, including the country's dramatic public finance situation, the adamant stance of certain leading states, the consequences of the international financial crisis (mid and late 2000s), the economic imbalances among EMU member states, and structural causes concerning the EMU's economic characteristics (Verde 2011, pp. 144–150). Consequently, there is by now a burgeoning literature that illustrates certain aspects of the GRFC. Our intention here is not to provide a detailed discussion of this literature, but it is necessary to briefly sketch out the complex amalgam of issues raised by the GRFC. These include the interplay of domestic and external/institutional factors and how they have shaped the crisis (Bitzenis et al. 2013; Sklias and Tzifakis 2013), domestic influences, such as weakened domestic institutions and the effects of the shadow economy (Featherstone 2011, pp. 195–200; Mitsopoulos and Pelagidis 2011; Tzogopoulos 2013, Chaps. 1–3; Bitzenis and Vlachos 2015), the intricacies of negotiation strategies and bargaining power (Tsebelis 2016; Zahariadis 2016, 2017), the dynamics and limits of the politics and policies of reforming public administration and the social sector (Kalyvas et al. 2012; Ladi 2012; Featherstone 2015; Petmesidou and Glatzer 2015; Theodoropoulou 2015), and deep structural causes of the crisis, such as falling profitability and the overaccumulation crisis (Mavroudeas 2014). Further, it has been suggested that the GRFC constitutes a noteworthy example of the 'politics of extreme austerity' (Karyotis and Gerodimos 2015) as well as a case of stateness under strain due to financial/economic adjustment and conditionality (Lavdas et al. 2013).

Likewise, attention has been paid to the effect of the GRFC on Greek foreign policy, political institutions, and the civil society (Kovras and Loizides 2014; Pappas 2014; Clarke et al. 2015; Katsanidou and Otjes 2016; Litsas and Tziampiris 2017). Another important focus of analysis has been the crucial role of the media in shaping domestic and external perceptions about the crisis and constructing prevailing discourses (Clements et al. 2014; Karyotis and Gerodimos 2015; Kyriakidis 2016; Takas and Samaras 2016). It should be noted that the discursive representation of the crisis in global media was far from monolithic, but it was clearly underpinned by Greece as a negative signifier and EU/Eurozone's 'Other'. From the outset, there was a tendency to frame Greece in negative terms invoking three major themes: corruption, lack of credibility/reliability, and 'irresponsibility'. This was accompanied by typical stereotypes regarding the Greeks based on excessive generalities or ironic comments, and less interest in domestic debates or alternative views (Antoniades 2013; Tzogopoulos 2013). In this regard, examining Eurozone discourses and narratives helps to illustrate key moves that shaped the EU response to the GRFC. One of the most important steps was the emergence of the politics of agency denial with regard to Greece, which was later replaced by the mantra of Greece 'as a special case'. This was followed by the politics of blaming and breaking the 'Grexit' taboo (Papadimitriou and Zartaloudis 2015).

The exit of Greece from the Euro was for the time averted thanks to the July 2015 agreement, but the very fact that Greece was portrayed as a possible outsider has had an important impact on how the EU decided to deal with the GRFC. First, as far as analogies with the nineteenth-century imperial rule and the management of the crisis are concerned, it is worth recalling certain policies and practices based on hierarchical and asymmetrical power relations between unequal parties (Eurozone members and Greece), including surrendering fiscal sovereignty in return for the provision of specific loan arrangements, and the central role of the creditors in monitoring the fulfillment of certain reforms and policies that conditions Greece as a member of the Eurozone. Remarkably, in one of his books before assuming office, Greece's current Minister of Foreign Affairs, Nikos Kotzias (2013), described the status of Greece in terms of the concept of 'debt colony'. In his view, there are certain analogies between the nineteenth-century imperial rule of European powers and the management of the GRFC that point to echoes of imperial rule, such as access to natural assets and resources, the central role of the creditors in monitoring key facets of the Greek economy and advancing/enforcing further privatization. This largely relates to the fact that the standards applied in the crisis management have been largely unfolded upon the myth of 'neo-liberal structural reforms as panacea' (Polychroniou 2015, p. 248). Comprehensive reflexivity over the nature and effects of such reforms was rather limited, especially if one considers the persistence of inequality and inefficiency in terms of precarious employment and social instability. In fact, the 'rescue' dimension of the respective programs of the European South has been more about protecting the European banking system than solving the actual economic problems of the corresponding nations (Polychroniou 2015, pp. 248–254).

Second, for all debates about EU solidarity, the idea of solidarity was somehow narrowly conceptualized, what is called 'restricted solidarity', in the sense that the bailout was influenced by proximity and homogeneity in economic, political, and cultural terms, with the main aim of maintaining macro-economic stability (Verde 2011, pp. 157–161). At the same time, the response to the crisis cannot be easily disentangled from Germany's hegemonic, albeit reluctant, position, evident in a burden-sharing and institutional design of asymmetrical interdependence, which provided a framework of asymmetrical bargaining power. Thus, it is not surprising that the elicited response, in many ways, reflected Germany's values related to a culture that emphasizes fiscal stability (Bulmer 2014; Schimmelfennig 2015). Notwithstanding what one thinks about Germany's contribution to the management of the GRFC, its obsession with stability, what is called 'ordoliberalism', led to the transformation of a nation's fiscal problem into a systemic sovereign debt crisis (Matthijs 2016). To be sure, it has been suggested (Ryner 2015) that the persistence of the EMU (despite various contradictions or social costs as well as of a discredited capitalism) can be better understood in terms of an 'ordoliberal iron cage' rather than merely an indication of a specific class or state dominance. Equally, in relation to the negotiations, it was apparent that asymmetrical and hierarchical power relations were also a reflection of Greece as a small country. This meant that there were few resources available in terms of bargaining power that could help the Greek government to formulate a more effective bargaining strategy (Zahariadis 2016, 2017). According to Tsebelis, EU's inflexibility (which was misconceived by the Greek side) and the unanimity rule as a means of turning multiple actors into veto players further complicated the process of managing the crisis (Tsebelis 2016).

Third, as was noted earlier, a crucial dimension of responding to the crisis was the construction of Greece as the EU/Eurozone 'Other', which has been embedded in the stigmatization of the European South. This involves the geopolitical projection of a core/periphery binary in economic and financial terms. But it also involves the reproduction of essentialist ideas about Greek culture premised on subtle racism and stereotypes that usually portray Greeks as 'corrupted', 'lazy', 'irresponsible', 'emotional', and so on, juxtaposed to essentialist qualities of Northern Europeans, such as 'industrious', 'rational', 'hard-working', 'responsible', and 'reliable' (Tekin 2014). Crucially, this has the effect of de-politicizing the crisis rather than focusing on economic differences or asymmetries, the historical evolution of political phenomena, and the salience of power politics (Leontidou 2012, 2014; Markantonatou 2013; Bitzenis et al. 2015; Van Vossole 2016).

Considering the above, framing the EU's response in binary distinctions has largely opened the way for hierarchical practices and policies that echo colonial legacies and the nineteenth-century SoC. This has important implications for at least three reasons. First, the stigmatization of Greece as the 'financially uncivilized Other' that needs to be civilized in economic terms, at least for now, has profoundly shaped the management of the GRFC, not the least because it has precluded other policies available. For instance, it is clear that an emphasis on economic growth, instead of an obsession with austerity measures, could have less detrimental effects to the most vulnerable population groups in Greece. But blaming the Greeks and their cultural qualities, that is, the 'culturalization' of what has largely been a systemic crisis, has led to the 'de-politization' of finding proper solutions, which, in turn, made easier the imposition of painful austerity measures that simply have not worked so far (Mylonas 2012). Therefore, civilizing narratives have interwoven with domestic and local politics (Constantopoulou 2016, p. 3).

Second, the repositioning of Greece as a semi-sovereign state points to different layers of sovereignty within the EU that has de facto demarcated the country as a second tier or failed state in terms of a standard of economic and financial civilization. But what should be added is that, despite efforts by non-European states to join the European international society, meeting the nineteenth-century SoC remained a moving target for the 'uncivilized' states to meet. A key question then that emerges is the extent to which Greece will continue to be suspended somewhere in the outer tier of the EU/Eurozone, regardless of whether it will be successful in restructuring the debt burden by complying with the criteria set by its creditors.

Third, returning to the concept of NPE, the GRFC has highlighted the limits of EU as a distinct cosmopolitan actor with normative power. Indeed, in the aftermath of the management of the GRFC, there is some scope of thinking the EU in terms of what Mikelis calls 'Neocolonial Power Europe' (Mikelis 2016). Consequently, is the EU still able to project its normative influence as an international actor by promoting certain values and norms, when one of its members has been constructed as a negative signifier? As Tekin notes, the ascent of power politics, the absence of a true cosmopolitan solidarity, the harsh treatment of Greece, and the EU's democratic deficit have rendered the EU project less appealing in its neighborhood (Tekin 2014, p. 35). Equally, the stigmatization and 'orientalization' that constructed Greece as EU's Other and solely responsible for the Eurozone crisis means that the EU is far from a cosmopolitan, post-national order (Tekin 2014).

Moreover, in relation to the GRFC, little effort was made to draw lessons from previous efforts of structural adjustment programs (Greer

2013). Equally, rather little attention has been paid to the need of crafting a conditionality strategy that is attentive to bureaucratic interests, administrative traditions, and cultural norms. As a result, a prevailing sense of forced adjustment contributed to the delegitimation of the conditionality strategy (Featherstone 2015). Hence, the EU failure to elicit the necessary substantive reforms has consequences for its ability to coordinate macroeconomic performance across a heterogeneous Eurozone, which marks an 'implicit challenge—to force adaptation—that has loomed for the EU since it embarked on the single market and the single currency' (Featherstone 2015, p. 310). As far as the hierarchical and asymmetrical nature of the EU's management of the GRFC is concerned, although a sort of condition might have been necessary and beneficial for fostering reforms, the lack of clear and full-blown safeguards (checks and balances) for all parties involved has reinforced the asymmetry of power politics and rendered the completion of the restructuring program a more formidable task for the Greek elites.

In this regard, our argument falls within the broader agenda of advancing a critique of the immaturity thesis. This is evident in the discourse of debt negotiations, which primarily attributes failure to specific peripheral actors unable to abide with systemic requirements, while paying less attention to structural deficiencies and the role of the system's gatekeepers. As a consequence of the immaturity argument, efforts to carve out a European institutional response to the crisis have emphasized the need to bring the immature states of Europe's periphery to the 'correct' path towards progress and economic recovery. But given the obvious limits of such efforts to date, a critique of this argument is necessary by taking into consideration exisiting asymmetries of power between EU member states and the role of agency and diversity among them (Dooley 2014).

Concluding Remarks

Despite the fact that the purpose of our analysis has been to elucidate certain aspects of the GRFC that have been downplayed in the relevant literature, our intention has not been to (over)simplify the complex external and internal factors that have shaped the management of the GRFC. Nor do we suggest that the causes of the crisis can be attributed only to how the EU decided to handle the GRFC. It is clear that Greek governments also bear responsibility in completing effectively the debt restructuring programs and fiscal adjustment. Yet, European and indeed EMU governance, especially regarding the management of the economic/financial and sovereign debt crisis may well be conceptualized as 'civilizing governance' in the sense that it is premised on a new civilizing mission or process. The logic of this civilizing governance can be described as 'comply to certain standards or suffer the consequences', echoing the legacies of imperial rule. As we have seen, this has been manifested in the demarcation between insiders and outsiders within the Eurozone that repositioned Greece as a negative signifier in the context of civilizational discourses and the collective pressure of a possible Grexit.

To be sure, we do not claim that the governance of the EU can be devoid of some sort of criteria and standards of conduct. Nor do we believe that any response to the EU should entail the unconditional provision of assistance. However, it is one thing to look for ways to improve the governance of the EU and another thing to consider the process of managing the GRFC and its outcomes to date in a constructive and reflexive way. After all, the Greek case helps to highlight certain features of the politics of conditionality that are relevant to other cases. For instance, there is evidence to suggest that financial assistance to African countries with the aim of facilitating poverty eradication has failed to reduce poverty alleviation because of the promotion of policies of regressive liberalization (Langan 2015).

Be that as it may, our main purpose has been to offer an alternative framework that helps to cast a revealing light on the enduring influence of civilizational discourse and hierarchical practices. Building on the concept of the SoC and borrowing ideas from postcolonial studies, we have argued that the construction of Greece as Eurozone's 'Other' through the distinction between Eurozone insiders and outsiders as well as the ways in which the EU responded to the crisis serve to highlight the continuing relevance of the logic of the SoC. Following from this, we also argued that the representation of Greece as a 'financially uncivilized Other' facilitated the introduction of ineffective austerity measures that have already caused much suffering among many Greek people. But the stigmatization of Greece as Eurozone's Other and the management of the GRFC have already challenged fundamental European values and norms, such as democracy and solidarity. Further, the EU's response to the GRFC raises important questions about whether the EU can still be seen as a distinct international actor with a normative influence in its periphery. Reinventing the EU amid several important challenges, such as the Eurozone crisis, the migration and refugee crisis, and Brexit, seems a daunting task. It is somehow ironic, therefore, that facing these challenges requires a stronger EU, but one that is genuinely 'united in diversity'.

REFERENCES

Anghie, A. (2004). *Imperialism, sovereignty and the making of international law.* Cambridge: Cambridge University Press.

Antoniades, A. (2013). At the eye of the cyclone: The greek crisis in global media. In P. Sklias & N. Tzifakis (Eds.), *Greece's horizons: Reflecting on the country's assets and capabilities. The Konstantinos Karamanlis Institute for Democracy Series on European and international affairs* (pp. 11–25). Berlin: Springer.

Bain, W. (2003). *Between anarchy and society: Trusteeship and the obligations of power.* Oxford: Oxford University Press.

Behr, H. (2007). The European Union in the legacies of imperial rule? EU accession politics viewed from a historical comparative perspective. *European Journal of International Relations, 13*(2), 239–262.

Behr, H., & Stivachtis, Y. (Eds.). (2016). *Revisiting the European Union as empire.* Abingdon: Routledge.

Bitzenis, A., Karagiannis, N., & Marangos, J. (Eds.). (2015). *Europe in crisis. Problems, challenges and alternative perspectives.* New York: Palgrave Macmillan.

Bitzenis, A., Papadopoulos, I., & Vlachos, V. A. (Eds.). (2013). *Reflections on the Greek sovereign debt crisis.* Newcastle Upon Tyne: Cambridge Scholars Publishing.

Bitzenis, A., & Vlachos, V. (2015). The fight against the shadow economy as an exit from the Greek sovereign debt crisis. In A. Bitzenis, N. Karagiannis, & J. Marangos (Eds.), *Europe in crisis: Problems, challenges, and alternative perspectives* (pp. 275–285). New York: Palgrave Macmillan.

Böröcz, J. (2001). Empire and coloniality in the 'eastern enlargement' of the European *Empire's* union. In J. Böröcz & M. Kovács (Eds.), *New clothes: Unveiling EU enlargement* (pp. 1–50). Shropshire: Central Europe Review.

Bowden, B. (2009). *The empire of civilization: The evolution of an imperial idea.* Chicago: University of Chicago Press.

Bowden, B., & Seabrooke, L. (2007). Global standards of market civilization. In M. Hall & P. T. Jackson (Eds.), *Civilizational identity: The production and reproduction of 'civilizations' in international relations* (pp. 119–133). New York: Palgrave Macmillan.

Bull, H., & Watson, A. (Eds.). (1984). *The expansion of international society.* Oxford: Clarendon Press.

Bulmer, S. (2014). Germany and the eurozone crisis: Between hegemony and domestic politics. *West European Politics, 37*(6), 1244–1263.

Buzan, B. (2014). The 'standard of civilisation' as an English school concept. *Millennium: Journal of International Studies, 42*(3), 576–594.

Buzan, B., & Little, R. (2014). The historical expansion of international society. In C. Navari & D. Green (Eds.), *Guide to the English School in International Studies* (pp. 59–74). Chichester: Wiley Blackwell.

Clark, I. (2009). Democracy in international society: Promotion or exclusion? *Millennium: Journal of International Studies, 37*(3), 563–581.

Clarke, J., Huliaras, A., & Sotiropoulos, D. A. (Eds.). (2015). *Austerity and the third sector in Greece*. Farnham: Ashgate.

Clements, B., Verney, S., & Nanou, K. (2014). We no longer love you, but we don't want to leave you': The eurozone crisis and popular euroscepticism in Greece. *Journal of European Integration, 36*(3), 247–265.

Constantopoulou, C. (2016). Introduction – Narratives of crisis: Myths and realities of the contemporary society. *French Journal for Media Research*, 5.

Del Sarto, R. A. (2016). Normative empire Europe: The European Union, its borderlands, and the 'Arab spring'. *Journal of Common Market Studies, 54*(2), 215–232.

Della Posta, P., & Talani, L. S. (Eds.). (2011). *Europe and the financial crisis*. Basingstoke: Palgrave Macmillan.

Donelly, J. (1998). Human rights: A new standard of civilization? *International Affairs, 74*(1), 1–24.

Dooley, N. (2014). Growing pains? Rethinking the 'immaturity' of the European periphery. *Millennium: Journal of International Studies, 42*(3), 936–946.

Featherstone, K. (2011). The Greek sovereign debt crisis and EMU: A failing state in a skewed regime. *Journal of Common Market Studies, 49*(2), 193–217.

Featherstone, K. (2015). External conditionality and the debt crisis: The 'troika' and public administration reform in Greece. *Journal of European Public Policy, 22*(3), 295–314.

Fidler, D. (2001). The return of the standard of civilization. *Chicago Journal of International Law, 36*(1), 137–157.

Foster, R. (2013). Tabula Imperii Europae: A cartographic approach to the current debate on the European Union as empire. *Geopolitics, 18*(2), 371–402.

Gong, G. W. (1984). *The standard of 'civilization' in international society*. Oxford: Clarendon Press.

Gong, G. W. (2002). Standards of civilization today. In M. Mozaffari (Ed.), *Globalization and civilization*. New York: Routledge.

Gravier, M. (2015). Imperial governance: Governing inwards or outwards? *Geopolitics, 20*(4), 814–835.

Greer, S. (2013). *(Why) Did we forget about history? Lessons for the Eurozone from the Failed Conditionality Debates in the 80s*. University of Michigan OSE Research Paper no. 11.

Hansen, P., & Jonsson, S. (2014). Another colonialism: Africa in the history of European integration. *Journal of Historical Sociology, 27*(3), 442–461.

Hobson, C. (2008). Democracy as civilisation. *Global Society, 22*(1), 75–95.

Ioannou, D., Leblond, P., & Niemann, A. (2015). European integration and the crisis: Practice and theory. *Journal of European Public Policy, 22*(2), 155–176.

Kalyvas, S., Pagoulatos, G., & Tsoukas, H. (Eds.). (2012). *From stagnation to forced adjustment: Reforms in Greece, 1974–2010.* London: Hurst and Company.

Karyotis, G., & Gerodimos, R. (Eds.). (2015). *The politics of extreme austerity: Greece in the Eurozone crisis.* Palgrave Macmillan.

Katsanidou, A., & Otjes, S. (2016). How the European debt crisis reshaped National Political Space: The case of Greece. *European Union Politics, 17*(2), 262–284.

Keene, E. (2002). *Beyond the anarchical society: Grotius, colonialism and order in world politics.* Cambridge: Cambridge University Press.

Koskenniemi, M. (2001). *The gentle civilizer of nations: The rise and fall of international law, 1870–1960.* Cambridge: Cambridge University Press.

Kotzias, N. (2013). *Greece, debt colony. European Empire and German Primacy.* Athens: Patakis. (in Greek).

Kovras, I., & Loizides, N. (2014). The Greek debt crisis and southern Europe: Majoritarian pitfalls? *Comparative Politics, 47*(1), 1–20.

Kyriakidis, A. (2016). Myths in the Greek crisis: 2009–2015. *French Journal for Media Research, 5.*

Ladi, S. (2012). *The Eurozone crisis and austerity politics: A trigger for administrative reform in Greece?* London: LSE Hellenic observatory GreeSE papers 57.

Langan, M. (2015). Budget support and Africa-European Union relations: Free market reform and Neocolonialism? *European Journal of International Relations, 21*(1), 101–121.

Lavdas, K., Litsas, S., & Skiadas, D. (2013). *Stateness and sovereign debt: Greece in the European conundrum.* Lanham: Lexington Books.

Leontidou, L. (2012). Reconstruction of the 'European South' in post-colonial Europe: *From Class Conflict to Cultural Identities.* In A. Afouxenidis (Ed.), *Inequality in the era of crisis. Theoretical and empirical investigations* (pp. 25–42). Athens: Propobos. (in Greek).

Leontidou, L. (2014). The crisis and its discourses: Quasi-orientalist attacks on Mediterranean urban spontaneity, informality and joie de vivre. *City: Analysis of Urban Trends, Culture, Theory, Policy, Action, 18*(4–5), 551–562.

Linklater, A. (2016). The 'standard of civilizer' in world politics. *Human Configurations, 5*(2). http://hdl.handle.net/2027/spo.11217607.0005.205.

Litsas, S., & Tziampiris, A. (2017). *Foreign policy under austerity. Greece's return to normality?* London: Palgrave Macmillan.

Manners, I. (2002). Normative power Europe: A contradiction in terms? *Journal of Common Market Studies, 40*(2), 235–258.

Markantonatou, M. (2013). *Diagnosis, treatment, and effects of the crisis in Greece a "special case" or a "test case"?* Max Planck Institute for the Study of societies discussion paper 13/3.

Matthijs, M. (2016). Powerful rules governing the Euro: The perverse logic of German ideas. *Journal of European Public Policy, 23*(3), 375–391.

Mavroudeas, D. (Ed.). (2014). *Greek capitalism in crisis. Marxist analysis.* London: Routledge.

Mikelis, K. (2016). Neocolonial power Europe? Postcolonial thought and the Eurozone crisis. *French Journal for Media Research, 5.*

Mitsopoulos, M., & Pelagidis, T. (2011). *Understanding the crisis in Greece: From boom to bust.* Basingstoke: Palgrave Macmillan.

Mozaffari, M. (2001). The transformationalist perspective and the rise of a global standard of civilization. *International Relations of the Asia-Pacific, 1*(2), 247–264.

Mylonas, Y. (2012). Media and the economic crisis of the EU: The 'culturalization' of a systemic crisis and Bild-Zeitung's framing of Greece. *TripleC (Cognition, Communication, Co-operation), 10*(2), 646–671.

Navari, C. (2013). Liberalism, democracy and international law: An English school approach. In R. Friedman, K. Oskanian, & R. P. Pardo (Eds.), *After liberalism? The future of liberalism in international relations* (pp. 33–50). Baskingstoke: Palgrave Macmillan.

Neumann, I. (2011). Entry into international society reconceptualised: The case of Russia. *Review of International Studies, 37*(2), 70–91.

Neumann, I., & Welsh, J. (1991). The other in European self-definition: An addendum to the literature on international society. *Review of International Studies, 17*(4), 327–348.

Nicolaidis, K., Vergerio, C., Fisher Onar, N., & Viehoff, V. (2014). From metropolis to Microcosmos: The EU's new standards of civilisation. *Millennium: Journal of International Studies, 42*(3), 718–745.

Nicolaïdis, K., & Whitman, R. G. (2013). Special issue on normative power Europe. *Cooperation and Conflict, 48*(2).

Pänke, J. (2015). The fallout of the EU's normative imperialism in the eastern Neighborhood. *Problems of Post-Communism, 62*(6), 350–363.

Papadimitriou, P., & Zartaloudis, S. (2015). European discourses on managing the Greek crisis: Denial, distancing and the politics of blame. In G. Karyotis & R. Gerodimos (Eds.), *The politics of extreme austerity: Greece in the Eurozone crisis* (pp. 34–45). Basingstoke: Palgrave Macmillan.

Pappas, T. (2014). *Populism and crisis politics in Greece.* New York: Palgrave Macmillan.

Paris, R. (2002). International peacebuilding and the 'mission civilisatrice'. *Review of International Studies, 28*(4), 637–656.

Patomäki, H. (2013). *The great Eurozone disaster. From crisis to global new deal.* London: Zed Books.

Petmesidou, M., & Glatzer, M. (2015). The crisis imperative, reform dynamics and rescaling in Greece and Portugal. *European Journal of Social Security, 17*(2), 157–180.

Polychroniou, C. J. (2015). Dead economic dogmas trump recovery: The continuing crisis in the Eurozone periphery. In A. Bitzenis, N. Karagiannis, & J. Marangos (Eds.), *Europe in crisis: Problems, challenges, and alternative perspectives* (pp. 241–257). New York: Palgrave Macmillan.

Ryner, M. (2015). Europe's Ordoliberal iron cage: Critical political economy, the Euro area crisis and its management. *Journal of European Public Policy, 22*(2), 275–294.

Schimmelfennig, F. (2015). Liberal intergovernmentalism and the Euro area crisis. *Journal of European Public Policy, 22*(2), 177–195.

Schmidt, S. (2012). Soft power or neo-colonialist power? – African perceptions of the EU. *Review of European Studies, 4*(3), 100–110.

Sepos, A. (2013). Imperial power Europe? The EU's relations with the ACP countries. *Journal of Political Power, 6*(2), 261–287.

Simpson, G. (2004). *Great powers and outlaw states: Unequal sovereigns in the international legal order*. Cambridge: Cambridge University Press.

Sklias, P., & Tzifakis, N. (Eds.). (2013). *Greece's horizons reflecting on the Country's assets and capabilities*. Heidelberg: Springer.

Stavridis, S., & Sola, N. F. (2011). The EU: What kind of international actor? In G. Voskopoulos & I. Kouskouvelis (Eds.), *Russia, the EU and the US as a security triangle: Action, interaction and challenges ahead* (pp. 23–51). Athens: Eurasia Publications.

Stivachtis, Y. (2008). Civilization and international society: The case of European Union expansion. *Contemporary Politics, 14*(1), 71–89.

Stroikos, D. (2014). Introduction: Rethinking the standard(s) of civilisation(s) in international relations. *Millennium: Journal of International Studies, 42*(3), 546–556.

Takas, E., & Samaras, A. (2016). Legitimation and de-legitimation processes of memorandum II in Greece: Facets of strategic framing in Greek parliamentary discourse. *French Journal for Media Research, 5.*

Tekin, B. C. (2014). Rethinking the post-national EU in times of austerity and crisis. *Mediterranean Politics, 19*(1), 21–39.

Theodoropoulou, S. (2015). National social and labour market policy reform in the shadow of EU bail-out conditionality: The cases of Greece and Portugal. *Comparative European Politics, 13*(1), 29–55.

Tosun, J., Wetzel, A., & Zapryanova, G. (2014). The EU in crisis: Advancing the debate. *Journal of European Integration, 36*(3), 195–211.

Towns, A. (2009). The status of women as a standard of civilization. *European Journal of International Relations, 15*(4), 681–706.

Tsebelis, G. (2016). Lessons from the Greek crisis. *Journal of European Public Policy, 23*(1), 25–41.

Tzogopoulos, G. (2013). *The Greek crisis in the media*. Ashgate: Stereotyping in the International Press.

Van Vossole, J. (2016). Framing PIGS: Patterns of racism and Neocolonialism in the Euro crisis. *Patterns of Prejudice, 50*(1), 1–20.

Verde, A. (2011). The Greek debt crisis: Causes, policy responses and consequences. In P. Della Posta & L. Talani (Eds.), *Europe and the financial crisis* (pp. 143–164). London: Palgrave Macmillan.

Vilpišauskas, R. (2013). Eurozone crisis and European integration: Functional Spillover, political spillback? *Journal of European Integration, 35*(3), 361–373.

Whitman, R. G. (Ed.). (2011). *Normative power Europe: Empirical and theoretical perspectives.* Basingstoke: Palgrave Macmillan.

Zahariadis, N. (2016). Values as barriers to compromise? Ideology, transnational coalitions, and distributive bargaining in negotiations over the third Greek bailout. *International Negotiation, 21*(3), 473–494.

Zahariadis, N. (2017). Bargaining power and negotiation strategy: Examining the Greek bailouts, 2010–2015. *Journal of European Public Policy, 24*(5), 675–694.

Zarakol, A. (2011). *After defeat: How the east learned to live with the west.* Cambridge: Cambridge University Press.

Zielonka, J. (2006). *Europe as empire: The nature of the enlarged European union.* Oxford: Oxford University Press.

CHAPTER 9

Greece in the Aftermath of the Economic Crisis Needs to Change Its Strategy in the International System: Choosing Between Melians and David

Revecca Pedi

INTRODUCTION

Apart from the severe economic and social consequences the economic crisis has had upon Greece, it also revealed Greece's inefficiency to respond effectively to challenges and pressures posed by the international system. At the international level, this inefficiency has been underpinned by claims about a failed or a failing state (Featherstone 2011; Litsas 2014; Summers 2015). At the domestic level, though, the dominant narrative has been one of victimization, emphasizing asymmetries of power and injustice. In his first interview after reaching a painful agreement with creditors for a

Thanks are due to Professor Katerina Sarri, Professor Ilias Kouskouvelis and the anonymous reviewer for their helpful comments on earlier drafts of this chapter. Any errors remain the author's responsibility.

R. Pedi (✉)
Department of International and European Studies, University of Macedonia, Thessaloniki, Greece

J. Marangos (ed.), *The Internal Impact and External Influence of the Greek Financial Crisis*, DOI 10.1007/978-3-319-60201-1_9

third bail-out, the Greek PM Alexis Tsipras (2015a) admitted that during the negotiations he was believing that justice would prevail over the power of the global financial markets. Thus, Greece's inefficiency has been concealed under what I call "Melians' narrative". Greek politicians and citizens have identified themselves with the citizens of Melos in their dialogue with the representatives of Athens. This narrative of the Greek economic crisis could be summarized by the Athenians' notorious response: "… that in human considerations justice is what is decided when equal forces are opposed, while possibilities are what superiors impose and the weak acquiesce to" (Thucydides (trans.) 1998, 5.89). Yet, these two opposite positions—as it often happens with the extremes—hide more than they reveal about the Greek economic crisis and the strategy of Greece in the international system and within the European Union (EU).

The aim of this chapter is to provide an alternative narrative about Greece's inefficiency, by taking into account the implications of the asymmetries of power in the Greek case and the options that Greece as a small state had in this context. It considers the hypothesis that had Greece followed a "small but smart" state strategy during the economic crisis, it would have avoided costly miscalculations. To this end, the period of negotiations between Greece and its creditors from the January 2015 to July 2015 is examined. Thus, the next section elaborates on the concept of the small state, looks at successful small state strategies and places the case of Greece into this context. To this background, the Greek strategy is then discussed. Finally, it is concluded that the Greek economic crisis proved the need for Greece to depart from its Melians' narrative and victimhood in its international relations towards cultivating a "small but smart" state mind-set.

UNDERSTANDING SMALLNESS

There is no consensus over the definition of small state, and scholars have used many different approaches: quantitative, qualitative, behavioural, based on perceptions, relative and residual (Pedi 2016). To cite but few examples, in the EU context, Panke (2012b, p. 330) argues that "Malta, Cyprus, Estonia, Latvia, Luxembourg, Slovenia, Denmark, Finland, Lithuania, Slovakia, Austria, Bulgaria, Sweden, Belgium, the Czech Republic, Greece, Hungary and Portugal have fewer than the average number of votes in the Council and thus, qualify as small states." Such a view concurs with Verdun (2013, p. 279), who suggests that "in the

EU context it is common to identify six large member states: Germany, France, Italy, United Kingdom, Spain and Poland." Wivel et al. (2014, p. 9) "define a small state as the weaker part in an asymmetric relationship, which is unable to change the nature or functioning of the relationship on its own." According to these definitions, Greece in the context of this study is by any means a small state.

Even when starting from different definitions, small state scholars explore the same states or group of states, agree on the factors that impact upon small states' behaviour, successes or failures and confine their attention to the same issues, looking for the implications of the asymmetry of power upon the states that are not great powers, namely, upon the states that cannot shape the international system (Pedi 2016). In this sense, the essence of smallness is vulnerability (Payne 2009). Small states owing to their limited resources and influence are more vulnerable than great powers to changes in the international system and to pressures emanate from such changes. Griffiths (2014, p. 48) sheds light on the causal relationship between vulnerability and smallness by stressing that the latter "exacerbates the impact of external shocks or diminishes the capacity to absorb them." Moreover, openness, a sine qua non for small economies, further increases vulnerability (Moses 2000). This interaction among size, openness and vulnerability has been reconfirmed during the recent economic crisis, as small EU member states have been more vulnerable than the bigger ones (Verdun 2013). However, the fact that small states are more vulnerable does not mean that they are impotent. Small states owing to their small size can adapt more easily to changes provoked by crises (Verdun 2013). In addition, they can compensate for their limitations and even succeed against a harsh environment, through forming special social arrangements and finding creative solutions (Katzenstein 1985; Baldacchino 2015). In this sense, small states, apart from being vulnerable, can also be resilient.

Small states that respond to crises, challenges and opportunities successfully are aware of their limitations, but they are not inhibited by them in their efforts to pursue their interests. They recognize that the international system is anarchical, competitive and a self-help system, and in this context, they acknowledge their limitations and priorities. Therefore, they try to safeguard and effectively exploit their own resources, while capitalizing on the resources of their allies, or of institutions such as the EU, in order to "punch above their weight". In other words, these states feel their vulnerability and they are constantly after ways to decrease it by maximizing their influence.

In the EU context, Pedi (2016) finds that the strategies of small states which maximize their influence involve undertaking innovative initiatives and norm or policy entrepreneurship that create value for all the involved parts, looking for consensus by playing the role of an "honest broker" or a mediator, forming alliances and/or networks and lobbying, holding a Chair, such as the Council's presidency, providing some needed expertise, good preparation and good knowledge of the issues concerned, credibility, consistency and commitment.

Panke (2012a, b), whose focus is on small state strategies in multilateral negotiations, concurs with the spirit of the above findings. She notes that equality is only theoretical even in cases where the "one state, one vote" principle is applied, as small states face significant limitations in resources and influence. She emphasizes the importance of prioritization, appropriate argumentation (legal, moral and normative, or technical and scientific) that fits with the context and addressees' prior beliefs, knowledge of the agenda, use of institutional opportunities and coalitions. According to Panke, when small states fail in negotiations, it is because of either lack of prioritization or due to a preference to follow bargaining strategies instead of persuasion. Thus, she concludes that "small states are neither per se power brokers nor are they per se political dwarfs in international negotiations" (Panke 2012a, p. 396).

In a different setting, bilateral negotiations, the combination of various factors such as the state of international system, leadership skills, domestic unity, geographic position and moral advantage are critical to the success of a small state (Pedi 2016). In addition, Keohane (1971), who explores the ways smaller allies had found to extract gains from the US during the Cold War, underlines, among others, the importance of a credible alternative and the threat of collapsing.

Concerning small states in the current economic crisis, different cases from Ireland, Estonia and Iceland show that political arrangements matter and that unity at both the political and societal levels is of utmost importance (Thorhallsson and Kirby 2012; Thorhallsson and Kattel 2013). Moreover, the role of reputation is highlighted (Jones 2013), as well as the significance of skilful leadership, able to anticipate events and foster change as Kouskouvelis (2015) notes with regard to Cyprus. Furthermore, scholars expect that the EU can provide shelter to its members (Thorhallsson 2010; Thorhallsson and Kirby 2012; Verdun 2013). Having the EU as a shelter, does not mean that small EU member states have not been seriously affected by the crisis. However, it is suggested that the EU can act as a security net, protecting small EU member states from a total collapse, while it comes at a cost in terms of autonomy (Thorhallsson and Kirby 2012).

Therefore, there are small states which prefer emulating David who used his flexibility and a well-calculated strategy to win over Goliath, to following the fate of the citizens of Melos. These states are usually and especially in an EU context called "small but smart" states (Wivel 2010). Smartness refers to an efficient use of means to achieve ends, namely, the maximization of their influence.

Under this perspective, initially the Greek economic crisis is neither exceptional nor unique. During the current economic crisis as well as in the past, several small states have suffered the implications of their vulnerability and most of them have recovered with varying degrees of success (Katzenstein 1985; Jones 2013; Thorhallsson and Kirby 2012; Thorhallsson and Kattel 2013). Although different small states have responded to the current economic crisis in different ways, research on small states reveals that size matters, but a state's resources of power and strategy are important too (Thorhallsson and Kirby 2012; Thorhallsson and Kattel 2013; Verdun 2013). Thus, what separates the Greek case from those small states that respond successfully to exogenous challenges is not that it is small and vulnerable, but that it has not been able to be resilient. Resilience according to Griffiths (2014, p. 57):

> has been taken to embrace two associated issues, namely the ability to with-stand an exogenous shock should one occur, and the ability to respond to a crisis should it develop. The first depends on mechanisms of flexibility and adaptability and the second depends on the quality of governance and the policy options available.

In the context of this chapter, we are interested in the latter and especially in the way that Greece dealt with its partners and creditors. Based on the above analysis, the next section investigates whether the Greek government followed a "small but smart" state strategy that could help Greece to maximize its influence at the negotiating table.

BACK TO GREECE: DID THE MELIANS HAVE A CREDIBLE STRATEGY?

During the six months from January 2015 to July 2015, the drawn-out political drama of the Greek crisis has unfolded intense and unpredictable events. The then newly elected SYRIZA-ANEL coalition government had promised to bring hope in Greece and Europe. PM Tsipras, young, left and uncorrupted, was expected to rock the status quo. He had pledged to tear up the memorandum, end austerity policies and force change in Greece and the EU. Both parties in their campaigns insisted that Greece could remain in the euro area without applying the devastating and onerous agreements with its creditors. However, six months later, the government had run out of money and asked from hospitals, universities and local governments to deposit their money to the Bank of Greece; capital controls were introduced and Greece found itself closer than ever to GREXIT; finally, PM Tsipras reached a painful agreement for a third bail-out which was worse than the proposal creditors had offered him earlier (Juncker 2015a). Of course, PM Tsipras and the SYRIZA-ANEL government are neither the first nor the last politicians who do not honour their pledges. However, the aftermath of their negotiations strategy, both the radical change of position by the governing coalition—government did not reach none of its goals—as well as the serious consequences upon the Greek society, economy and the country's reputation reveal that the Greek government's strategy has been seriously miscalculated.

Explanations for the reasons why the Greek government chose such a strategy vary. It was believed that as a professor of Game Theory, Varoufakis had turned his theory into Greece's negotiating strategy (Giugliano 2015). Thus, for Featherstone (2016) was Varoufakis, the then Finance Minister, who put forward a Game of 'Chicken'; namely, a game that refers to two drivers who drive towards each other: he who will swerve first, to avoid the crash, will be considered a coward, a 'chicken', and will miss; if both twist, then both will face the consequences; if both of them insist, then the cost can be death for both (Kouskouvelis 1997). Even in this case the Greek side should have taken into account the asymmetry of power, as Greece and its creditors would not belong to the same category of vehicles and therefore even a crash would have affected them differently. Tsebelis (2016, p. 29) offers a different perspective; PM Tsipras had to respond to three different games: the first was about the Greek voters, the second concerned the opposition in his own party and the third refers to the multiple actors with whom Tsipras had to negotiate in the EU context. As a result, he notes, "[T]he Greek 'strategy' is a mess of random and contradictory messages from Greek government officials, resulting from trying to coordinate across these different games." Zahariadis (2016, pp. 13–14) suggests that the Greek government chose a "hard bargaining" strategy, instead of a "soft bargaining" one, the type of bargaining previous governments, for three reasons: (a) more resources initially, as the economic situation of Greece was slightly better in comparison with the previous two rounds of negotiations, (b) a perceived better best alternative to negotiated agreement and (c) more domestic constraints. He also adds that "SYRIZA's ideology and feedback effects from previous negotiations rounds" played a role. Zahariadis (2016, p. 17) concludes that "[W]eakness limits choice." Thus, the question whether it was weakness or a series of bad choices because of which the Greek strategy failed begs for an answer.

Being the weaker part at the negotiating table, the Greek government was seeking to maximize its influence. Therefore, we should ask whether the Greek government's choices were compatible with a "small but smart" state strategy. To answer this question, based on the above analysis, we confine our attention to factors such as Greek government's ability to estimate the state of the international system, arguments and mind-set of the Greek side, its level of preparation, experience and understanding of the negotiations' context, existence of allies and other resources such as reputation, unity, Greece's geography and leadership.

The International System

The Greek government aspired to play off the powerful actors in the system against one another by looking for alternative sources of support, beyond the West. From Russia, PM Tsipras (quoted in Chu 2015) stated that:

> We are at the centre of a storm, of a whirlpool. But you know we live near the sea—we are not afraid of storms, we are not scared of open seas, of going into new seas. We are ready to go into new seas to reach new safe ports.

This statement has been perceived by many commentators as a signal to his EU partners that Greece is not afraid of a GREXIT and was looking for alternative solutions. Earlier from Moscow the Greek PM had openly expressed his opposition to the EU's sanctions on Russia (Tsipras 2015b), a position also shared publicly and in the EU circles by his Minister of Foreign Affairs, Kotzias (Higgins 2015).

Although such a strategy has been successful for small states during the Cold War (Keohane 1971), it seems that it was not the currency in the international system anymore, as there was little competition among the great powers in the system, and even less over the Greek case. After all it was known that Russia's dire economic situation would not permit supporting Greece. What is more in 2013 when Cyprus counted on financial aid from Russia, as its own 'Plan B', the Cypriot efforts to draw support from Russians proved futile (Kouskouvelis 2015). So, Cyprus' miscalculation should have been alarming.

Yet, it was not only that the Greek government could not extract any gains from a supposed special relationship with Russia, but also that the other major players in the system insisted that Greece should conform with the EU's order. Remarks made by President Obama (2015) in the Q&A session of a Joint with the Brazilian President Press Conference at the White House are telling:

> What we've been encouraging both the Greek government and our European partners to do is to continue to negotiate and find a pathway towards a resolution. [...] In layman's terms for the American people, this is not something that we believe will have a major shock to the system. [...] So it's something that we take seriously, but it's not something that I think should prompt overreactions. And so far, I think the markets have properly factored in the risks involved.

In a similar vein, the Chinese Prime Minister stated from Brussels that "We would like to see Greece staying in the euro zone..." because as he argued "[I]t is in China's interest" (quoted in Emmot 2015). That said, the Greek government had already sent alarming and confusing signals to both the United States and China. By passing a law that could lead to the early release of the notorious terrorist Savvas Xiros provoked the Americans. The then US Ambassador to Greece reacted by saying that "If Savvas Xiros—or anyone else with the blood of American diplomats and U.S. Mission members on their hands— leaves prison, it will be seen as a profoundly unfriendly act" (quoted in Bouras 2015). He also revealed that such concerns were made clear to the Greek PM by the US Secretary of State John Kerry (Bouras 2015). At the same time, the ambivalence of the Greek government on the COSCO's investment in the port of Piraeus had puzzled the Chinese (Smith 2015). Therefore, it seems that the Greek government had misread the international system and its potential for best alternatives to the agreement with its creditors.

Argumentation and Mind-Set of the Greek Side

The Greek government wanted to reframe negotiations; it was seeking a political solution, instead of a technical and therefore it used political arguments. Its main positions were first that austerity policies were wrong and therefore the EU should put an end to austerity starting from Greece; second that the Greek government had a fresh and clear mandate by the Greek people not to accept any agreement, so the creditors should recognize the will of the Greek people. Only days before reaching agreement for a new bail-out in his speech in front of the Members of the European Parliament, PM Tsipras (2015c) insisted on those two arguments. As he put it:

> …Europe–our common European project–the European Union, will either be democratic or will face enormous difficulties surviving, given the difficult conditions we're experiencing.
>
> […] we should all acknowledge that the primary responsibility for the difficulties that the Greek economy is experiencing today, for the difficulties that Europe is experiencing today, is not the result of choices made in the last five months, but in the five years of implementing programs that did not end the crisis.

Yet, both arguments were doomed to fail. First, reframing was hard to be achieved, because it presupposes resonance with the addresses' prior beliefs (Panke 2012b) and such a condition did not exist. Second, for any argumentation to be successful, Panke (2012b) notes that it should fit the context of the negotiations. Thus, the Greek government's political arguments were perceived as irrelevant to negotiations which for the rest of the participants were technical. Moscovici (2015) claims that he had warned Greek Finance Minister Varoufakis that his ideas were appropriate for a conference of leftists, but Schauble Germany's Federal Minister of Finance, a Christian Democrat politician and untiring advocate of austerity, and others would not be persuaded by academic lecturing on Keynes. Yet, the then Greek Finance Minister had invested in a strategy of "creative imprecision" (Tagaris 2015). Even Georgiadis, Finance Minister of Cyprus at the time, did not support the Greek line at the Eurogroup and stated that he was unsure about what the Greek government was asking for (Kathimerini 2015). Third, for all the value that the debate on the EU's democratic deficit has in this case (Featherstone 2016), in the eyes of the rest European leaders the Greek government was suggesting that they should respect the rights of the Greek voters more than the interests and rights of their own electorates. Nonetheless, the Greek government did not consider that some of those European leaders had already taken austerity measures in their respective countries. If they had given into the Greek demands, they would have to pay high political cost in their countries and even sacrifice their political careers.

Furthermore, the Greek government, on the one hand, was arguing that its proposal created value for the whole of the EU and its citizens, and, on the other, was blackmailing its partners with its collapse. Such a stance has been problematic for two reasons. First, it created a deficit of credibility. The Greek government did not act as an honest broker seeking a mutually beneficial compromise, but as a radical force wanting to upset the status quo no matter the costs. Second, the threat of collapse was not credible. As Keohane (1971) argues, a small state can threaten a powerful ally with its collapse but not for ever. This time the EU had been prepared. Such a fact has been proved first by the reaction of the markets in the announcement of the Greek referendum and second by the informal but actual proposal for a GREXIT from the creditors' part. What is more, Greece has already run out of money and time.

Therefore, it seems that the Greek negotiations team did not have the necessary experience in international negotiations, was not very well prepared and lacked understanding of the context. Both Featherstone (2016) and Tsebelis (2016) advocate that this lack of knowledge and understanding was critical for the Greek failure. As Tsebelis (2016, p. 27) notes, "[T]he Greek leadership did not understand that the negotiating deck was stacked in the EU's favor, and wasted time learning the obvious." To this background and under a small state perspective, the Greek government had not understood that for all the problems that such a development creates for democracy in the EU and Europe, the EU comes as a shelter, but with a cost in autonomy for small states (Thorhallsson and Kirby 2012).

Allies

One would assume that Greece could find some support among other small states hit by the crisis and austerity or among the larger states in the North, France and Italy, where Social Democrats were in power. Although France, Italy and the United States did not approve the Greek strategy, they acted, at different stages of the negotiations, as bridge-builders between Greece and Germany and between Greece and the EU, for their own reasons. The rest have been either indifferent to the Greek pleas or critical of the Greek strategy. Even Cyprus, a permanent ally of Greece, kept its distance from the Greek demands. Domestic politics should not be underestimated in this context. Among the European supporters and friends of the Greek coalition government were anti status quo politicians, such as Podemos in Spain. Thus, for example, the then Spanish PM Rajoy, who was already following an austerity programme in his country, had every reason to oppose the Greek proposals. In addition, other countries, like the Baltic states, have been alarmed by the pro-Kremlin position Greece took from the very first days of the SYRIZA-ANEL government.

On the institutions front, the Greek strategy upset even the Commission that was assumed to be a supporter of Greece. President Jean Claude Juncker (2015b) stated that he felt betrayed to add that:

> After months and months of discussions and debate, we were once more determined, patient, around a table working for the best possible agreement. This momentum has been broken unilaterally by the announcement of the referendum and above all by the intention to campaign on a 'no' to this agreement and above all by not telling the whole truth.

Given the above analysis, it should not come as a surprise that the Greek government isolated itself and rendered the relationship between Greece and the EU bilateral, one against all.

Reputation, Unity and Geography

Greece's image as the cradle of democracy, the land of the invaluable ancient Greek culture, has provided Greece a special position among its allies and the international public opinion. However, during the economic crisis, the reputation capital of Greece has evaporated. Its place was taken by a series of stereotypes. Greeks were described as lazy, corrupted, tax evaders, data cookers and free riders, totally irresponsible people who do not deserve to be members of the Eurozone. Although we know that Greeks were not alone in manifesting such a behaviour in the EU and even within the Eurozone (Featherstone 2011; Jones 2013). However, "[G] iven its reputation for vice, Greece is an obvious scapegoat. The Greeks are not only unlucky in being so poorly equipped to handle the crisis, they are also unlucky in being stereotyped as Greeks," as Jones (2013, p. 303) notes. Nonetheless, the Greek government's brinkmanship strengthened the stereotyping narrative. According to Kori Schake (2015), "[T]he reck-lessness of Finance Minister Yanis Varoufakis seems to personify the cri-tique." Thus, the moral advantage that offered the coalition government broad public support at the domestic level was vastly outweighed by the stereotypes about Greece at the international level. In such a context, the argument that Greece was bullied by more powerful players, although legitimate, lost its power due to Greece's already damaged reputation.

Concerning unity, Greek politics have always been divisive and prone to populism (Vasilopoulou et al. 2014). Besides, economic crisis and the austerity programmes impacted heavily upon the political system in Greece. Political polarization increased, mainly around memorandum, and changes in the political landscape were dramatic, especially after the 2012 double elections (Freire et al. 2014). In a sense for Greece to achieve a state of consensual politics was next to the impossible. Fioretos (2013) argues that even at times of economic crisis when vulnerability is high, it is impossible for the Greek political system to achieve unity due to historical reasons. Thus, he concludes that conditions of political and social unity that helped other small states to respond effectively to economic crises were not expected in Greece. Indeed, the four different coalition governments formed during the current crisis have been more an outcome out of necessity and concurrence of political interests rather than a sign of political system's or voters' maturity. In any case, it was too little and too late.

During the period under consideration, lack of unity became an even bigger problem, because there was no unity even within the Greek gov-ernment. At least two different groups were promoting different agen-das. First, the hardliners, whose leading figure was Energy Minister Panagiotis Lafazanis, wanted to remain loyal to their pledges, believed that Greece had many other alternatives, and they would go as far as leav-ing the Eurozone and even the EU. This group of MPs and Ministers abandoned SYRIZA after the agreement. Second, the circle around the PM Tsipras preferred an agreement with Greece's creditors and Greece to remain in the Eurozone. Even this circle was divided to those who favoured a more consensual approach and others who suggested a pro-brinkmanship strategy (Antoniou 2015), making PM Tsipras to change his positions during the negotiations many times (Moscovici 2015). However, the Greek PM was determined to keep his party united and his government in power; therefore, he chose the referendum option as an exit strategy. Euclid Tsakalotos, then chief negotiator and afterwards Greece's Finance Minister, admitted that as the agreement "would never have been ratified by Parliament and would have brought down the government," a referendum was the only way forward (quoted in ekathimerini.com 2015). However, the referendum damaged social and political unity even more.

Geography is the only factor that accidentally has played a positive role for Greece during the negotiations. Greece's location and circumstances in its vicinity strengthened the voices of those among the Europeans and the Americans who were against a GREXIT. According to Reuters (2015):

> The United States has added its voice to calls for a deal this weekend, concerned at the geopolitical consequences if Greece were to be cut loose and become a failed state in the fragile southern Balkans, adjoining the Middle East. 'No one wants to see a North Korea in southeastern Europe,' a European Commission official said.

Leadership

A "small but smart" state strategy requires "smart" leadership. Kouskouvelis (2015) has actually suggested that leadership is what makes a small state "smart" or not and he associates "smartness" with maximization of influence and change. Although a charismatic leader himself at the domestic level, by any account PM Tsipras' leadership at the international stage has not been smart. The above analysis has revealed a series of miscalculations. Tsipras (2015a) himself has admitted that he might have made mistakes, but he tried any possible solution he thought could save Greece and he did not lie to the Greek people. In the light of our small state analysis, the major pitfall of the Greek leadership has been its mistaken priorities. PM Tsipras was hostage to its pre-electoral pledges and intra-party balances, and what is more he lacked international experience. For that reason, his focus was more on the domestic than on the international stage. He underestimated that time and power were not on his side. Moreover, as his strategy sought to satisfy many different and controversial demands (Tsebelis 2016), it lacked coherence and therefore credibility. Thus, it could not be effective.

That said, PM Tsipras and the SYRIZA-ANEL coalition government were not alone in resorting to populism. Vasilopoulou et al. (2014, p. 400) note that:

the need to provide successful solutions to what is primarily an economic problem with international dimensions presented Greek actors with a political dilemma: how to implement fast and effective structural change, while not compromising their own position in the status quo. The answer: by diverting political accountability through a populist rhetoric of blame-shifting. Given the development of a populist democracy in the metapolitefsi era, this is unsurprising and the most likely option available to Greek political actors.

In this sense, the Greek economic crisis showed that the lack of an entrepreneurial leadership, able to make painful choices, find creative solutions and effect change in order to avert further losses has been a major disadvantage for Greece. Moreover, developments concerning the Greek politics and leadership and the interplay between the domestic and the international levels during the economic crisis were only the first signs of a political tradition that later became an international trend: 'post-truth politics'.

Conclusion

This chapter shed some new light on public and scholarly beliefs about the strategies of the Greek governments during the crisis. It suggested that the Greek economic crisis revealed the inefficiency of Greece to respond effectively to pressures emanating from the international system and put forward the hypothesis that had Greece followed a "small but smart" state strategy, it would have avoided miscalculations that prolonged and aggravated the economic crisis. Evidence from the period of the third bail-out agreement shows that the Greek strategy diverged from a "small but smart" state strategy and reconfirms the initial hypothesis. If the Greek government had checked its strategy against the requirements of a "small but smart" state strategy it would probably have paid more attention to the state of the international system, had a better understanding of the implications of power asymmetries in the international system and the EU, the importance of appropriate argumentation, credibility, reputation, allies, unity and geography. Greek leadership's prioritization and focus on the domestic level was also mistaken.

Therefore, this chapter's main proposal is that Greece should depart from its victimhood mind-set and "Melians' narrative" and understand that the international system is first and foremost a self-help system. To increase its influence, Greece should emulate David and adopt a "small but smart" state approach in its international relations. Such a change will enable it to follow strategies that could help Greece to respond effectively to the challenges of current crisis and even prosper. That said, the responsibilities of other actors such as the EU or the International Monetary Fund (IMF) regarding the crisis in the euro area and the mismanagement of the Greek economic crisis should not be underestimated. Yet, the focus is on the way Greece played the cards in hand and the lessons that can be learnt from its failures for the future.

REFERENCES

Antoniou, D. (2015). *Slaughter at the Maximus court.* Kathimerini. (in Greek) Retrieved from http://www.kathimerini.gr/821633/article/epikairothta/politikh/sfazontai-sthn-aylh-toy-ma3imoy

Baldacchino, G. (2015). *Entrepreneurship in small Island states and territories.* New York: Routledge.

Bouras, S. (2015). New Greek law could release prominent left-wing terrorist. *Wall Street Journal.* Retrieved from http://www.wsj.com/articles/new-greek-law-could-release-prominent-left-wing-terrorist-1429548014

Chu, B. (2015). Greece crisis: Alexis Tsipras woos Vladimir Putin as Greeks rush for their savings. *Independent.* Retrieved from http://www.independent.co.uk/news/world/europe/greece-crisis-alexis-tsipras-woos-vladimir-putin-as-greeks-rush-for-their-savings-10333104.html

ekathimerini.com. (2015). SYRIZA's Tsakalotos says referendum was called to stave off government collapse. Retrieved from http://www.ekathimerini.com/198871/article/ekathimerini/news/syrizas-tsakalotos-says-referendum-was-called-to-stave-off-government-collapse

Emmot, R. (2015). China's premier offers Europe investment, wants Greece in Euro Zone. *Reuters.* Retrieved from http://www.reuters.com/article/us-eu-china-idUSKCN0P813T20150629

Featherstone, K. (2011). The JCMS annual lecture: The Greek sovereign debt crisis and EMU: A failing state in a skewed regime. *JCMS: Journal of Common Market Studies, 49*(2), 193–217.

Featherstone, K. (2016). Democracy and institutional weakness: The Euro-crisis trilemma. *JCMS: Journal of Common Market Studies, 54*(*Annual Review*), 48–64.

Fioretos, O. (2013). Origins of embedded orthodoxy: International cooperation and political unity in Greece. *European Political Science, 12*, 305–319.

Freire, A., et al. (2014). Political representation in bailed-out southern Europe: Greece and Portugal compared. *South European Society and Politics, 19*(4), 413–433.

Giugliano, F. (2015). Varoufakis faces challenge of turning game theory into triumph. *Financial Times*. Retrieved from https://www.ft.com/content/0b340146-b20e-11e4-b380-00144feab7de

Griffiths, R. T. (2014). Economic security and size. In C. Archer, A. Bailes, & A. Wivel (Eds.), *Small states and international security: Europe and beyond* (pp. 46–65). Abingdon: Routledge.

Higgins, A. (2015). Greece steps back into line with European Union policy on Russia sanctions. *The New York Times*. Retrieved from http://www.nytimes.com/2015/01/30/world/europe/european-union-russia-sanctions-greece.html

Jones, E. (2013). Getting to Greece: Uncertainty, misfortune, and the origins of political disorder. *European Political Science, 12*, 294–304.

Juncker, J. K. (2015a). Interview to Arte Thema: Grèce, le jour d'après. Retrieved from https://www.youtube.com/watch?v=CBnvVZVq3Fk&t=40s

Juncker, J. K. (2015b). Juncker on Greece: "I feel betrayed". *EurActiv Youtube channel*. Retrieved from https://www.youtube.com/watch?v=i77zvp6wZFY

Kathimerini. (2015). And Cyprus in line with Brussels. *Cyprus Kathimerini*. Retrieved from http://www.kathimerini.gr/803968/article/epikairothta/politikh/kai-h-kypros-se-grammh-vry3ellwn

Katzenstein, P. J. (1985). *Small states in world markets: Industrial policy in Europe*. New York: Cornell University Press.

Keohane, O. (1971). The big influence of small allies. *Foreign Policy*, (2), 161–182.

Kouskouvelis, I. (1997). *Decision making, crisis, negotiation*. Athens: Papazisis. (in Greek).

Kouskouvelis, I. (2015). Smart' leadership in a small state: The case of Cyprus. In A. Tziampiris & S. Litsas (Eds.), *The Eastern Mediterranean in transition: Multipolarity, politics and power* (pp. 93–117). Abingdon: Routledge.

Litsas, S. N. (2014). The Greek failing state and its "smart power" prospects: A theoretical approach. *Mediterranean Quarterly, 25*(3), 52–73.

Moscovici, P. (2015). Interview to Arte Thema: Grèce, le jour d'après. Retrieved from https://www.youtube.com/watch?v=CBnvVZVq3Fk&t=40s

Moses, J. (2000). *Open states in the global economy: The political economy of small-state macroeconomic management*. New York: Springer.

Obama. (2015). Remarks by President Obama and President Rousseff of Brazil in joint press conference. The White House Office of Press Secretary. Retrieved from https://www.whitehouse.gov/the-press-office/2015/06/30/remarks-president-obama-and-president-rousseff-brazil-joint-press

Panke, D. (2012a). Small states in multilateral negotiations. What have we learned? *Cambridge Review of International Affairs, 25*(3), 387–398.

Panke, D. (2012b). Being small in a big union: Punching above their weights? How small states prevailed in the vodka and the pesticides cases. *Cambridge Review of International Affairs, 25*(3), 329–344.

Payne, A. (2009). Afterword: Vulnerability as a condition, resilience as a strategy. In A. Cooper & T. Shaw (Eds.), *The diplomacies of small states* (pp. 279–285). London: Palgrave Macmillan.

Pedi, R. (2016). Theory of international relations: Small states in the international system. Doctoral dissertation, University of Macedonia, School of Social Sciences, Humanities and Arts, Department of International Relations, Thessaloniki.

Reuters. (2015). Euro zone leaders: Greece must do more to earn rescue. Retrieved from http://www.reuters.com/article/us-eurozone-greece-idUSKBN-0P40EO20150712

Schake, K. (2015). The political tragedy of the Greek economic crisis. *Foreign Policy.* Retrieved from http://foreignpolicy.com/2015/05/12/the-political-tragedy-of-the-greek-economic-crisis-default-europe-tsipras/

Smith, H. (2015). Greece's port in a storm: Anger as Syriza stops China extending hold on Piraeus. *Guardian.* Retrieved from https://www.theguardian.com/world/2015/feb/09/greece-syriza-stops-china-extending-hold-piraeus

Summers, L. (2015). Greece is Europe's failed state in waiting. *Financial Times.* Retrieved from https://www.ft.com/content/9c27c84c-1751-11e5-8201-cbdb03d71480

Tagaris, K. (2015). Greece's "creative ambiguity" won extra lifeline, says finance minister. *Reuters.* Retrieved from http://www.reuters.com/article/eurozone-greece-varoufakis-idUSL5N0W14HU2015022

Thorhallsson, B. (2010). The Icelandic crash and its consequences: A small state without economic and political shelter. In R. Steinmetz & A. Wivel (Eds.), *Small states in Europe challenges and opportunities* (pp. 199–214). Farnham: Ashgate.

Thorhallsson, B., & Kattel, R. (2013). Neo-liberal small states and economic crisis: Lessons for democratic corporatism. *Journal of Baltic Studies, 44*(1), 83–103.

Thorhallsson, B., & Kirby, P. (2012). Financial crises in Iceland and Ireland: Does European Union and euro membership matter? *JCMS: Journal of Common Market Studies, 50*(5), 801–818.

Thucydides. (1998). *The Peloponnesian war* (trans. S. Lattimore). Indiana: Hackett.

Tsebelis, G. (2016). Lessons from the Greek crisis. *Journal of European Public Policy, 23*(1), 25–41.

Tsipras, A. (2015a, July 15). Interview of Prime Minister Alexis Tsipras to ERT 1. *Prime Minister of Greece.* Retrieved from http://primeminister.gr/2015/07/15/13887

Tsipras, A. (2015b). Joint press conference with prime minister of Greece Alexis Tsipras. *President of Russia.* Retrieved from http://en.kremlin.ru/events/president/news/52024

Tsipras, A. (2015c). Prime Minister Alexis Tsipras' speech to the European Parliament. *Prime Minister of Greece*. Retrieved from http://primeminister.gr/english/2015/07/08/prime-minister-alexis-tsipras-speech-to-the-european-parliament/

Vasilopoulou, S., Halikiopoulou, D., & Exadaktylos, T. (2014). Greece in crisis: Austerity, populism and the politics of blame. *JCMS: Journal of Common Market Studies, 52*, 388–402.

Verdun, A. (2013). Small states and the global economic crisis: An assessment. *European Political Science, 12*, 276–293.

Wivel, A. (2010). From small state to smart state: Devising a strategy for influence in the European Union. In R. Steinmentz & A. Wivel (Eds.), *Small states in Europe: Challenges and opportunities* (pp. 15–29). Farnham: Ashgate.

Wivel, A., Bailes, A. J. K., & Archer, C. (2014). Setting the scene small states in international security. In C. Archer, A. Bailes, & A. Wivel (Eds.), *Small states and international security: Europe and beyond* (pp. 3–25). Routledge: Abingdon.

Zahariadis, N. (2016). Bargaining power and negotiation strategy: Examining the Greek bailouts, 2010–2015. *Journal of European Public Policy*, 1–20. doi:10.1080/13501763.2016.1154977

A Comparative Analysis of the Greek Financial Crisis and the IMF's Bailout Programs: An East Asian View

Hee-Young Shin

INTRODUCTION

For many East Asian social scientists, the current financial and economic crisis in Greece is like a never-ending nightmare over again. This is because the 'Troika's' (European Commission, European Central Bank (ECB), and the International Monetary Fund (IMF)) policy response to the current Greek financial crisis is not at all different from what the 'Wall Street-Treasury-IMF complex' (Wade and Veneroso 1998) did to Thailand, Indonesia, and South Korea during and after a similar financial crisis in the late 1990s. Just as the current financial crisis in Greece originated from the vagary of foreign capital flows that were directly associated with a global spread of the US subprime mortgage-led financial crisis in 2008–2009, foreign investors' drastic withdrawal from East Asian countries resulted in a series of domino crises in currency markets in the late 1990s. At that time, the IMF under heavy political influences from the US Treasury Department and the army of Wall Street banks played an equivalent role in East Asia, as that

H.-Y. Shin (✉)
Raj Soin College of Business, Wright State University, Dayton, OH, USA

© The Author(s) 2017
J. Marangos (ed.), *The Internal Impact and External Influence of the Greek Financial Crisis*, DOI 10.1007/978-3-319-60201-1_10

161

of the Troika in Greece nowadays. The Wall Street-Treasury-IMF complex imposed a strict bailout conditionality and a series of austerity-oriented policy measures in the name of 'saving' Asian economies, just as the Troika nowadays has been imposing the same conditionality to Greece in the name of 'helping' Greece. However, it has been clear that the Troika is actually creating a humanitarian crisis on a massive scale in this country now, just as the Wall Street–Treasury–IMF complex did in East Asia in the 1990s.

Since the eruption of the initial sign of the financial crisis in Greece, the Greek society has undergone a series of different policy arrangements in dealing with the Troika's bailout conditionality and threats from international creditors. The financial crisis in East Asia also engendered a similar policy regime change that took a variety of forms, including collapse of former military dictatorships that were partially responsible for the financial crisis, a temporal peaceful transition toward a new civilian government, and the reversal of this transition by another military coup and the rise of authoritarian regime, exemplified by both Thailand and Indonesia. Quite recently, the Greek economic crisis has been eclipsed by a massive influx of refugees, multiple terrorist attacks and contempt in Western Europe, and by the 'Brexit' referendum in the UK. While European mass media and international journalists have diverted their attention away from Greece in this process, ordinary Greek people have disproportionately borne unnecessary socioeconomic pain and despair largely imposed by the Troika's misguided bailout programs. Just as some natural disasters such as earthquakes and the tsunami that devastated Indonesia in the early 2000s should not mask the systematic failure of the IMF's bailout programs in this country, many geopolitical and coincidental tragic incidents surrounding the European continent should not be used as distracting excuses for the policy-induced humanitarian crisis in Greece nowadays.

This chapter examines the origin and process of the ongoing economic crisis in Greece from a comparative perspective, paying close attention to the detrimental effect of the Troika's austerity policies in Greece. For this purpose, the chapter is organized as follows: in the next two sections, the author traces and examines the origin and process of the current financial crisis in Greece and the IMF's roles. In Section 'Revisiting the East Asian Financial Crisis in the Late 1990,' the author contrasts the Greek financial and economic crisis with that of East Asia in the late 1990s. The observation in these sections strongly suggests that (1) drastic capital outflows from a country in the absence of regional and/or international regulatory arrangements are the most destabilizing factor that created the financial crisis in both Greece and East Asia, and (2) the IMF and the Troika's austerity-oriented bailout programs have exacerbated the problem of a vicious cycle of economic contraction and increasing sovereign debt burden in Greece. Drawing upon this observation, the author proposes a series of reform agendas that may be applicable to both the regional and international levels in Section 'Policy Lessons for Sovereign Financial Stability and Reforming the Global Financial System.' In this section, the author calls for the need of (1) reversing myopic financial liberalization policy and the premature transfer of fiscal and monetary authorities to a supranational entity, (2) extending and granting the US Chapter 11 bankruptcy provision to sovereign states, (3) creating an effective regional and international lender of last resort, and (4) completely overhauling the existing austerity-oriented bailout conditionality in favor of economic growth and development. The Section 'Conclusion' concludes the discussion in this chapter.

THE ORIGIN AND PROCESS OF THE CURRENT FINANCIAL AND ECONOMIC CRISIS IN GREECE

Let us examine what happened in Greece for the last 6 to 7 years and identify some of the distinctive patterns in this financial and economic crisis. The first and initial stage of the Greek financial crisis dates to late 2009, when the then newly elected Pan-Hellenic Socialist Movement (PASOK) government revealed that former conservative governments intentionally concealed the true magnitude of the fiscal deficit and the government debt. As part of the Eurozone membership requirements, all Eurozone member countries, including Greece, were required to meet a series of 'convergence criteria,' which include the individual member country maintaining not more than 3% of fiscal deficits and 60% of public debts (European Commission 2015). The PASOK government officials found that the former conservative government had not accurately recorded the true liability and in some cases intentionally covered up the actual size of fiscal deficit and debts, by adopting a questionable accounting technique aided by a notorious American investment bank Goldman Sachs (Armitage and Chu 2015; Reich 2015).

Under normal circumstances, this revelation could have ended up as a minor scandal. The time in which this news was reported, however, was in no sense a 'normal' financial circumstance. The year of 2009 was just 1 year after the collapse of the American investment bank, Lehman

Brothers. The flourishing of unregulated subprime mortgage lending in the US housing market, together with massive over-the-counter transactions of opaque private-labeled mortgaged- and asset-backed securities throughout the world instantaneously brought down the entire banking system in the United States and core Eurozone economies. Under these circumstances, the revelation that the Greek government had actually accumulated more debts than initially thought inevitably jolted the Eurozone financial markets. The banks and non-bank financial companies in core Eurozone economies instantaneously froze their lending to Greece and ran on many other peripheral economies in the Eurozone such as Spain, Portugal, and Italy. The Greek stock price index fell sharply and borrowing cost on Greek government bonds rapidly rose to an intolerable level. Three major American crediting agencies (Fitch, S&Ps, and Moody's) lowered their credit ratings of the Greek government bonds, amplifying portfolio investors' concerns for credit and default risks even further. Simply put, a series of chain events like these were the immediate causes of the initial financial crisis in Greece (BBC News 2012).

Of course, the problem did not end there. The second stage of the Greek financial crisis resurfaced 1 year after the Greek government agreed to accept the first 3-year standby loan agreement with the IMF. As part of this bailout agreement, the Greek government had started implementing pension cuts and tax reforms. The government also announced a preliminary privatization program in early 2010, defying massive domestic resistance and protests against the austerity measure. In return, the European creditors released the first two tranches (15 billion euros each) out of the initially proposed total bailout funds. In late May of 2011, however, the Greek government announced that the government might not be able to achieve its 3% of fiscal surplus target, citing 'adverse economic fallout' and 'contraction of tax base and revenues' (IMF 2011). An American credit rating agency, Moody's, downgraded the Greek bonds from B1 to Caa1 (which is effectively 'junk' status), and the 10-year government bond interest rates sharply rose to 16.25% at one point.

European finance ministers hurriedly pressed the Greek government to fasten its efforts to impose 'structural reforms' to gain credibility and confidence from foreign creditors, threatening to rescind additional tranche releases (IMF 2011). As the Eurozone financial market abruptly swelled into another instability in this way, however. European finance ministers overturned their hardline position and attempted to expedite Greek debt restructuring negotiations.

As this negotiation was stalled and frequently suspended due to disagreement among creditors, European finance ministers came up with an ad hoc idea of providing 8.7 billion euros of emergent funds to bridge the shortfall in the Greek government debt repayment. They also agreed to provide another 3-year extended standby bailout fund to Greece by 2014, totaling 109 billion euros (37 billion euros in each tranche) on top of the remaining tranches of the first bailout fund (IMF 2012a). Unfortunately, these measures turned out to be too late and too timid. Even though it seemed to help stabilize Southern European sovereign bond markets (notably, in Spain, Portugal, and Italy) temporarily, they failed to address the fundamental debt sustainability problem in Greece that foreign creditors were mostly concerned.

The end of the second stage in this Greek tragic drama had its own Greek characteristics. By the time the Greek parliament was required to approve this second bailout conditionality, the Greek Prime Minister Papandreou announced that he would rather hold a general referendum, asking whether ordinary Greek citizens would be willing to accept the harsher second bailout conditionality. As this plan was announced, the European financial markets plunged again. Angela Merkel (Chancellor of Germany) and Nicholas Sarkozy (then President of France) pressed George Papandreou to resign from the post, citing that his 'defiant' move endangered the hard-earned consensus among creditors. After having 2 to 3 days of tumultuous political clamor, the members of second majority party, the New Democracy (ND) in the Greek parliament impeached the publicly elected Greek prime minister. After expelling George Papandreou, the ND right-wing party and some opposition leaders in the PASOK agreed to hold a general election. In the following two elections held in May and June 2012, the ND ultimately formed an allied government with a majority parliamentary seat. This coalition government elected Antonis Samaras as its new prime minister, and it pledged to implement the agreed second bailout conditionality thoroughly.

The last and concurrent stage of the Greek drama is coincided with an unexpected electoral victory of SYRIZA, the Coalition of the Radical Left in the 2015 January election. After experiencing the failed austerity-oriented bailout program, the Greek voters wanted to change the course. They wanted to say 'no more austerity' and the majority of Greek citizens voted for Syriza in the election, which had actively campaigned for renegotiation over the bailout terms. The Syriza gained 36.34% of the total ballots and occupied 149 parliamentary seats, shrinking the second leading ND party's seats to only 76. One of the main campaign agendas and Syriza's party programs was that Greece's new government would renegotiate the bailout terms so that the Greek economy and people would have some 'breathing space.' They claimed that they would be able to gain much more concession from Eurozone creditor countries by even leveraging Greece's potential 'exit' from the Eurozone. The new Prime Minister, Alexis Tsipras, nominated Yanis Varoufakis as finance minister to renew negotiations with the German counterpart. The overall negotiation process between Greece and the Troika was tumultuous, sometimes involving multiple suspensions of negotiation schedules, personal blaming, and of course overreacted responses in Eurozone financial markets. At one point, Alexis Tsipras called for a referendum, asking whether Greek citizens would be willing to accept another round of bailout conditionality. He also replaced the prime minister to refresh the air over the negotiation table. The Syriza government introduced temporary bank closing and capital controls to prevent chaotic capital outflows by domestic citizens (McSweeney and Rankin 2015; Blackstone et al. 2015). After a majority of Greek citizens voted 'No' to harsh bailout conditionality in the referendum held in July of 2015, however, Alexis Tsipras shockingly overturned the course and hurriedly signed the third bailout terms without receiving any concessions from the German finance minister, a chief negotiator from creditor countries. The Prime Minister, Alexis Tsipras, survived in another election held in September after this humiliating negotiation outcome, but the Greek economic crisis continues.

It was not clear at that time why the Syriza government suddenly overturned its original renegotiation strategies and literally betrayed the public's overwhelming supports for a 'no more austerity' stance. In one interview, the former Finance Minister Varoufakis indicated that Greece's leftist government was not at all prepared to leave the Eurozone, just as the majority of the Greek public did not want to exit from the Eurozone (Varoufakis 2016). In addition, Tsipras and his cabinet members naively believed that their 'parallel legislative program' would somehow alleviate apparent socioeconomic costs and social pains inevitably expected to result from a harsher third bailout conditionality (Panagiotidis 2016; Landy and Harrison 2015). However, the Troika rejected the Syriza's social spending program, threatening the termination of the additional tranche release.

THE ROLE OF THE IMF AND THE TROIKA IN THE CURRENT CRISIS IN GREECE

Unfortunately, during the entire process of the Greek financial and economic crisis, the Troika simply exacerbated the initial financial problem. Rather than helping and saving the Greek economy, it has played a critical role in triggering a full-blown spread of financial instability into painful socioeconomic crisis in Greece (BBC News 2015; Giannitsis and Zografakis 2015; Matsaganis 2013; Mitrakos 2014).

In the IMF's country report (known as 'Article IV consultation') issued in both January and December of 2007, IMF economists highly praised the Greek government's 'financial market liberalization' policy and optimistically projected a sustained economic growth in Greece. They argued that the Greek economy had grown remarkably thanks to sustained inflows of foreign private capital to the country and corresponding growth of household and corporate credit. They also praised the Greek government's efforts to enhance 'the competitiveness in domestic banking and financial industry' by following Eurozone-wide financial sector liberalization policies (IMF 2007a, b).

The IMF's extremely fragrant attitude toward the Greek economy, however, was drastically reversed during the first half of 2009. Suddenly, the IMF report began to warn that the Greek economy might enter into recession as foreign financial capital flew out of the country. Even though Greece did not have any direct exposure to toxic mortgage-backed securities, the report observed that banks' balance sheets would quickly deteriorate, posing serious 'downside risks' to the Greek economy, as foreign private lending dried up (IMF 2009).

This reversed diagnosis of the Greek economy, from the author's point of view, should have served an important historical moment to realize the danger of myopic financial market liberalization policy, which both the IMF and European policy makers in Frankfurt and Brussels have strongly advocated for a decade and mandated as an important precondition for joining in the Eurozone. The initial financial market instability that surfaced not only in Greece, but also in many other southern European peripheral economies should also have vindicated the need of emergency capital control measures. The IMF and the Troika should have come up with a series of financial regulatory arrangements including the control for capital outflows with which an individual government and monetary authority in the region withstands the vagary of short-term international financial flows.

Rather than doing so, the IMF imposed a series of bailout condition- alities (IMF 2010a, b), when the Greek government ultimately reached a deal with the IMF in May of 2010. This austerity policy stance, as it turned out, exacerbated initial financial troubles in Greece. In the face of rapid foreign capital outflows, the Greek government and the European monetary authorities should have adopted a strong capital control mea- sure to insulate systemic damages that this myopic capital outflow can pose to the stability of the Greek financial system. At that time, foreign private creditors drastically reversed their portfolio decisions and competitively withdrew their prior investment from Greece, not because they came to realize that the Greek government mismanaged its foreign liability per se, but mainly because they feared that they might lose their portfolio if they had not done so. Thus, the natural and sensible way to prevent this panicky herd behavior was to introduce temporal capital control and to create an orderly debt repayment mechanism, in which both creditors and debtors renegotiate the maturity and the terms of debt repayment. They could have discussed a debt rollover, debt maturity extension, and even a substantial reduction in the debt outstanding in an orderly man- ner, without endangering the stability of the entire financial system in the Eurozone. If this negotiation potentially involved too many private par- ties (i.e., transnational creditors headquartered in the UK, Germany, and France), the IMF or ECB could have played a role as a leading negotiator on behalf of multiple private creditors.

It seemed also necessary for the Greek government to adopt a series of countercyclical fiscal and monetary policies to alleviate socioeconomic pain caused by financial crisis and economic recession. The Greek govern- ment should increase its revenues if it wants to repay previously incurred debts, and the only sensible way to achieve this goal is to help the pri- vate sector economy grow substantially in a sustainable way. This in turn requires that the Greek government adopt countercyclical expansionary fiscal policies to forge rapid economic recovery. When it comes to actual policy instruments, the Greek government should have incurred more deficits and debts temporarily to finance the government-sponsored work projects, infrastructure building and renovation, and increases in its social and educational spending, in order to complement a substantial reduction and deficiency in private aggregate demand.

The Troika's bailout conditionality contained exactly opposite measures to this basic economic principle. The imposed standby agreement erroneously mandated the Greek government to achieve fiscal surpluses during the culminating period of the financial crisis and completely failed to address how to set up and manage an orderly debt repayment mechanism over a long period of time (IMF 2010c, d). The Greek government repeatedly failed to meet the mandated target to achieve fiscal surplus because the unmitigated recessionary spiral wiped out the existing tax base and revenues. As the financial crisis hit the real sector of the Greek economy, the private sector suffered from the recession. Precisely for that reason, the Greek government experienced a reduced tax revenue. Under these circumstances, the Troika forced the Greek government to achieve fiscal surplus. The Greek government could have achieved this urged fiscal target by radically slashing its basic necessary social spending temporarily. However, the same austerity policy has pushed the Greek economy spiraling downward further, ultimately making it impossible for the Greek government to repay its existing debts.

Despite these repeated failures in the Greek bailout programs, the IMF and Troika have imposed the same nonsensical austerity-oriented bailout conditionality over again. The medieval surgeon who made coughing patients crippled and bleeding dangerously now expects them to run and fly. This is what the modern-day medieval surgeon, the IMF and the Troika, has done to the Greek economy. They have never thought about the apparent fact that austerity measures that they have insisted are the very same barriers that make it impossible for the Greek government to repay its debts. As the Greek chief negotiator, Yanis Varoufakis, once reflected, Wolfgang Schauble, the German finance minister, and many other ministers from creditor countries did not listen to whatever the economically sensible debt relief and debt repayment plan that the former Greek finance minister proposed in vain (Varoufakis et al. 2013). They put their unfounded 'Christian ethics'—'debtor should be punished at all cost' far ahead of any sensible economic recovery proposal (Varoufakis 2015). For this reason, the IMF and Troika are responsible for the current ongoing economic and humanitarian crisis in Greece.

Under the ND party-led, pro-Troika coalition government that has thoroughly implemented the second bailout conditionalities, the Greek economic situation deteriorated seriously. The government has successively cut the pension payment to retirees and salaries for public employees by 25% during the last 6 years. They also drastically reduced educational and social spending, including the long-lasting government subsidies for food and nutrition supports for elementary school students. Under the Troika's close monitoring, the government also has come up with a series of expedite privatization plans for public utility enterprises such as water, electricity, and onshore gas and oil drilling companies (IMF 2012b, 2013, 2014). The end outcome of this austerity is simply a prolonged recession and debt deflation. As we can see from the following series of charts that capture Greece's GDP growth rates and industrial production activities, the Greek economy has been pushed into a serious economic contraction, whose level is unseen in any advanced capitalist market economy since the Great Depression in the 1930s (see Figs. 10.1 and 10.2).

According to the IMF and Troika's rosy economic forecast, the Greek economy will soon quickly recover, once the Greek government committed itself to cutting its profligate expenditures. Unfortunately, the Greek government has not only missed the Troika's annual fiscal targets multiple times, but also has incurred an increasingly high public debt burden

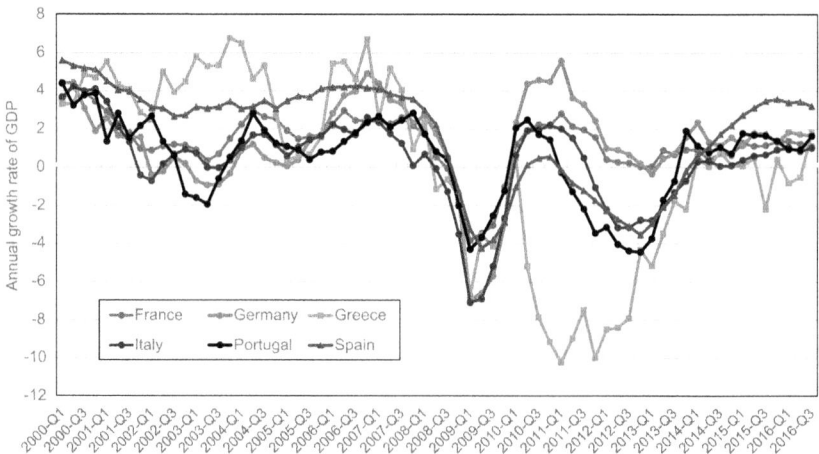

Fig. 10.1 Growth rate of real GDP in selected Eurozone economies, 1Q of 2000–3Q of 2016. Source: OECD statistical data ((OECD 2016), quarterly GDP (indicator). doi:10.1787/b86d1fc8-en (Accessed on 07 December 2016))

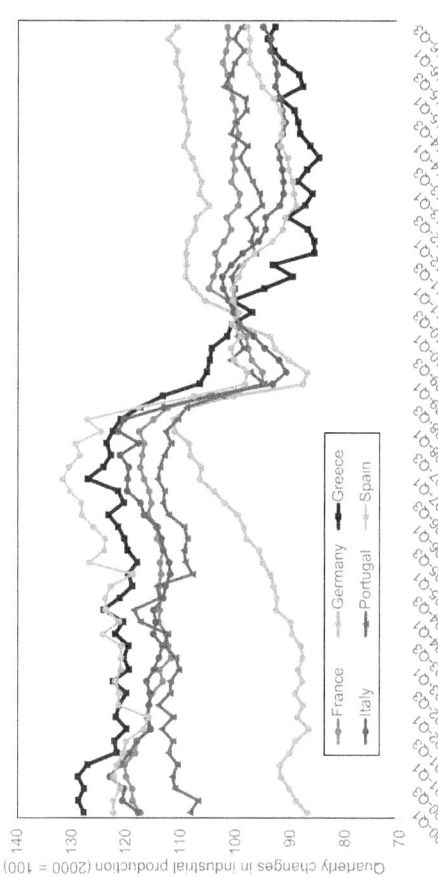

Fig. 10.2 Changes in industrial production activities in selected Eurozone economies, 1Q of 2000–3Q of 2016. Source: OECD statistical data ((OECD 2016), industrial production (indicator). doi:10.1787/39121c55-en (Accessed on 07 December 2016))

measured by the government debt to GDP ratio. Ironically, this is not because the pro-Troika government in Greece has cheated the Troika repeatedly, but precisely because the government has thoroughly implemented what the Troika imposed onto Greece. Under the circumstances of serious economic downturn, private aggregate demand (both household consumption and corporate investment) fall. In the absence of the government's countercyclical policy measures, the economy must fall into a deeper downward spiral. The Troika's austerity-oriented bailout conditionality has simply reinforced this downward spiral, making it impossible for the Greek economy to achieve any meaningful debt repayment through economic recovery. The ultimate result borned by Greek citizens is a massive humanitarian crisis, a combination of prolonged and severe economic recession, a rising unemployment rate, accompanied by an unabated debt payment burden (see Figs. 10.3 and 10.4).

In early 2015, the newly elected Syriza government attempted to change this course, by promising renegotiations with the Troika over the bailout terms. At one point, Alexis Tsipras and his team called for a referendum to ask whether the ordinary Greek public would be willing to accept harsher austerity policies, and the overwhelming majority of the Greek citizens strongly backed for the Syriza government's negotiation strategies. The Greek prime minister also attempted to implement so-called 'parallel programs' that he hoped would offset the devastating impacts of the Troika's harsher bailout conditionality. The Troika immediately rejected this effort. As it turns out, however, even the IMF's economists did not believe the viability and effectiveness of the Troika's bailout program (IEO 2016; Assange 2016; Nunevar 2016). It is also revealed that less than 5% of the Troika's bailout loans went to the Greek government's budget and most of them have been simply used to pay back the existing debts and interest the private creditors in Germany and France (Rocholl and Stahmer 2016). One may wonder, then, why the Troika is imposing the same austerity program repeatedly, if it uses the tranches of bailout funds to repay the Greek debt. One may also argue that the Troika could have bought up the entire Greek government debts from many private creditors and initiated the negotiation with the Greek government over the potential debt rollover and debt reduction. If the Troika had done so early on, the current Greek financial and economic crisis as we now know would not have existed from the beginning.

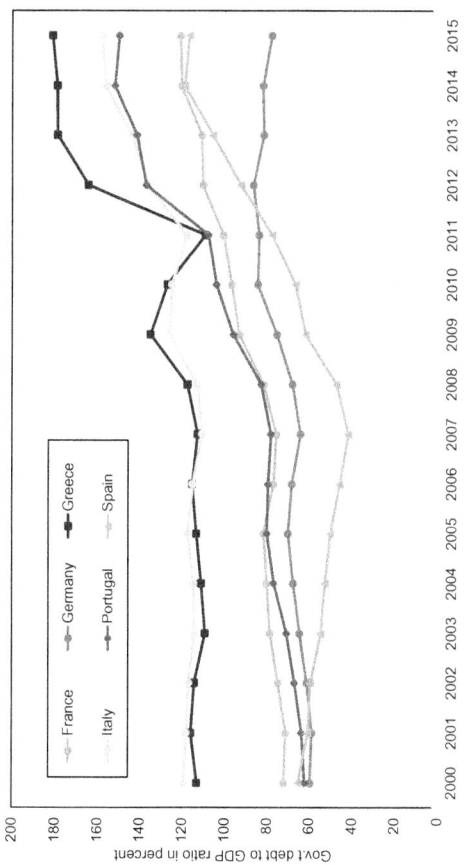

Fig. 10.3 Government debt to GDP ratios in selected Eurozone economies, 2000–2015. Source: OECD statistical data ((OECD 2016), general government debt (indicator). doi:10.1787/a0528cc2-en (Accessed on 07 December 2016))

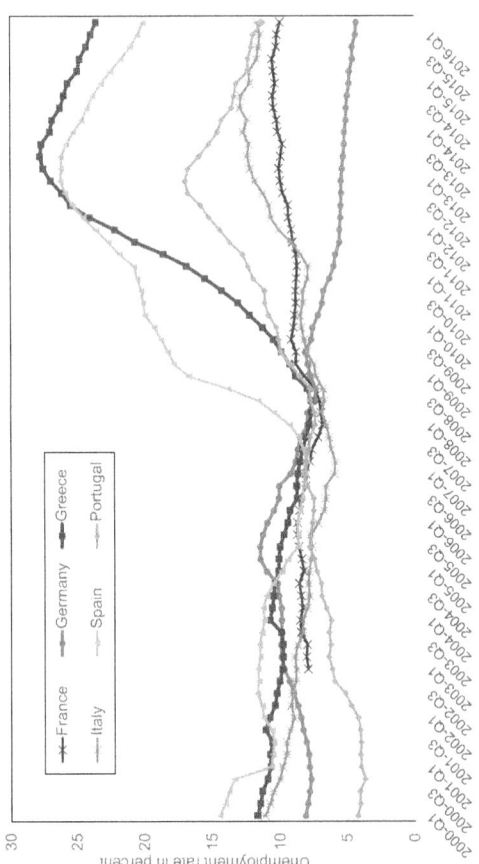

Fig. 10.4 Official unemployment rates in selected Eurozone economies (1Q of 2000–2Q of 2016). Source: OECD statistical data ((OECD 2016), unemployment rate (indicator). doi:10.1787/997c8750-en (Accessed on 07 December 2016))

Revisiting the East Asian Financial Crisis in the Late 1990s

Unfortunately, this artificial humanitarian crisis is not historically unprecedented. Many East Asian economies in the late 1990s had undergone a similar tragic experience. From the mid-1997, some East Asian countries experienced a region-wide currency market turmoil, which ultimately brought down governments of Thailand, Indonesia, the Philippines, and South Korea to the IMF bailout negotiation table.

The immediate cause of this currency market crisis was a heavy devaluation pressure associated with drastic capital outflows. Foreign portfolio investors (banks, institutional, and individual investors) massively invested in these countries, partly because of a strong economic performance during booming years and partly because of low interest rate environments in most advanced capitalist economies at that time. Foreign investors' substantial increases in Asian portfolio in turn were made possible, because of most East Asian governments' successive capital account liberalization policies since the late 1980s onward.

During the heyday of finance-led globalization, monetary policy makers in advanced economies and in international financial institutions popularized the idea that opening domestic financial markets to foreign investors would offer a chance for developing countries to finance their domestic investment and economic growth. Foreign investors, in turn, would earn higher rates of return by purchasing various financial assets issued in developing countries. In this way, financial market liberalization and the government's *laissez faire* approach to financial markets in developing countries were praised to be conducive to economic growth in these countries (McKinnon 1973; Shaw 1973; Williamson 1983; IEO 2005; Marangos 2009).

Under the influence of this orthodox doctrine known as 'Washington Consensus,' most Asian governments and monetary authorities competitively liberalized their financial markets, by allowing foreign investors to purchase financial assets and real estate property freely, in addition to holding majority ownership stakes in financial firms in this region. Monetary authorities in this region also changed their securities law, lifting restrictions on the type of financial instruments that domestic financial institutions could sell and restrictions on the volume and type of foreign exchange transactions (Azis 2006; Dekle and Pradhan 1997; Johnston et al. 1997; Chang et al. 1998).

One immediate consequence of this financial market liberalization was a substantial increase in capital flows into the Asian region and a resultant real exchange rate appreciation. The total magnitude of portfolio investment drastically rose to an unprecedentedly high level between 1993 and 1997, and most of this portfolio investment flowed into asset markets, creating both equity and real estate bubbles. According to a series of reports published by the Bank of International Settlements (BIS) that track the volume of international capital flows afterward, a total $378.1 billion of foreign capital flowed to all parts of East Asia (even excluding Singapore and Hong Kong) by the end of 1997 (BIS 1997–1999). The flipside of the coin is that recipient domestic entities in the Asian region were continuously incurring foreign liabilities. Banks and non-bank financial companies massively increased the volume of consumer credit and corporate lending in order to recycle their short-term foreign capital. According to the same compiled data, the private sector (banks and non-bank financial companies)'s foreign liabilities occupied more than 80% of the total foreign debt by the end of 1997, compared to less than 20% of public debt.

Of course, there was an additional complicating factor specific to the Asian region. That was a massive increase in the volume of yen carry trade. Since the burst of its own real estate bubble in the early 1990s, the Japanese Central Bank (Bank of Japan) had maintained near-zero interest rate policy in the hope of reviving the depressed domestic economy. This low interest rate in Japan in turn attracted massive foreign equity flows that invested in booming Asian property markets after borrowing cheap money from the Japanese financial sector. This short-term portfolio investment known as carry trade generated bubbles in both equity and real estate markets, which ultimately burst during the onset of the currency crisis in East Asia.

As foreign banks and creditors began to worry about the region's debt sustainability, they drastically reversed their lending decisions and began cutting their loans as competitively as they did when they purchased Asian portfolio. All of sudden, foreign short-term capital began to flow out of East Asian countries, leading to successive currency devaluation and banking crises in the region. The day of reckoning came to reign shortly. In the face of rapid capital outflows, monetary authorities in this region abandoned their quasi-fixed exchange rate regime and allowed their currencies to fall freely. As the value of Thai Baht, Indonesian Rupiah, Malaysian Ringgit, and Korean Won fell almost simultaneously, foreign liability situations deteriorated further. This is because Thai and Indonesian banks and non-bank financial companies borrowed short-term foreign capitals in the form of loans that were denominated in foreign currencies (i.e., in US dollar term and/or Japanese Yen). This means that indebted Southeast Asian countries needed to pay back these foreign loans, not in terms of their own currencies, but in terms of US dollars. Thus, drastic and competitive foreign capital outflows that led to currency devaluation also meant that highly indebted private banks and corporations in these countries could not find any other short-term solutions but to declare corporate bankruptcy in the face of rapidly deteriorating balance sheet and rising foreign debt liability.

Governments in Asian countries ultimately resorted to the IMF's bailout programs, after failing to defend the stability of their currencies for months. In exchange for receiving emergency financial assistance under the standby loan agreement, Asian governments had to accept highly stringent conditionality that was, in substance, the same as what the Troika has imposed on Greece nowadays (IMF 1999a, b, 2000, 2002). As in the case of Greece, however, the IMF's East Asian bailout programs also failed to stabilize the currency market turmoil in the region. Instead of providing a framework for an orderly debt resolution mechanism, the IMF's imposition of austerity-oriented policy measures worsened the financial situation, ultimately spreading the initial currency market instability into severe economic recession.

The IMF claimed that increasing interest rates as part of the East Asian bailout conditionality was the only way to stabilize the currency market and to prevent further depreciation of regional currencies (Lane et al. 1999; IMF 1999c, 2000). However, there was no empirical evidence that supported the stable correlation (not to mention, causality) between interest rates and exchange rates, especially during the culminated currency crisis period (IEO 2003). The most effective alternative way to prevent further decline in currencies associated with capital outflows is for the Asian governments and private creditors to devise a coherent and speedy mechanism to reach an agreement on how to repay the private debts orderly under the government guarantee. Once agreed, foreign creditors would have no longer had an incentive to cut their credit line competitively, which triggered the initial currency market turmoil in the first place.

The IMF also claimed that maintaining fiscal surpluses in the government budget, which was the second part of the bailout conditionality, was necessary in restoring the credibility of the government. In response to heavy criticisms of this nonsensical measure, the IMF economists even argued that mandating to achieve fiscal surplus in East Asia did not contribute to a sharp private sector contraction after the crisis (Lane et al. 1999). However, the Asian financial crisis was unrelated to public sector deficits, thus there was no need at all to rein in the government's fiscal position in the name of restoring foreign investors' confidence. The government can and should expand, rather than reduce, its economic functions to complement the drastic reduction in private sector investment and ultimately to pull the economies out of recessions. Otherwise, the economy would fall into a deeper recessionary spiral, as it actually happened in both East Asia then and Greece. Indeed, the relaxation of the IMF's rigid requirement for maintaining fiscal balance and the partial implementation of expansionary fiscal policies adopted by the government in varying degrees since late 1998—the exact opposite fiscal policy stance from what the IMF imposed—explained much of the rapid economic recovery in both Malaysia and Korea afterward. Of course, this partial relaxation of the IMF's bailout conditionality was not made by the IMF's voluntary choice, but became possible partly because of Malaysia's unilateral introduction of capital control measures that jolted the entire IMF's East Asian bailout programs and partly because of the coincidental leadership change and related uncertainty surrounding the IMF's programs during that time (for empirical studies of the effectiveness of capital control in Malaysia and other countries, see Ariyoshi et al. 2000; Edison and Reinhart 2000; Government of Malaysia 1999).

Last but not least, the IMF's blind emphasis on 'corporate governance reform' was one of the most destabilizing factors in the crisis in East Asia. The IMF economists repeatedly claimed that the structural weakness in the Asian banking sector and 'cronyism' in corporate governance were the root causes of the financial crisis in East Asia, and thus that any reform measure should target this fundamental governance problem (Lane et al. 1999; IMF 2000). This attitude is quite similar to the Troika's blind emphasis on the urgent need of 'structural reform' in Greek government and banking sectors. However, this diagnosis was highly dubious from the beginning in East Asia, and it became increasingly clear that the currency crisis was largely driven by self-fulfilling expectations on the part of myopic foreign investors. The magnitude and the direction of foreign capital flows were largely exogenous to East Asian economies, and the deterioration of Asian banking and financial balance sheets was a direct consequence of the redirection of short-term capital flows. Thus, various indicators of 'structural weakness' that the IMF economists enumerated were not the *cause*, but the *result* of the currency market turmoil. Even if this claim of

'Asian cronyism' were to be correct, it does not follow that the IMF and any other international lenders should mandate the governance reform *a priori*. Instead, the IMF should have provided an orderly debt resolution mechanism that addressed how to repay private sector foreign debts as the foremost important priority at the culmination of the currency crisis. Prioritizing governance reform was like putting the cart ahead of the horse, which was nonsensical from any sound economic reasoning.

The IMF's East Asian bailout program, in this way, completely failed to contain the regional currency crisis. The IMF bailout program in East Asia not only contributed to making economic situations even worse by amplifying the initial currency market turmoil into a full-blown banking crisis and a far more severe post-crisis economic recession, but also destabilized the political and socioeconomic stability in the East Asian region. By confusing the priority of resolving the immediate debt repayment concern with the long-term structural reform agenda, the IMF policy endangered a series of bank runs that transformed the initial currency shock into a series of banking crisis and financial collapse. Ultimately, the IMF's failed bailout programs in East Asia triggered a series of sovereign debt crises in other parts of the world. Sovereign debt crises in Russia and Brazil in 1999 ensued, followed by another sovereign debt crisis in Argentina in 2001.

Policy Lessons for Sovereign Financial Stability and Reforming the Global Financial System

It is ironic to see that the same old institutions are playing exactly the same role in the current European financial and economic crisis: the IMF and the Troika preaching the benefit of the same old neoliberal ideology before the crisis and imposing the same old misguided policies based upon a nonsensical and outdated model after the crisis. However, it is not only tragic but also farcical to see that the IMF is playing the exactly same role in Greece, even after it publicly apologized multiple times for its failed bailout programs in East Asia and for its blind advocacy of unfounded benefits of financial liberalization. It is even more striking to recognize that the IMF once published highly unorthodox papers on the benefit of capital control measures during the culminated period of the financial crisis in recent years (Ostry et al. 2010, 2011; Gallagher 2010). Betraying its own modest proposals, the IMF has behaved in exactly the same way in Greece as it once did in East Asia, causing the same humanitarian crisis all over again.

During the recent financial crisis in the United States, the IMF and many other international financial institutions largely sidestepped from the international monetary policy-making process. Just as the US monetary authorities completely failed to detect the initial sign of the financial crisis associated with subprime mortgage lending and the proliferation of over-the-counter transactions of mortgage-backed securities, the IMF had no idea of what was happening in the US housing market. It has not even mandated the US monetary authority to adopt the rule that it used to impose on many developing countries. As it turns out, the United States was the only advanced country that had not signed the IMF-led multilateral initiative on financial stability assessment program (Bryant and Guha 2008; Torres 2008). It is also striking to see how the US policy makers quickly abandoned the long-lasting austerity-oriented post-crisis response and structural adjustment rules that they have long upheld whenever there was a financial crisis in many developing countries. This time, the US Federal Reserve (Fed) and the Department of Treasury adopted a series of expansionary monetary and fiscal policies whose policy target and direction were exactly opposite from what they once preached in many East Asian countries 20 years ago.

The US Treasury under the leadership of Robert Rubin and Lawrence Summers and the US Fed under Alan Greenspan during the late 1990s used the IMF's East Asian bailout program as a powerful instrument to liberalize the Asian financial sector further, transplanting the American financial system in many East Asian countries. Imposing unnecessary and costly monetary and fiscal austerity policies and demanding a complete privatization of the transportation, water, and energy sector in East Asia were the prime examples that show how the IMF's East Asian bailout program disproportionately benefited the interest of Wall Street bankers and multinational corporations.

During and after the recent financial crisis in the United States back in 2007–2008, the US Treasury and the Fed have adopted exactly opposite policy measures that they once vehemently opposed in East Asia. Rather than mandating a high interest rate in the name of bringing in confidence in the financial market, the Fed has quickly lowered the federal funds rate, operated various emergency liquidity programs, and adopted massive asset purchase programs known as 'quantitative easing' multiple times to drive down and maintain long-term interest rates artificially. The US Treasury in turn introduced and implemented a series of expansionary fiscal policy measures, including the Troubled Asset Relief Program (TARP) and the

American Recovery and Reinvestment Act (ARRA), rather than cutting the government's fiscal expenditures (for a complete list of fiscal and monetary policy measures adopted during the recent financial crisis in the United States, see Blinder and Zandi 2010). These emergency policy measures turn out be exactly opposite to the Wall Street-Treasury-IMF complex's bailout programs imposed in East Asia 20 years ago and to the Troika's austerity programs imposed in Greece these days. This double standard or outright reversal of the post-crisis policy response led one prominent American economist to deplore 'American crony capitalism' (Palley 2008).

This cronyism, however, is not unique to the US financial system. The IMF policy makers and the European financial regulators, who have continued to fail to detect and prevent the global spread of the financial crisis, who did not have any problem in injecting huge amounts of emergency liquidity into their own sovereign financial system on a massive scale, and who have preferentially rescued their own state-owned banks and non-bank financial companies, now have imposed the exact opposite austerity policy measures to the very victim of the same financial crisis. According to their 'scientific economic principles,' the need of 'structural reform' applies to Greece, but not to German or French or Swedish banks; the Greek government's 'profligate spending' should be harshly punished, but the same Christian ethics does not apply to banks in the creditor countries. This stark contrast in policy response and the post-crisis economic management in Greece (and East Asia) vis-à-vis in the United States and the core Eurozone economies, and the IMF's differential roles played in each of these cases should serve as a moment of revealing truth.

One set of important policy lessons that we should learn from these experiences is to recognize the grave danger of financial liberalization policies and of a premature relegation of sovereign policy autonomy to a supranational entity. As long as individual governments cannot control the speed, magnitude, and direction of short-term capital flows, any financial market liberalization should not be adopted. As long as the existing global financial system persistently fails to provide symmetric provision of long-term financial resources for growth and development, and thus as long as the global financial system lacks an effective international lender of last resort function, any decision to transfer domestic monetary and fiscal authority to a supranational entity should be cautiously adopted or even avoided.

As an alternative, properly reformed international financial institutions should expand special drawing rights (SDR) to its member states regardless of their country size and respective contribution, and should actually play a role as an effective international lender of last resort. The World Bank (if it should exist) or regional development banks in turn should increase the volume of their low-cost long-term loans to developing countries, so that the governments in these countries can safely rely on them to increase their public investment in infrastructure and educational systems. In the context of Eurozone, this means that the member countries should agree upon the need of creating a common fiscal authority and a regional development fund, both of which are designed to mitigate and reduce uneven regional economic development among the member countries in the medium and long run.

In the face of an urgent need of currency and financial crisis management, international financial institutions should coordinate an orderly debt restructuring management, in which both creditors and borrowers voluntarily agree to such measures as debt rollover as well as debt swap (Stiglitz and Guzman 2015). The IMF and the Troika should allow an individual government to adopt emergent policy measures including capital controls to prevent devastating runs on the country. If the country ultimately requested the bailout fund, the IMF and the Troika's conditionality should include developmental policies and criteria, rather than sticking to the prevailing austerity-oriented policy prescription. Under this new institutional framework:

- The Troika should set up a formal monitoring and enforcement mechanism in order to stop an unnecessary run on the country and to prevent free riders among foreign investors during the early stage of financial crisis;
- The Troika should coordinate and target to expand domestic and regional aggregate demand by helping the country and the region adopt coordinated expansionary fiscal and monetary policies.
- The Troika's financial program should also allow the government to provide an unlimited and unconditional provision of domestic liquidity for the monetary authority to prevent a sharp freeze in the domestic interbank market from causing a complete breakdown of the financial system;
- Post-crisis financial sector restructuring may be inevitable to clean up bad loans and to create a sounder financial system. During the culmination of a financial crisis, however, it is necessary for the government to temporarily ease or suspend the international capital adequacy rules in order to prevent banks from drastically cutting much needed corporate and household credit;

- The individual government can set up separate financial facilities through recapitalized financial institutions under the government's conservatorship to help ease credit constraints placed on otherwise solvent non-financial corporations and households. In this case, international financial institutions and regional central banks should support this effort, rather than doing otherwise;
- The crisis-stricken country or entity should be given rights to take full advantage of an internationally extended Chapter 11 bankruptcy protection mechanism that would enable them to shield and protect themselves from panicky creditors' herd behaviors.
- As in the area of trade and industrial policy, the individual government should have sufficient 'policy space' for adopting different financial regimes and measures for managing short-term capital flows. This requires a fundamental change in our notion of capital controls, which should be understood as a legitimate component in a series of 'macro-prudential' preemptive measures to stabilize the economy.

Conclusion

The main goal of this chapter is to examine the current financial and economic crisis in Greece and the role played by the IMF and Troika based upon the experience of the East Asian financial crisis in the late 1990s. This comparative analysis of the two crises strongly suggests that the myopic and premature liberalization of domestic capital accounts in the absence of proper fiscal and monetary sovereignty is the common cause of financial crises in both regions. In addition, the Troika's misguided bailout conditionality exacerbated economic situations, rather than helping the government withstand the early sign of the financial problem, just as the Wall Street–Treasury–IMF complex's response had a detrimental effect on many East Asian countries back in the late 1990s.

One important lesson we should learn is that we do not have any adequate sovereign debt resolution mechanism at the international level. In the absence of this effective arrangement for the sovereign debt crisis management, we may continue to see repeating currency and banking crises associated with drastic capital flows. The East Asian financial crisis in the late 1990s and the current ongoing humanitarian crisis in Greece have clearly shown how fundamental flaws inherent in the prevailing global financial system and the lack of decisive will for policy reform can seriously harm societies.

For many developing countries, the analysis in this chapter should also serve as a clear warning sign for adopting myopic financial liberalization that the IMF and foreign creditor countries have sold to them for decades. In the absence of a fundamental policy reform in the international financial arena, the maxim for many policy makers in developing or peripheral countries would be to 'do as they do, not as they say.' After all, we are still living in an era of 'kicking away the ladder,' one nineteenth-century Prussian political economist Friedrich List once used to describe the dominant international trade and financial regime at that time. In this continued era of kicking away the ladder, the dominant system and rules are designed to exclusively benefit the center, the rich, the powerful, and the creditor at the expense of the periphery, the poor, the powerless, and the debtors.

REFERENCES

Ariyoshi, A. et al. (2000). Capital controls: Country experiences with their use and liberalization. *IMF Occasional Paper*, No. 190.

Armitage, J., & Chu, B. (2015). Greek debt crisis: Goldman Sachs could be sued for helping hide debts when it joined euro. *The Independent 10*. Retrieved from http://www.independent.co.uk/news/world/europe/greek-debt-crisis-goldman-sachs-could-be-sued-for-helping-country-hide-debts-when-it-joined-euro-10381926.html

Assange, J. (2016, March 19). IMF internal meeting predicts Greek 'disaster', threatens to leave Troika. *Wikileaks.org*. Retrieved from https://wikileaks.org/imf-internal-20160319/transcript/page-1.html.

Azis, I. J. (2006). Indonesia's external liberalization: Policy dynamics and socio-economic impact. In L. Taylor (Ed.), *External liberalization in Asia, post-socialist Europe and Brazil* (pp. 180–188). Oxford: Oxford University Press.

Bank for International Settlements (BIS). (1997–1999). *The maturity, sectoral and Nationality Distribution of International Bank data* (the author's own compilation of data based upon the BIS report on *The Maturity, Sectoral and Nationality Distribution of International Bank* issued in Jan. 1997, July 1997, Jan. 1998, May 1998, Nov. 1998, May 1999).

BBC News. (2012, June 13). Timeline: The unfolding Eurozone crisis. Retrieved from http://www.bbc.com/news/business-13856580

BBC News. (2015, July 16). How bad are things for the people of Greece? Retrieved from http://www.bbc.com/news/worldeurope33507802

Blackstone, B., Stamouli, N., & Forelle, C. (2015, June 28) Greece orders banks closed, imposes capital controls to stem deposit flight. *Wall Street Journal*. Retrieved from http://www.wsj.com/articles/SB11064341213388534269604581075703841095260

Blinder, A. S., & Zandi, M. (2010). How the great recession was brought to an end. Unpublished Report. Retrieved from https://www.princeton.edu/~blinder/End-of-Great-Recession.pdf

Bryant, C., & Guha, K. (2008, April 10). IMF rejects criticism over global turmoil. *Financial Times*.

Chang, H.-J., Park, H.-J., & Yoo, C.-G. (1998). Interpreting the Korean crisis – Financial liberalization, industrial policy and corporate governance. *Cambridge Journal of Economics, 22*(6), 735–746.

Dekle, R., & Pradhan, M. (1997). Financial liberalization and money demand in ASEAN countries: Implications for monetary policy. *IMF Working Paper*, WP/97/36.

Edison, H. J., & Reinhart, C. M. (2000). Capital controls during financial crises: The case of Malaysia and Thailand. *Board of Governors of the Federal Reserve System International Finance Discussion Papers*, No. 662.

European Commission. (2015). Adopting Euro – Who can join and when? Retrieved from http://ec.europa.eu/economy_finance/euro/index_en.htm

Gallagher, K. P. (2010, March 1). Capital controls back in IMF toolkit. *The Guardian*.

Giannitsis, T., & Zografakis, S. (2015). Greece: Solidarity and adjustment in times of crisis. *Macroeconomic Policy Institute Study* no. 38. Berlin: Macroeconomic Policy Institute.

Government of Malaysia. (1999). White Paper: Status of the Malaysian economy. Government of Malaysia.

Independent Evaluation Office (IEO). (2003). *Evaluation report – The IMF and the recent capital account crises: Indonesia, Korea, Brazil*. Washington, DC: IMF IEO.

Independent Evaluation Office (IEO). (2005). *Evaluation report – The IMF's approach to capital account liberalization*. Washington, DC: IMF IEO.

Independent Evaluation Office (IEO). (2016). *Evaluation report – The IMF and the crises in Greece, Ireland, and Portugal*. Washington, DC: IMF IEO.

International Monetary Fund (IMF). (1999a). The IMF's stand-by Agreement and Financial Assistance for Thailand, Aug. 1997–Sep. 1999. The author's compilation of the Thai government's Letter of Intent with the IMF, IMF's Article IV for Thailand, and the IMF's Press Release. Retrieved from http://www.imf.org/external/country/THA/index.htm

International Monetary Fund (IMF). (1999b). The IMF's Stand-by Agreement and Extended Funding Facility for Indonesia, Nov. 1997–Jul. 1999. The author's compilation of the Indonesian government's Letter of Intent with the IMF, IMF's Article IV for Indonesia, and the IMF's Press Release. Retrieved from http://www.imf.org/external/country/idn/index.htm

International Monetary Fund (IMF). (1999c). *IMF-supported programs in Indonesia, Korea, and Thailand: A preliminary assessment*. Washington, DC: IMF.

International Monetary Fund (IMF). (2000). The IMF's stand-by agreement and extended Funding Facility for Korea, Dec. 1997–Jul. 2000. The author's compilation of the Korean government's Letter of Intent with the IMF, IMF's Article IV for Korea, and the IMF's Press Release. Retrieved from http://www.imf.org/external/country/kor/index.htm?pn=17

International Monetary Fund (IMF). (2002). The IMF article IV consultation with Malaysia, 1998–2002. The author's compilation of the IMF's article IV for Malaysia and the IMF's Press release. Retrieved from http://www.imf.org/external/country/MYS/index.htm

International Monetary Fund (IMF). (2007a, January 25). IMF executive Board concludes 2006 article IV consultation with Greece public information notice (PIN). *International Monetary Fund Press Release.*

International Monetary Fund (IMF). (2007b, December 10). Greece: 2007 article IV consultation; preliminary conclusions of the mission. *International Monetary Fund Press Release.*

International Monetary Fund (IMF). (2009, May 25). Greece: 2009 article IV consultation concluding statement of the mission. *International Monetary Fund Press Release.*

International Monetary Fund (IMF). (2010a, May 2). Staff-level agreement: Europe and IMF agree €110 billion financing plan with Greece. *International Monetary Fund Press Release.*

International Monetary Fund (IMF). (2010b). IMF reaches Staff-level agreement with Greece on €30 billion Stand-by arrangement. *International Monetary Fund Press Release.*

International Monetary Fund (IMF). (2010c, August 06). Greece: Letter of Intent, Memorandum of economic and financial policies, Technical Memorandum of Understanding, and Memorandum of Understanding on specific economic policy conditionality by European Commission and European central bank. *International Monetary Fund Press Release.*

International Monetary Fund (IMF). (2010d, December 08). Greece: Letter of Intent, Memorandum of economic and financial policies, and Technical Memorandum. *International Monetary Fund Press Release.*

International Monetary Fund (IMF). (2011, July 04). Greece: Letter of Intent, Memorandum of economic and financial policies, and Technical Memorandum of Understanding. *International Monetary Fund Press Release.*

International Monetary Fund (IMF). (2012a, March 15). GREECE program: IMF Board approves €28 billion loan for Greece. *IMF Survey Online.*

International Monetary Fund (IMF). (2012b, December 21). Greece: Letter of intent, Memorandum of economic and financial policies, and technical memorandum of understanding. *International Monetary Fund Press Release.*

International Monetary Fund (IMF). (2013, January 16). IMF Executive Board Completes First and Second Reviews Under Extended Fund Facility

Arrangement for Greece and Approves €3.24 Billion Disbursement. *International Monetary Fund Press release.*

International Monetary Fund (IMF). (2014, May 14). Greece: Letter of Intent, Memorandum of economic and financial policies, and Technical Memorandum of Understanding. *International Monetary Fund Press Release.*

Johnston, B., Darbar, S. M., & Echeverria, C. (1997). Sequencing capital account liberalization: Lessons from the experiences in Chile, Indonesia, Korea, and Thailand. *IMF Working Paper Series,* WP/97/157.

Landy, J., & Harrison, T. (2015, March 24). What's next for Greece? – Debating Syriza's options. *The Nation.* Retrieved from https://www.thenation.com/article/whats-next-greece-debating-syrizas-options/

Lane, T., Ghosh, A., & Hamann, J. (1999). IMF-supported programs in Indonesia, Korea, and Thailand: A preliminary assessment. *IMF Occasional Paper* no. 178.

Marangos, J. (2009). The evolution of the term 'Washington consensus'. *The Journal of Socio-Economics, 38*(1), 198–208.

Matsaganis, M. (2013). The Greek crisis: Social impact and policy responses. *Friedrich Ebert Stiftung Report.* Berlin: Friedrich Ebert Stiftung.

McKinnon, R. I. (1973). *Money and capital in economic development.* Washington, DC: The Brookings Institutions.

McSweeney, R., & Rankin, J. (2015, July 20). Greek banks reopen for first time in three weeks. *The Guardian.* Retrieved from https://www.theguardian.com/world/2015/jul/19/greek-banks-reopen-first-time-three-weeks-queues-expected.

Mitrakos, T. (2014). *Inequality, poverty and social welfare in Greece: Distributional effects of austerity.* Bank of Greece Working Paper no. 174. Athens, Greece: Bank of Greece.

Nunevar, D. (2016, September 30). Why the IMF must go beyond *Mea Culpa* over Greece. *Social Europe.* Retrieved from https://www.socialeurope.eu/2016/09/imf-must-go-beyond-mea-culpa-greece/

Ostry, J. D. et al. (2010). Capital inflows: The role of controls. *IMF Staff Position Note.* SPN/10/24.

Ostry, J. D. et al. (2011). Managing capital inflows: What tools to use? *IMF Staff Discussion Note* SDN/11/06.

Palley, T. (2008, March 31). The fed and crony capitalism. *The American Prospect.* Retrieved from http://prospect.org/article/fed-and-crony-capitalism

Panagiotidis, S. (2016). The Greek government's parallel program. *Transform Europe.* Retrieved from http://www.transform-network.net/blog/blog-2016/news/detail/Blog/the-parallel-program-of-the-greek-government.html.

Reich, R. (2015, July 16). How Goldman Sachs profited from the Greek debt crisis. *The Nation.* Retrieved from https://www.thenation.com/article/goldmans-greek-gambit/

Rocholl, J., & Stahmer, A. (2016). Where did the Greek bailout money go? *European School of Management and Technology (ESMT) Working Paper* WP-16-02. Berlin: European School of Management and Technology.

Shaw, E. S. (1973). *Financial deepening in economic development.* New York: Oxford University Press.

Stiglitz, J. E., & Guzman, M. (2015, June 26). A rule of law for sovereign debt. *Social Europe.* Retrieved from https://www.socialeurope.eu/2015/06/a-rule-of-law-for-sovereign-debt/

Torres, H. (2008, April 7). Why the IMF missed the subprime story. *The New York Sun.*

Varoufakis, Y. (2015, July 15). Behind Germany's refusal to grant Greece debt relief. *The Guardian.* Retrieved from https://www.theguardian.com/commentisfree/2015/jul/10/germany-greek-pain-debt-relief-grexit

Varoufakis, Y. (2016). On Greece, Syriza, Podemos and the democracy in Europe movement – Yanis Varoufakis interview in el Mundo. Retrieved from https://yanisvaroufakis.eu/2016/01/24/on-podemos-greece-and-diem-interview-in-el-mund0/

Varoufakis, Y., Holland, S., & Galbraith, J. K. (2013). A modest proposal for resolving the Eurozone crisis. Retrieved from https://yanisvaroufakis.eu/euro-crisis/modest-proposal/

Wade, R., & Veneroso, F. (1998). The Asian crisis: The high debt model versus the Wall Street-Treasury-IMF complex. *New Left Review, 228,* 3–23.

Williamson, J. (Ed.). (1983). *IMF conditionality.* Washington, DC: Institute for International Economics.

CHAPTER 11

Commonalities Between the 'Bookends' Financial Crises of Mexico 1994 and Greece 2007

Jesús Muñoz

FACTS IN 'MODERN' FINANCIAL CRISES

Both the number and the recurrence of financial crises have augmented in the world. This 'tradition' started in 1982. However, then there were 'old fashioned' external debt crises, whereas 'modern' financial crises have occurred since the 1990s. Crises have wiped out advances in development and provoked a decrease in wealth along with contagion. They are the negative effect of ´rapid´ globalization, an indicator of poor governance and the result of the fragility in both financial and productive systems, especially in the developing world.

Modern financial crises slightly differ from old-style financial crises on the basis of the development level of the world financial system. The former are produced by external debt, whereas the latter are basically generated by both private and public indebtedness. Both produce initial false expectations arising from previous booms. For this reason, modern financial crises are also the consequence of heterogeneous risk takers.

J. Muñoz (✉)
Universidad Anáhuac, Mexico City, Mexico

© The Author(s) 2017
J. Marangos (ed.), *The Internal Impact and External Influence of the Greek Financial Crisis*, DOI 10.1007/978-3-319-60201-1_11

189

Table 11.1   'Modern' financial crises

Year	Country/región
1982[a]	México
1992–1993	European Union
1994	Mexico
1997	East Asia
1998	Russia
1999	Brazil; Ecuador
2000	Argentina
2001	Turkey
2007	Western Europe (mainly Greece and Spain), United States

[a]An old-fashioned debt-type crisis

All crises have consequences on local economies and on the world economy. Crises have spread out throughout the world as can be seen in Table 11.1. However, crises are not only linked via contagion: They all have similar characteristics in terms of development, rescues and bailouts, and normally failed management. Strong economies emerge stronger after crises, whereas strong non-financial economies do not suffer crises. See Table 11.1.

Eventually, Mexico returned to the path of development, whereas uncertainty prevails about the future of Greece, since effects and response on the part of the European nation seem to be lagged. Although details vary, developments are similar. Even though recovery in Greece is lagging probably due to disagreements in responses to the explanation of consequences in Greece, these disagreements do not imply a qualitative change in perspective as will be demonstrated latter. See Table 11.2.

México 1994: A Currency (Financial) Crisis

The Mexican case was considered as unique at that time. Latin America had enjoyed a temporary boom, starting in 1989 after the Brady Plan for reducing external debt was implemented. Thereafter, confidence was restored and most Latin American countries experienced a temporary boom as a response to the former 'lost decade'. Mexico received large inflows of portfolio capital since 1988. Growth was high between 1989 and 1994 in the face of scarce knowledge of risks. Expectations were also positive partly due to the signing of the North American Trade Agreement (NAFTA) in early 1994. The prevailing exchange rate soundness was

Table 11.2   Real growth in Mexico and Greece circa crises

Year	(%)	Year	(%)
1994	4.4	2003	5.9
1995	−6.2	2004	4.4
1996	5.2	2005	2.3
1997	6.8	2006	4.6
1998	5.0	2007	3.0
1999	3.8	2008	−0.1
2000	6.6	2009	−3.2
2001	0.0	2010	−3.5
2002	1.4	2011	−6.9
2003	4.1	2012	−10.2

Source: Banco de México, *Indicadores Económicos y Financieros* (2016); IMF *Data & Statistics* (2016); website of the European Central Bank (2016)

based on a high level of international reserves, and inflation was in 1993 at the single-digit level. Ratings improved.

However, growth was based on shaky foundations. Dornbusch's warnings in 1993 on overheating were unheeded. In 1994, the public sector issued *Tesobonos* (inflation-indexed public bonds) to hide its borrowing. After some political events, the Peso was devalued at the end of that year as reserves were depleted in the face of loose monetary policy. Portfolio capitals left. Investment was stagnating and both unemployment and indebtedness soared.

The Peso had been de facto pegged to the US Dollar since 1987 due to a stabilization program, but immediately after the US economy diverged. Consequently, the economy used private over-lending for sustaining growth (Edwards and Sevastano 1998; Calvo and Reinhart 2000; Tornell et al. 2004). The ensuing crisis proved that the banking system—privatized in 1991—was institutionally weak, due also to appetite for short-term profits. Speculation arose at the end of 1994 after investors perceived bad fundamentals, for example, the current account exhibited an unsustainable deficit. After years of real appreciation, authorities suddenly widened the exchange band up to 13.5% instead of 2.5% in December 1994. Mini-devaluations ensued.

Both intellectual and practical confusion prevailed. A rescue package was set in March 1995, amounting to an unprecedented 51.6 billion Pesos (20 billion Pesos for repaying the Tesobonos-debt), which immediately cut monetary, inflationary and exchange pressures. Gross Domestic Product decreased (Table 11.2 above) while the domestic management of the crisis was not adequate. Authorities opted for an insurance deposit, a temporary recapitalization program and a restructuring of foreign-currency denominated credits. It took some years for the banking sector to resume growth, after being sold to foreign investors around 1997. The industrial sector was unevenly affected after 1995. In the short term, non-competitive sectors benefitted. In the social arena, both inequality and migration to the United States increased both in quantitative and qualitative terms. This means that although migration has been increasing prior to the crisis, its growth reached higher levels and previously non-affected persons decided to migrate after the crisis. Finally, Mexico generated 'contagion' into other emerging economies, especially into Argentina.

Overvaluation in this case in the form of a peg to the US Dollar is an artificial resource for demonstrating apparent success in macroeconomic management and only feasible in the short term, thereby producing excessive short-term speculation. Contagion arose and speculation re-emerged as modern investors consider 'similar' countries as equally attractive. Since 1995 the Peso floats, although with some discretionary interventions in the face of international contagion. After 1996, the Mexican economy resumed growth. In 1997, monetary policy was devoted to reduce both inflation and interest rates, while fiscal policy was reformed in order to 'permanently' reduce the budget deficit. Thereafter, the Mexican economy has exhibited an increasing pattern in terms of growth.

Similar Subsequent Crises

Local financial deficiencies received attention in the identification of emerging market currency crisis in the late 1990s after the Mexican ('Tequila') crisis was partially understood. As of 1997, pegs still promoted both un-hedged inflows and indebtedness in some regions. Nonetheless, prudential regulation was not an issue at the time, as banks were still undercapitalized, whereas strategic privatization of insolvent public entities was going on. At the end, pegged exchange rates were replaced in the main Latin American countries.

On the basis of the Mexican 1994 crisis, many theoretical and empirical models were created. After investors walked away from Latin America, the target was East Asia with booming economies, relatively developed financial systems and high productivity levels. Problems in fundamentals in this new region along with weak policies were not visible. Other crises ensued (see Table 11.3) preceded by a fixed exchange regime.

Table 11.3 Financial crises between 1994 and 2001

Country/region	Date	Causes	Outline
East Asia	July 1997	Pegs, private deficit, banking crisis	Explosion and 'contagion'
Russia	August 1998	Under-performance, default, speculation	Control and 'contagion'
Brazil	January 1999	Peg, weak fundamentals, public deficit, default	Control
Turkey	September 2000	Budget deficit	Control
Argentina	December 2001	Collapsing currency board	Recession and 'contagion'

Source: Own synthesis

Greece 2007

There are many articles on the unfolding of the Greek crisis in 2007. The approach to be used here is the outlining of some of its key elements to contrast them with the unfolding of the Mexican crisis of 1994, especially around 2007 in the aftermath of the financial crisis. There are hundreds of papers and blogs on the late developments of the Greek financial crisis. The focus here is to unearth the main elements in a financial crisis for outlining a contrastable complex system. Starting from 1991, the first years of the European Union (EU) were promissory. However, country situations would soon prove to be very distinct. Greece under-reported its statistics on the budget deficit, when it was accepted by the EU in 2000 (Fig. 11.1), as it exceeded during that year the 3% limit as a proportion of its GDP.

Financial products were developed with the help of large banks, as it was revealed in 2010. Back in the early 2000s, liabilities were hidden. This situation fueled government spending after entering a boom. Public debt soared, hitting 120% of GDP in 2010. After 2007, doubts arose about Greece ability to pay its sovereign debt.[1] At the end, rescue programs were set in motion, but unlike in the Mexican case, they were lagged and uncertain.

Other Eurozone countries agreed a rescue package of 35 billion Euros in loans. A second bailout amounting to 130 billion Euros was agreed in 2012, subject to financial reforms and austerity. There was uncertainty about the timing of resolution of the crisis despite relative progress on planned policy

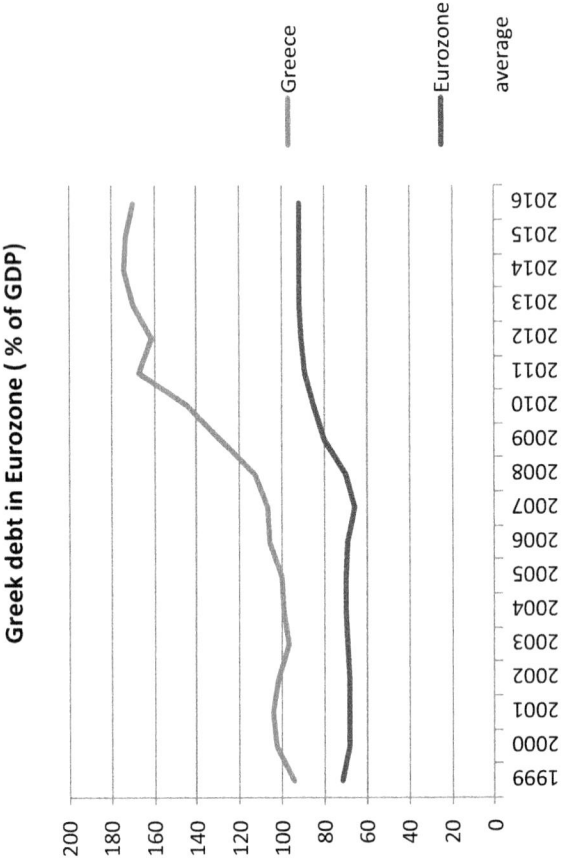

Fig. 11.1 Greek debt in comparison to Eurozone average. Source: Eurostat 2014, *estimates

reforms. Actually, activity in the Eurozone had been soft during the late 2010s (IMF 2012, 2013), and this was not helpful for Greece. Policy actions faced two challenges in order to reduce the risks of prolonged stagnation and the arising of new bubbles: Steady fiscal consolidation and financial reform, like in Latin America. Likewise, further challenges were taking steps toward full banking union and a greater fiscal integration. These actions were intended to restore confidence, reverse capital flights and reintegrate the Hellenic nation into the Eurozone. A productivity new agenda and fiscal policy reforms were both required (IMF 2013).

The Greek Debt

As of 2013, Greece achieved progress in terms of both structural reforms and tax collection in order to avoid wage and jobs cuts. Privatization was needed as well as efforts to meet targets and structural benchmarks. Greece continued to adjust through recessionary rather than productivity changes, but this was necessary at that stage. The fiscal gap must have been closed. Interest rates were decreased, maturities were lengthened and the Greek debt was re-transferred back to the country.

The plan was to reduce debt to 124% of GDP by 2020. However, relief and financing from European partners are required for success.

Table 11.4   The Greek economy after the crisis

Concept	Index	2009	2010	2011
GDP deflactor index	2005 = 100	113.4	114.6	115.8
Consumer prices index	2005 = 100	111.9	117.2	121.1

Source: *International Financial Statistics* (2013), International Monetary Fund

Table 11.5   Greece: Real gross debt (% of GDP) after the crisis

2007	2008	2009	2010	2011
107.45	112.6	128.9	144.5	165.4

Source: *International Financial Statistics* (2013), International Monetary Fund

A longer period was needed for fiscal adjustment, while an appropriate reception of debt relief was required to resume growth. The country modified its fiscal program, even more than say Spain (see IMF 2012, p. 62). The crisis in Greece was caused by excessive government expenditure combined with over-lending and a de facto peg to the euro. Risk was underpriced and derivatives proliferated. Greece like Spain in the late 2000s possessed an unstable financial system unlike those of Germany or the United Kingdom. Mortgage prices were the speculative vehicle or triggering factor in the subprime crisis of 2007, whereas currency expectations were the mobile in 1994. Once again, the impact of financial crises was on confidence and investment levels in the midst of disorganized finance. In the next two subsections, the situation in Western Europe is discussed as an introduction to crises theories.

Recent Insights About the Greek Crisis

Greece announced in October 2009 that it understated its deficit. Therefore, a new crisis arose in 2010. There were three international bailouts and austerity was mandatory. The Greek economy was built on excessive budget deficits exactly like the Mexican economy between 1988 and 1994. Resolutions have taken more than 8 years. The viability of the Eurozone is questioned. Keynes's organicist lessons in the *Economics Consequences of the Peace* (1919) had been forgotten. Keynes had claimed that interactions were necessary. Bailout is for paying debts and (external) debt relief (7.5 billion Euros). The International Monetary Fund (IMF) and Germany are the main creditors. They are committed to debt payments until 2018. The argument was that there must be limits to financing. The Greek economy shrank by 25% in 5 years, with unemployment at 25%. There also was a political escalation of the crisis as well as political upheaval in 2015, and bailout deals were undertaken.

There also was a reduction in deposits coupled with a default on 1.5 billion Euros to the IMF. As of 2015, there was a banks' collapse and claims for leaving the EU. There also was a proposal due to June 2015 about reforms for attaining debt sustainability. Since 2008, Greece debt had shot up. IOUs (non-negotiable debt instruments) were the means for repayment. In that context, bail-in means taking money from depositors, and bailout comes from loans. In those years, Greece was not allowed to default, but concessions were insufficient. With the euro as a string currency, the Greek budget weight increased.

Contagion was not only about perceptions but also about rising borrowing costs. There was both irresponsible spending and borrowing. The cause of the crisis was unsustainable budget deficits, and the triggering moment was the fall of Lehman Brothers. There will be borrowing from the EU in the face of a budget deficit lower than 3%. As mentioned before, the EU and the IMF granted Greece a bailout amounting to 110 billion Euros conditioned to austerity reforms in 2008, and one amounting to 130 billion Euros in 2012. After 5 years, Greece owed 340 billion Euros, but no referendum was held up until July 2015.

THE EUROZONE

The Northern Western hemisphere crisis affected the developed countries. The ultimate consequence in the United States was a financial system bailout amounting to approximately $29 quadrillion (Felkerson 2011), being a rescue program related to the Federal Reserve System response and to the safety net provided by the US government (Wray 2009), similar in principles to the Mexican insurance deposit. As of 2009, the Eurozone was the source of concern in terms of increasing risks to the global financial system, just as Latin America was in the nineties. Although crisis intervention methods are still in use in many economies of Western Europe, they delay world safeness.

According to Hannsgen and Papadimitriou (2012), a Keynesian response related to stimulus was necessary to counterbalance the then-current measures in Europe, since austerity is recessionary and non-sovereign currency nations do not require wage or employment cuts, implying that deficit cuts are not the solution. If countries are to resume growth, a virtuous cycle is required. Like in Keynes's models, money must not be retired from the circular income flow. It exacerbates problems. In fact bailout agreements were undertaken in Greece, Ireland and Portugal.[2] As finance was still out of control, new bailouts were undertaken by the IMF, the European Central Bank and the EU. New debt rules were also set in motion.

The appropriate management of fiscal policy generates financial stability. Austerity only provokes decreases in consumption, investment and tax collections. Recessive effects spread out across Europe in 2009. Hence, system dynamics has to be modified. Austerity policies also produce diminishing profits (cf. Hannsgen and Papadimitriou 2012). Both temporary stimulus programs and permanent automatic stabilizers were needed in the face of an inflexible currency system. Stable interest rates and costs of servicing debt could break the vicious cycle. Fiscal stimulus enhances aggregate demand and employment, whereas central banks provide solvency. A balanced budget is not necessary in times of crisis. Financial crises arise when many entities pay their debts with borrowed money calling for public bailout. Further at that moment, austerity measures were unpopular at the Euro zone (cf. Hannsgen and Papadimitriou 2012). These points will be clearer after the main theories of financial crises will be outlined in the next section.

THEORIES OF FINANCIAL CRISES

The purpose of this section is to distinguish the elements that trigger and aggravate a financial crisis for understanding modern financial crises from a conceptual perspective beyond the historical facts. Thus, this is the background for applying this knowledge to the cases in point in this chapter. There may be conflicting crisis narratives in domestic countries since 1982. Nevertheless, the understanding of theoretical–practical patterns in financial crises is the path for avoiding financial turmoil and instability in social systems by identifying their mechanics, preventive factors and policies.

This analysis is conducted in terms of: The Orthodox (exogenous) theory, the Minsky (endogenous) model and a complex system framework, highlighting the qualitative and historical aspects of crises. Their consideration as three varieties of a single explication may play a role in the comprehension of the avoidance of crises. This uniqueness in approach is based on the fact that there have been identical causes, effects and responses to crisis in different regions. For grasping the essence of all financial crises, it is necessary to consider that both balance-of-payments-crises (circa 1979) and currency crises (occurring in the 1990s) are special cases of orthodox financial crises (which took hold in the 2000s).

Orthodox (Exogenous) Theory

In this view, the roles of both Efficient Market Hypothesis and *laissez faire* are relevant. In other words, equilibrium and stability are the rule. In addition, orthodoxy shyly states that over-lending (McKinnon and Pill 1996) coupled with pegs is one of the causes, even though strangely enough money and debts have no place in the Neo-classical tradition. Main causes are excessive spending (like in heterodox theories of crisis), excessive lending, de facto pegs, and failing industrial and banking sectors (cf. Dornbusch 1999; McKinnon and Pill 1996), but these events constitute the exception. Finally, crises are the result of 'moral hazard' (Krugman 1999), which generate financial runs—panic—and contagion.

In this perspective, an inefficient financial system does not allocate real investment in an appropriate manner, thus more financial liberalization, transparency and regulation are required for attaining a competitive international environment. Part of de-regulation is the successful securitization of future flows. At any rate, financial disruptions bring about recessions and retard economic development, thus altering income distribution (Baldacci et al. 2002). They also increase general unemployment in the short run affecting expectations, like in Diaz Alejandro (Diaz-Alejandro 1985) and in Dornbusch's overshooting models.

According to the first-generation models, the currency is devalued in order to sustain the economy after domestic problems, but devaluation is considered as an external shock (Krugman 1979). The second-generation models contend that devaluing after destabilizing speculation is a policy choice (Obstfeld 1994). The third-generation models state that banking and currency crises occur simultaneously after either real or imaginary shocks (Kaminsky and Reinhart 1999). Finally, the fourth-generation models (Krugman 1999; Dornbusch 2001) state that the main effect of currency crises is on corporate balance sheets. In all cases, investment halts produce recessions and disrupt productive systems. However, all these models consider that economies rapidly return to equilibrium, and hence for them vulnerability is an exceptional phenomenon.

In a word, crises are caused by the effect of extraordinary (exogenous) events on macroeconomic variables which are normally under control. This view proposes as a remedy more of the same: An increase in global assets cured by more *laissez faire* and development (Tornell et al. 2004). Actually, indebtedness increases during the crisis. There are also empirical studies about crises in the orthodox tradition, for example about expectations and stock markets for the case of Mexico (see Becker et al. 2002). Expectations are rational and stock markets are stable.

Heterodox (Minskyan or Endogenous) Theory

This opposing explication includes the concept of heterogeneous risk takers (cf. Wray 2007), in an attempt for explaining crises by contending that problems are endogenous and that economic systems implode after booms. While Keynes was aware of the effect of uncertainty on investors, and thence on economic stability, Minsky's consideration of the genesis of financial turmoil related to the dichotomy investors-debtors is the key for understanding financial crises. In both paradigms, investment is halted and then both debt deflation à-la-Fisher and recessions arise (along with inflation). All theories of financial crises state that investment is the culprit of crises, but the orthodox view is silent about deficiencies in de-regulation and the overstating of financialization (money-manager capitalism).

This is the reason why Minsky's analyses of stages and his Financial Fragility Hypothesis (Minsky 1982) are hereby used, not mentioning that facts have proven that booms generate their own busts. Neither Keynes (in this sense a heterogeneous economist) nor Minsky believes that the economic system is self-regulating. The Minsky model is about an internal crisis, but it also explains the mechanics of financial crises. Crises are endogenous: Booms turn into busts via excessive indebtedness, which progresses through the speculative, hedge and Ponzi stages. The 'Minsky moment' arrives when investors borrow for paying their debts. For Minsky, such institutions as Big Government and the Central Bank soften the impact of crises (Minsky 1982).

Finally, future flows must be carefully securitized. This environment is recessionary as money is retired from the circular income flow. This is obviously applicable to the case of Mexico 1994 and Greece 2007. Minsky's own expression for financial crises is 'It', which perhaps means that crises arise after economies implode. Other interrelated causes of financial crises are the excessive appetite for financial profits, de-supervision and investors' bullish attitude in the face of lax regulatory attitudes (cf. Wray 2009). These *laissez-faire* type causes arose since the 1970s. Hence, all these explanations reveal common patterns in financial crises.

Complex Systems (Comprehensive) Theory

In appearance, financial crises are solely the result of misguided policy interventions in markets. An innovative alternative approach is that crises may be seen as arising from a complex—dynamic and unstable—system. This is one of the messages of Keynes the 'organicist' in *The Economic Consequences of the Peace*: Problems and developments are comprehensive and are hence spread out into all elements in a system.

A complex system is thus an integral dynamic framework for explaining and predicting phenomena fueled by a mobile. The interrelations among elements are multidirectional, and the whole is different from the sum of the parts. Complexity is related to the concepts of 'the fallacy of composition' or *organicism (everything is interrelated in modernity)*, which is at the core of Keynes's philosophy. Dynamic complex systems are comprised by causes, interrelations, mobiles (or triggering factors in orthodox theory), consequences and solutions. Some constituents may be larger, more interrelated with others and more relevant than others. The linkages among the elements of financial crises are macroeconomic, microeconomic and financial variables. An example is the evolutionary dichotomy of indebtedness and investment. The mobile of financial crises is related to heterogeneous risk and is referred to speculative vehicles: the Mexican exchange rate or the mortgages price for Greece, but the cause is economic mismanagement.

The orthodox simplistic mode of thought is derived from the Classical-Newtonian paradigm, with *atomism* at its heart. Atomism is axiomatic. It considers systems as comprised by homogeneous agents linked by unidirectional relationships, with an inherent tendency to equilibrium with exceptional deviations. Obviously, organicism stands for the opposite perspective. By integrating the pieces of the crises into a complex system, organic, financial crises may be prevented or at least understood. For example, confusion between causes, triggering factors and symptoms may be avoided and speculators may not be blamed as the culprits of crises, since they simply manage speculative vehicles in their own benefit.

Comparison of the Financial Crisis of Mexico 1994 and Greece 2007 and Proposal of Guidelines

No country is equal to any other, but some social processes may be similar in some of them at least in certain stages of development. It is thus hereby suggested that common patterns between Mexico and Greece are found in the genesis of the crises, that is, excessive spending, de facto pegs and over-lending (in orthodox terms, cf. McKinnon and Pill 1996) or indebtedness (in Minsky's parlance). Main differences are solely related practicalities (expediency), for example, the effectiveness of rescue packages, as in the case of the EU.

In the issue of financial crises, differences among emerging countries are superficial since most financial and industrial systems are vulnerable. Whether they are propelled by currency problems (in East Asia) or subprime-crises (in Greece or Spain), they are financial crises. Examples were provided in Table 11.1. In addition, all financial crises may result from or are aggravated by misleading or unchecked remedial policies (as rising interest rates in East Asia), acts, measures and accords. In the 'Tequila Crisis', the lack of adequate surveillance of credit, market and operational risks enhanced the crisis. But this also happened in Brazil 1999.

According to all theories, crises reduce investment and activity, the financial system becomes even more fragile (especially in Minsky's view) and bad economic performance arises. At the end, financial crises bring about adjusting shocks to all economies, wherein some productive sectors are more affected than others (cf. Tornell et al. 2004). Appropriate macroeconomic management must be achieved bearing in mind that investment (both real and financial) is the key for growth attainment. Nonetheless, investment is the consequence of (as well as the pre-condition for) stability. Nevertheless, in the heterodox view, both the Mexican and the Greek crisis were caused by internal—non-random—motives and those causes are comprehensive, like in the complex system paradigm. Hence, policy guidelines based on both observational–historical (Section 'Facts in "Modern" Financial Crises') and theoretical–practical (Section 'The Eurozone') insights are now outlined for the cases in point. The objective is proving the existence of a general pattern and hence a general long-term and structural remedy for financial crises.

Policy Suggestions for Financial Crises

These suggestions arise from selecting the best recommendations generated by the three varieties of models of financial crisis. Orthodox insights may be used for inferring such policy suggestions as corrective measures on either spending or assets issuance. As a part of those measures, the use of tight fiscal policies in many countries is necessary but may complicate matters, due to contagion in terms of recessionary scenarios. This is the standard recipe for mitigating the effects of crises as can be seen in specialized reports of the IMF. Since new views in terms of factor ordering as a method are required for solving the problem, it is necessary to analyze rescue policies.

Even though pegged currencies (Peso and Euro), speculative vehicles (the exchange rate and mortgage prices), development levels, speculative circumstances and stages vary, a common policy implementation is at the heart of the solution. The crucial point for minimizing a hard aftermath of all crises is a reform in macro policies, financial institutions and rating agencies. This is a permanent solution. Policy guidelines must consist in all cases of domestic comprehensive solutions for financial crises, for example, more transparency and modernization in financial systems. In terms of the real sector, most emerging economies need to enhance their productivity (in terms of diversification) and informational levels.

Perhaps a more realistic conduction of local policies must be set in motion in order to attain stability. Risk propensities and prevailing uncertainty must be monitored. The implementation of co-operative, realist guidelines and modified academic assumptions thus will reduce the probability for crashes in the aftermath of booms. The debate between sudden and gradual liberalization of financial systems must be at the heart of the topic. In Mexico, sudden liberalization propitiated bad management and sudden capital inflows, revealing at the end domestic vulnerability. In a sense, this was also the case of the south of the EU. The design of opening policies must also consider short-term problems. The notion of integration at all costs must be revised before its implementation. It seems that all economies have to pay a price for becoming modern, especially the emerging economies, the so-called orthodox *original sin hypothesis*.

In the face of bullish attitudes in financial markets, regulators must take measures in terms of limiting the issuance of financial instruments. Central banks must play a leading role in this issue by means of interventions in the business cycle according to Heterodox models. In heterodox parlance, both central bankers and regulators must act as circuit breakers. Nevertheless, such orthodox remedies as limiting the creation of financial instruments with foreign institutions which were implemented in Greece by orthodox economists were palliative. Preventive and long-term regulatory policies must soften the impact of financial crises. This is one of the main messages of Minsky. Summarizing, a key issue of Minsky's legacy is related to the interrelated concepts of Big Government, and the trilogy of spender, lender and employer of last resort (which goes beyond the scope of this investigation).

The Greek crisis is obviously an indicative part of the world—Global North—crisis. The United States must play a leading role in the solving of the crisis by taking an efficient stand in fiscal policy. However, misguided German-style austerity measures which entail contractions must be discarded in favor of policies related to the sovereign currency system combined with Keynesian fiscal policies, in order to enhance aggregate demand (cf. Hannsgen and Papadimitriou 2012). Retiring money from the circular income flow is against common sense. Suggested policy guidelines aimed to counter the effects of fiscal retrenchment must be an 'actual' feasible target rate in the budget as well as policies rules added up to automatic stabilizers for enhancing spending, even at the price of an increase in the budget by implementing aid policies. Financial innovation must be set in motion in order to increase household spending, instead of household indebtedness, which is one of the main causes of all crises. No tight policies must be followed. Bond-purchasing programs are insufficient. Finally, only controlled variables must be targeted (cf. Hannsgen and Papadimitriou 2012).

CONCLUSIONS

Some analysts argue that comparisons show nothing. Actually, comparative economic systems may highlight salient elements to be targeted in prevention programs. Whereas emergent economies are prone to crises since they are capital importers implying an implosion, developed economies are also subject to implosion due to the size of their economic systems. Pattern equalization is thus confirmed by the identification of key factors related to prevention. Indeed, 'contagion' (in the orthodox sense) or 'commonalities' (in the heterodox sense) are larger among developed economies due to financial homogeneity. The problem may be solved by adopting an integral perspective. In all cases, financial speculation is the mobile, triggered by underlying deficiencies. Turbulence is the rule, since no automatic equilibrium exists and *laissez faire* is excessive in volatility episodes. Finally, disparities among countries do not cause crises, as suggested by orthodox authors (cf. Caballero 2006) in all models generations.

The existence of crises also challenges both conventional microeconomic wisdom and the use of method in economics. However, complex systems and heterodox views are innovative methods for crisis solution. This investigation attempted to prove in historical terms that financial crises are not a random effect, so that economic reasons (mainly debt, spending and lagged investment) were hereby reviewed in order to detect patterns based on two examples. A generalized pattern was found: Crises are endogenously determined but revealed by external events. Hence, the subprime crisis of 2007 was not different, as some researchers conclude after using a Minskyan approach (cf. Dymski 2010). All 'modern' crises can be analyzed departing from the dichotomy between investment and debt, which is at the heart of their unfolding. A higher abstraction level is required: All meteorites are different but have the same origin.

Therefore, the conventional notion that crises are isolated—random—episodes is challenged with the use of both a heterodox (Minskyan) framework and a complex system model. A historical perception was also helpful. The insights undertaken in this investigation also allowed the identification of guidelines. Another Minsky's insight—based on Keynes—is that only fiscal stimulus can provide a solution for 'modern' financial crises. Neither randomness nor atomism exists in financial crises. Most financial systems are immaturely sophisticated. About avenues for future research for the purpose of financial crises prevention, key variables, especially those in the financial sector, both at the entrepreneurial and the country levels must be analyzed but considering their internal connections and evolution, not only as leading indicators as it used to be done in the 1990s.

NOTES

1. Although debt in developed countries is high, they possess strong and developed financial, industrial and public sectors.
2. The latter two countries almost approached default in 2010, resembling the situation of Latin America in the early 1980s (cf. the Policy Brief of Levy Economics Institute, 2012).

REFERENCES

Banco de México. (2016). Indicadores Económicos y Financieros. http://www.banxico.org

Baldacci, E., de Mello, L., & Inchauste, G. (2002, June). Financial crises, poverty and income distribution. *Finance & Development, 39*(2), 1–6. International Monetary Fund.

Becker, R., Gelos, G., & Richards, A. (2002). Devaluation expectations and the stock market – The case of Mexico in 1994/95. *International Journal of Finance and Economics, 7*(3), 195–214.

Caballero, R. J. (2006). On the macroeconomics of asset shortages. MIT and NBER, the 4th ECB Central Banking Conference on *The Role of Money: Money and Monetary Policy in the Twenty-first Century*, Frankfurt, November.

Calvo, G. A., & Reinhart, C. (2000, November). *Fear of Floating.* NBER Working Paper No. 7993. Washington, DC: National Bureau of Economic Research.

Diaz-Alejandro, M. (1985). Good-bye financial repression, hello financial crash. *Journal of Development Economics, 19*(1), 1–24.

Dornbusch, R. (1999, June). *A primer on emerging market crises*. NBER Working Paper No. 8326. Washington, DC: National Bureau of Economic Research.

Dornbusch, R. (2001, June). *A primer on emerging market crises*. NBER WP No. 8326, pp. 1–12. Retrieved from www.nber.org/chapters/e10649.PDF

Dymski, G. (2010). Why the subprime crisis is different: A Minskyan approach. *Cambridge Journal of Economics, 34*(2), 239–255.

Edwards, S., & Sevastano, M. A. (1998). *The morning after: The Mexican Peso in the aftermath of the 1994 currency crisis*. NBER Working Paper No. 6516. Washington, DC: National Bureau of Economic Research.

European Central Bank. (2016). Statistics. www.ecb.europa.eu.

Felkerson, A. S. (2011). *$29,000,000,000,000: A detailed look at the fed's bailout by funding facility and recipient*. Working Paper No. 698, Annandale-on-Hudson, NY: The Levy Economics Institute of Bard College.

Hannsgen, G., & Papadimitriou, D. B. (2012). Fiscal traps and macro policy after the Euro Zone Crisis. Public Policy Brief No. 127. Annandale-on-Hudson, NY: The Levy Economics Institute of Bard College.

International Monetary Fund. (2012, October). World economic and financial surveys, restoring confidence and progressing on reforms. www.imf.org.

International Monetary Fund. (2013, February 20). Transcript of a press briefing, by William Murray. Deputy Spokesman, External Relations Department, *International Monetary Fund*. www.imf.org.

International Monetary Fund. (2016). IMF Data & Statistics. www.imf.org/external//data.htm.

Kaminsky, G., & Reinhart, C. (1999). The twin crises: The causes of banking and balance-of-payments problems. *American Economic Review, 89*(3), 473–500.

Krugman, P. (1979). A model of balance-of-payments crises. *Journal of Money, Credit, and Banking, 11*, 311–325.

Krugman, P. (1999). Balance sheets, the transfer problem, and financial crises. *International Tax and Public Finance, 6*(4), 459–472.

McKinnon, R., & Pill, H. (1996). Credible liberalizations and international capital flows: The 'overborrowing syndrome'. *NBER Chapters in Financial Deregulation and Integration in East Asia NBER-EASE, 5*, 7–50.

Minsky, H. P. (1982). *Can 'it' happen again? Essays on instability and finance*. Armonk: Sharpe.

Obstfeld, M. (1994). The logic of currency crises. Banque de France, *Cahiers Economiques et Monetaires, 43*, 189–213.

Tornell, A., Westermann, F., & Martínez, L. (2004). *The positive link between financial liberalization, growth, and crises*. NBER Working Paper No. 10293. Washington, DC: National Bureau of Economic Research.

Wray, L. R. (2009). The rise and fall of money manager capitalism: A Minskyan approach. *Cambridge Journal of Economics, 33*, 807–828.

CHAPTER 12

Restructuring Accounting Education: The Key to Avoiding Another Financial Crisis in Greece

Dimitrios Siskos and John Marangos

INTRODUCTION

During the last decade, many authors connected the recent financial crisis in Greece with accounting omissions and manipulations in financial statements both in public and in private sector based on unethical behavior (Brewer et al. 2014). In Greece, "creative accounting" was practiced many years before crisis despite the comprehensive accounting regulations (Baralexis 2004). The concept of "creative accounting" describes how accounting professionals make use of their knowledge in order to manipulate the figures in the annual accounts (Rada 2014). Research also highlighted the lack of the necessary fiscal consolidation during the past 15 years, when Greece was experiencing high growth rates, in relation

D. Siskos (✉)
Swiss Management Center University, Zug, Switzerland

J. Marangos
Department of Balkan, Slavic and Oriental Studies, University of Macedonia, Thessaloniki, Greece

© The Author(s) 2017
J. Marangos (ed.), *The Internal Impact and External Influence of the Greek Financial Crisis*, DOI 10.1007/978-3-319-60201-1_12

to the continuous false reporting of fiscal accounting data (Kouretas and Vlamis 2010). All of these issues had undermined Greece's credibility. For example, in mid-October 2009, the newly elected government announced that the budget deficit for 2009 was estimated to be 12.7% of gross domestic product (GDP), while the previous government was arguing in September 2009 that deficit would not be higher than 6.5% of GDP (Kouretas and Vlamis 2010). At the same time, large companies overstated profits to satisfy the demand for external financing, while the small companies understated profit in order to reduce company taxes (Baralexis 2004). Moreover, auditors detected manipulation in accounts for depreciation, forecast payment defaults, forecast staff severance pay, participation in other companies and fiddling accounts for tax purposes (Spathis et al. 2004).

The connection between the recent financial crisis and accounting irregularities is documented also on a global scale. It is widely known that the "credit crunch", which began in the USA in August 2007, turned into a crisis when Lehman Brothers went bankrupt in September 2008 (Allen and Moessner 2011). The findings suggested that Lehman acted unethically by violating credibility standards in its use of Repo 105 transactions and violating the accounting requirements by manipulating financial statements. Repo 105 is an aggressive and deceitful accounting off-balance sheet device which was used to temporarily remove securities and troubled liabilities from Lehman's balance sheet, while reporting fallaciously its quarterly financial results to the public (Jeffers 2011). Consequently, it is efficient to act proactively in restructuring accounting education, which could serve this purpose and prevent future accounting omissions and serious malpractices of ethics. Therefore, Ravenscroft and Williams (2004) rightly wonder who trained the professionals involved in all of these scandals, exactly what were they trained to do and how should educators modify the content and teaching methods? Marangos (2002) stressed that the survival of the economics education would depend on how successful economics is in adjusting to the new conditions and on altering the emphasis of teaching materials from being hypothetical to incorporate problem-solving techniques. The last ascertainment should be considered seriously in Greece, as according to the framework of Economic Chamber, graduates from departments of economics can become accounting professionals. Nevertheless, many US schools or educators recognized an opportunity for growth in response to the scandals and made changes to their curriculum (Titard et al. 2004). However, in Greece, the curriculum has not changed and thus it is essential to redefine the education of accounting along with the role that accountants play in financial markets.

Accounting education is strongly related to the recent financial crisis in Greece, since some of the main root causes of the crisis were accounting omissions and manipulations in financial statements all embraced by unethical actions (Brewer et al. 2014). The recent financial crisis in Greece, epitomized by the recession of 2009, raises the question of whether and how should accounting educators respond. To prevent a future financial crisis, the accounting professors in Greece should consider certain changes in the accounting curriculum with the purpose of preparing finest and ethical professionals. This new curriculum should cultivate the necessary skills and competencies to the future accounting professionals in line with contemporary developments in areas such as ethics, forensic accounting, information systems, auditing and green accounting (Santouridis et al. 2014). Accounting education, as one of the most significant parts of the broader area of financial science, should take lead into adjusting its structure to fulfill the gap between what is taught in higher learning education and the skills required for success in accounting profession (Brewer et al. 2014).

The importance of this study is crucial to many fields, including the economy, unemployment, society's coherence, development and competitiveness. Since it was accounting education which trained the professionals, whose actions was one root cause of the recent financial crisis, it is rather plausible to connect accounting education with the financial crisis. As such, the value of an updated accounting education curriculum becomes extremely critical and important for the society given the large consequences of the recent financial crisis. By now, the tectonic damage left by the recent financial crisis of 2009 in Greece has been well documented. According to the Hellenic Statistical Authority (2015) figures, during February of 2015, the percentage of employed people was 74% of the total available workforce, while the percentage of unemployed was 26%. Employment rose by 1.6% compared with February 2014 and decreased by 4.2% compared to February 2012 (Aspridis et al. 2013). Many Greeks suffered big pay cuts, tax hikes and reduced pensions imposed by successive governments on the orders of international lenders. Unfortunately, the harsh austerity measures imposed on the Greek public since the depths of country's financial crisis have led to a sustained increase in suicides, 26.5% increase in 2011 compared to 2010 and 43% compared to 2007, the year before the crisis began (Aspridis et al. 2013).

Last, Greek births have fallen by 10% since 2007 compared with 2012, while the Greek immigrants to countries mainly in Western and Northern Europe and America exceed approximately 120,000 people during the first two years from the beginning of the crisis (Aspridis et al. 2013). Since 2015, more than 200,000 Greeks have left the country due to the financial crisis hit (Smith 2015).

Literature Review

Santouridis et al.'s (2014) study determined the strengths and weaknesses of higher accounting education in Greece, and our study involves interviews with academic staff and practitioners in order to evaluate the current structure of the accounting curricula. The chapter also aims to elaborate further on the curricula strengths and weaknesses, and to devise a new educational framework which would prevent another financial crisis.

Greek secondary-school students are not introduced to accounting courses until the final year of their studies when an introductory course is offered among many other optional courses (Feldmann and Rupert 2012). According to Feldmann and Rupert (2012), after completing secondary school, students who choose to continue to tertiary education take part in the Pan-Hellenic examinations to enter a free public university or choose to continue to a private college. Their scores in this examination define their acceptance from the public institutions. After graduation, the students can work as accountants both for the public and for the private sector. Some students choose to start their own accounting businesses, while others prefer to pursue postgraduate studies in accounting (Manganaris and Spathis 2012).

In Greece, three types of higher educational institutions provide accounting programs: the public University sector, the public higher Technical sector and private Colleges. Public higher institutions are permitted to operate under the endorsement of the state, while institutions of higher learning are accredited branches of foreign universities mainly with UK origins. Meanwhile, all higher education institutions in Greece provide three types of accounting degrees: Bachelor, Master and Doctoral degrees. The duration of the accounting courses at tertiary level institutes is four years. After the last major reform that took place in the beginning of 2013, the Greek higher education map includes 22 Universities, 15 Technical Universities and 39 Colleges (Santouridis et al. 2014).

According to a research by Santouridis et al. (2014), the accounting programs were firstly introduced in Centers of Higher Technical Education (KATEE), which were the precursors of Technical Universities (TEI) in the 1970s. The first accounting and finance programs appeared in universities at the early 1990s. The same study stressed that accounting and finance modules were included only in the curricula of business administration and economics university departments. Today, four-year accounting and finance programs are offered by 3 Universities (AEIs) and 11 Technical Universities (TEIs). The same research reveals the curriculum for each program, as classified into six disciplines, which, apart from Accounting and Finance, were Economics, IT and Mathematics, Management, Law or other. The accounting and finance modules cover on average approximately 63% of the total number of modules offered in both the Universities and the TEIs, while Management and IT cover the rest.

Regarding the concept of business ethics, the curricula review process showed that it is very limited if present at all, while forensic accounting was absent from the curriculum of all tertiary departments. The examination of the auditing modules' outlines unveiled that they include some elements of business ethics, while for green accounting, a single relevant module was found in the curriculum of a university department.

The review of the leading accounting literature has, however, clearly shown that very little research has been published reporting the connection between financial crisis and accounting education in Greece (Olson 2011). It actually seems that the accounting society may learn much by trying to understand the function, or roles, accounting in action have had in the beginning of the global financial crisis in 2008 and has in the current financial crisis (Olson 2011).

Available research on themes surrounding accounting education in Greece, either directly or indirectly, is divided into research before crisis and after the crisis (Livanos 2010; Santouridis et al. 2014; Venieris and Cohen 2004). Research before crisis is mostly focused on technical enhancements as introducing accrual and management accounting modules in Greek Public Universities (Venieris and Cohen 2004) or incorporating auditing courses throughout education curriculum. Previous studies have shown that graduates who have had an understanding of conventional accounting remained far behind features that were demanded by the industries or markets (Arnold 2009). There is strong research evidence showing that the recent financial crisis in Greece came partially from accounting omissions and manipulations in financial statements all embraced by unethical actions (Brewer et al. 2014; Kermis and Kermis 2011; Santouridis et al. 2014). Conventional accounting education in Greece resulted into producing professionals with poor qualifications.

In contrast, in the post-crisis era, literature shows a significant increase in research output focused specifically on restructuring accounting education to prevent accounting omissions and serious malpractices of ethics (Parker 2001). Skills and competencies necessary for the future accounting professionals have been discussed largely by many other authors (Brewer et al. 2014; Filos 2010). Nonetheless, altering the content and teaching methods in the current accounting curricula still remains under speculation in Greek tertiary education. However, the whole venture is young and still at an early stage of development.

METHODOLOGY

The methodology of this study was qualitative. More specifically, a descriptive phenomenological approach was used to achieve the purposes of this study: to explore perceptions of stakeholders concerning problems with current accounting education in Greece, and to examine to what extent accounting education is "fit for purpose" in terms of developing professional accountants that can meet the needs of enterprises and society. The number and extent of studies that assessed accounting education by using phenomenological approach is limited; the current study advances accounting research in new horizons and with a different perspective.

The detailed descriptions provided by 25 participants, 10 accounting professionals and 15 accounting professors, in this study clarified the role of accounting education in Greece in the post-crisis era and provided a foundation for developing finest and ethical professionals. The questionnaires were used in the first stage, followed by interviews on a sample to serve as a check and to fill out certain features of the questionnaire. Interaction among techniques in this way is typical of qualitative research. Ideally, there was a qualitative "check" on a sample of questionnaire replies to see if respondents were interpreting questions in the way intended. Due to the differences in the two populations, professors and professionals, it was required to implement two sampling procedures. As such, with an aim to listen to the experiences of those individuals, the current research employed two strategies for sampling: purposeful and criterion sampling. During the purposeful sampling strategy, the researchers invited via e-mail the individuals to ensure that they are able to share personal knowledge and inform an understanding of the research problem (Creswell 2007). In order to make sure that criterion sampling would unbiasedly work, it was important for the participants to share certain characteristics: (a) for the 15 professors: have a minimum experience of three years in teaching accounting courses, hold a Ph.D. degree and work in different universities or colleges in Greece; and (b) for the 10 professionals: hold a bachelor degree in accounting, work as accountants for at least five years in Greece and work in different companies or are self-employed.

The 15 accounting professors represented the 3 different cultures of tertiary education in Greece. Thus, three of them work in private colleges, six of them work in AEIs and six of them work in TEIs. Among the 15 professors, 4 are females. The ten professionals represented all different cultures of working environments. Three of them work in the industry sector, five of them work in the services sector, one of them also works in the Economic Chamber of Greece and the last one works in the Ministry of Defense.

The researchers conducted face-to-face interviews with participants, which took place in Thessaloniki. The interviews of the ten professionals were conducted in a quiet and private place outside their workplace. Each interview took approximately 30–40 minutes and was digitally recorded to make sure that participants' perspectives are captured accurately. The researchers allowed the participant to take any direction he or she wanted to explore in his or her experience. With the aim to better understand initial responses, the researchers asked some sub-questions, which helped to clarify and to go deeper into the participants' experiences. Throughout the interview, the researchers, in addition to digitally recorded audio, took notes.

Regarding the 15 selected accounting professors, the questionnaires were initially used, followed by interviews on a sample as a check and to fill out certain features of the questionnaire replies. Interviews served as a qualitative "check" on a sample of questionnaire replies to see if respondents were interpreting items in the way intended. As such, questionnaires were mailed in February 2014 by the researchers to each of the 15 faculty members selected for the study, accompanied by the Individual Informed Consent form. The questionnaire included 6 demographic questions, 20 multiple choice questions and 16 open-ended questions. All of them focused on gaining information on the professors' "lived experiences" in accounting education and its impact on accounting profession. Recipients were requested to complete and to return the questionnaire to the researchers as soon as possible. Wherever was geographically possible, the researchers went to the professors' office rooms on the university campus to conduct interviews based on their questionnaires' responses, eliciting supplementary information about research. This enabled the researchers to develop a level of detail about the place and to be highly involved in actual experiences of the participants. The interviews principally focused on gaining supplementary information on the questionnaires' responses about accounting education and its impact on accounting profession.

Although it was time demanding, transcript-based analysis was used for the transcription of the recorded interviews. The interviews were tape-recorded, with permission of the participants, and then the tapes were transcribed verbatim. Some notes were taken by the researchers in order to assist in accuracy and transcription, but the note taking was limited to allow the researchers to focus on the participants and their answers to the prompts. The recorded interviews were transcribed into text format using Microsoft Word, and then were loaded in a qualitative research software program NVivo 2.0 to organize and code them. The data analysis of the questionnaires consisted of examining the surveys for correctness and completeness, coding and keying data into a database in Google Drive and performing an analysis of descriptive responses according to frequency distributions and descriptive statistics. A constant comparison analysis was effectively served to compare findings. Following the three major stages of constant comparison analysis, the researchers initially used open coding to separate data into small units, attaching a code to them. The data were analyzed separately, once for the professionals and the other for professors. Then, axial coding was used to group these codes into categories. The researchers used the meaning of analysis context as the unit of analysis for coding and also looked for description. This means that the data were not coded sentence by sentence or paragraph by paragraph, but coded for meaning. Following, the researchers compared specific incidents of data, developing concepts that express the content of the participants. Generally, all identifying information was deleted to ensure confidentiality. In most transcripts, there were problems with expressions in Greek and grammatical errors, but all interviews were transcribed just as the research participants spoke.

Discussion of the Results

Consistent with previous studies concerning accounting education in Greece (Filos 2010) and abroad (Beresford 2005; Wyatt 2004), the results showed that accounting education in tertiary level in Greece do not correspond to the real requirements of the accounting profession. Particularly, the implication was that the accounting professionals, who were asked to evaluate the current structure of accounting education in Greece in regard to the accounting profession, encountered difficulties in defining positive effects, while most of them recognized educational deficiencies. Similar to other studies, the study showed that changes in economy caused by globalization and the emergence of information as a critical response to crisis have changed significantly the requirements for the accounting profession in Greece (Kermis and Kermis 2011). Participants found that the current accounting education structure in tertiary education in Greece provides only the understanding of the basic accounting principles and that this is not sufficient enough to face the market demand, which are consistent with the findings of Beresford (2005) and Parker (2001). In the Beresford study (Beresford 2005), major accounting firms had increasingly called for adjusting accounting education to reflect the realities of the current work environment as another way to create accounting professionals. In his work, Parker (2001) discussed the restructuring that took place in the accounting profession over the last years and has not been reflected in the education of accounting. The findings of the present study support the study of Gabbin (2002), indicating that many practicing accountants perceived as the accounting education graduates get today to be outdated and in desperate need of an overhaul.

Consistent with previous studies concerning the perception of the accounting profession (Gabbin 2002; Pekdemir and Pekdemir 2013), the results of the current study criticize accounting curriculum and accounting educators for not providing students with a full sense of professional identity, an appreciation of their ethical and legal duties or an understanding of the profession's demands and risks. Similar to Pekdemir and Pekdemir (2013), most accounting professionals reported that their perception about the accounting profession in regard to its effect on the society, to the difficulty level and to the nature of the duties they perform has been changed dramatically since they were students. In Gabbin's (2002) study, most accounting professionals who participated in interviews argued that if they were completing their own education over again, they would choose not to major in accounting.

Moreover, most accounting professionals found the teaching of accounting they had in university uninteresting. This finding is consistent with a previous study of Byrne and Willis (2005) which indicated that the accounting professionals found to hold a traditional view of the teaching of accounting considering it boring, definite and precise. The findings also support the literature (Belias and Koustelios 2013). In the study of Belias and Koustelios (2013), it was found that the teaching of accounting has been done, mostly, by conventional teacher-centered methods rather than modern student-oriented applications and techniques, while the transmission of knowledge and information has been realized with the usual form of lectures.

Consistent with previous studies by Brewer et al. (2014), Ravenscroft and Williams (2004) and Santouridis et al. (2014), the results showed that the recent financial crisis had great effect on the accounting profession. Both accounting professionals and professors mostly argued that there were many ethical lessons learnt from the financial crisis in Greece of 2009. Most of them stood in moral lessons learnt, while less stood in technical conclusions. This finding can be related to the conduct of serious malpractices of business ethics in the banking and finance sector, which brought the role of accounting professionals into the center of widespread debates (Santouridis et al. 2014). It is also noticeable that the study found that there are serious ethical dilemmas throughout the upper level management of accounting profession. This finding also supports previous literature, which describes discussions of individuals facing dilemmas—"do I do the 'right' thing and risk my job or do I conspire tacitly with my superior to do something immoral and keep my job and become economically successful?" (Ravenscroft and Williams 2004, p. 19). As such, similar to the results of the two previous surveys, almost all of the professors and practitioners recognized the need to develop the accountants' profile on an ethical basis after the Greek crisis of 2009. Mintz (1997) indicated that accounting graduates should be aware that recruiters in the profession look, mostly after crisis, for values such as honesty, reliability, trustworthiness and a willingness to honor the public trust and public interest. However, there is limited evidence of response to calls to include ethical issues (Parker 2001; Ravenscroft and Williams 2004). Only a few ethical decision-making models emphasized the role of education on ethical decision making (Pimentel et al. 2010).

Moreover, the majority of professors and professionals strongly agreed that the recent financial crisis in Greece brings about more interest and demand for ethical accountants and recognized the utility of such educational reform describing the benefits for the society and the accounting profession. These findings are consistent with Pain's study (2003), who described ethics and morality as a highly practical invention because society expects business and its leaders to fit within contexts that endow human activity with meaning, prescribe standards of behavior and establish expectations of how we should treat one another.

The results of the study showed that most professors have already considered altering the content of the accounting curricula and the teaching–learning mechanisms after the crisis of 2009, while in the same time, they believe that the Greek universities should integrate new courses in their accounting curricula. The findings are partially consistent with Ravenscroft, Williams' study (2004) who concluded that the recent financial scandals raise the question of whether and how accounting educators should respond. However, the findings of a study by Arnold (2009) resulted that accounting academics failed to anticipate the global financial crisis of 2008, because of the persistent gap between the world of academic research and the world of accounting in action. In particular, Parker (2001, p. 388) concluded, "Recent accounting scandals and regulatory responses had made very little impact on the content of the accounting curricula in universities". The "undisturbed curriculum" continues to be accounting standards and compliance-driven, with ethics and social responsibility being comparatively neglected (2001, p. 388).

Following a research made by Santouridis et al. (2014), the study also examined new content on areas such as ethics, forensic accounting, auditing and green accounting. Specifically, Santouridis et al. (2014) identified the gaps and weaknesses of the current traditional curricula and the development of the orientations of a new curriculum in Accounting and Finance Education. The findings of the present study are also consistent with previous literature (Bekiaris et al. 2013; Filos 2010) that accounting professors and professionals expect an increased future demand for ethics and auditing skills. However, the findings are inconsistent with Rezaee et al.'s (2003) study showing that accounting professors and professionals expect that the future demand for forensic accounting will remain the same. In contrast, Rezaee et al. (2003) indicated that the demand for forensic accounting is expected to increase. However, similar to Buckhoff and Schrader's study (Buckhoff and Schrader 2000), the findings showed that high-profile financial statement fraud cases in Greece revealed the intention from the professors to encourage students on career opportunities in forensic accounting (less) and auditing (more). Moreover, the findings revealed an intention from the professors to include green or environmental accounting as part of the accounting education in Greece.

The findings are consistent with the literature reporting that the ethics, forensic accounting and green accounting are not contained often in the current content of the accounting curricula, while auditing course is the only of the four examined areas that is being offered frequently (Santouridis et al. 2014). However, it is noteworthy to refer that a high percentage of universities offer ethics modules. The study showed that most accounting curriculums offer only auditing modules corroborating a previous study of Massey and Van Hise (2009) who claim that this happens due to the lack of space in the curriculum, instructional resources and faculty members' discomfort in teaching such courses due to a lack of formal training. Indeed, the results indicated that only few accounting programs offer separate ethics, forensic accounting and green courses, and most of them are integrated through other accounting courses. However, this finding contradicts Rezaee et al.'s (2003) study, which stated that this approach has a few major impediments: first, adding such modules to existing accounting courses can overburden faculty and students alike in dealing with courses already saturated with related materials; second, accounting faculty may not wish to add new topics to their courses primarily because of their own lack of comfort with these accounting topics; finally, instructors may have to consolidate some of the existing accounting subjects in order to add the new accounting topics.

The study also revealed that most accounting departments, which currently do not offer any ethics and forensic accounting coverage, are planning to do so within five years. This finding should be considered along with Bean and Bernardi's (2005) study who found that an initial course in ethics, rooted in philosophy and ethical reasoning, should be a required course prior to taking a discipline-specific ethics or forensic accounting course in the basic curriculum. Consistent to a model for integrating ethical-oriented courses into the accounting curriculum presented by Carroll (2000), the results showed that ethics and forensic accounting should be offered in both graduate and undergraduate level. Specifically, the model includes (a) half a semester of the Introduction to Accounting to general business ethics for the undergraduate level, (b) integration of ethics into each and every accounting course throughout the curriculum for both graduate and undergraduate level and (c) developing a capstone course at the senior level that deals with complex issues of business social responsibility and professional responsibility for graduate level.

Consistent with the literature, the results of the study indicated that the most important learning mechanism in teaching ethics, forensic accounting, auditing and green accounting courses is case studies (Farrell 2005; Green and Calderon 2005; Lockhart and Mathews 2000; Xia et al. 2012). Research projects, guest speakers and textbooks are also considered important teaching methods. Field trips to professional organizations and correctional facilities are viewed as a slightly important teaching technique. In Farrell's study (2005), which considered accounting ethics as an established academic discipline, it was found that a useful approach for a business ethics course is to understand and describe how ethical decisions are made and the environment that influences ethical decision making. Green and Calderon (2005), who studied the effect of plausible simulations on the ability of the students to recognize management fraud, concluded that students taught with lifelike simulations had a better understanding of the calculated risks involved and better competence in applying professional standards as well as confidence in the results. Xia et al. (2012) used business games to teach auditing courses, in which players explore all the components of a complex situation, in contrast to the traditional classroom setting. Lockhart and Mathews (2000) encouraged teaching strategies such as the use of remedial modules and case studies for environmental accounting education, recommending a four-part framework that allows students to examine green accounting within both the conventional and the expanded model of accounting.

Accounting professors' experiences influenced their opinion about the potential obstacles in integrating ethics, forensic accounting, auditing and green accounting education into the accounting curriculum in Greek tertiary education. Similar to Rezaee et al. (2003), the responses showed that the main obstacles in integrating the above modules in the accounting curriculum are: lack of financial resources, lack of faculty interest, lack of instructional material and lack of administration interest and support. The findings of this study support studies (Rezaee et al. 2003) that the primary obstacles facing delivery of the above courses are institutional in nature (i.e., faculty, funding, administration), and not because of a perceived lack of demand by employers and students.

The results also highlighted the importance of integrating additional modules to develop non-technical skills and to improve students' perception about the accounting profession. Consistent with the literature by Kermis and Kermis (2011) and Leone (2008), the study resulted that soft skills are important for the new generations of accountants in Greece due to the current developments in the profession. Specifically, the study showed that such skills would improve interpersonal relations and encourage team working as well as problem solving. The study of Kermis and Kermis (2011), which focused on the transition from Generally Accepted Accounting Principles (GAAP) to International Financial Reporting Standards (IFRS), increased the need for accountants with strong soft skills because of IFRS's requirement to apply principles rather than comply with rules. Leone (2008) highlighted that their biggest challenge, besides technical training, may be mastering the soft skills such as judgment, critical thinking and analysis, integrity and openness, as well as how to make transparent disclosures. Participants also suggested that soft skills should be part of accounting education in the tertiary level and, hence, need to be integrated within the accounting curricula.

The findings also revealed the importance of an introductory accounting course in shaping perceptions of accounting studies and the profession of accountancy in general. In terms of generating best practices and consistent to previous literature (Manganaris and Spathis 2012; Marriott and Marriott 2003), the study concluded that an introductory course of accounting would improve Greek students' perception about accounting and thus it could create more conscious students. In the study of Manganaris and Spathis' (2012), the results revealed that students' perceptions of the accounting profession mirror the traditional stereotypical image of accountants. Marriott and Marriott (2003) highlighted the importance of an introductory accounting course in shaping perceptions of accounting studies and the profession of accountancy with regard to undergraduate students.

The study also focused on the strategy that accounting education needs to devise in the post-crisis era. Driven from the findings of previous studies (Brewer et al. 2014; Eleren and Kayahan 2007), the results showed that accounting professionals ask for a more holistic and less technocratic accounting education, ask for interaction with other areas of management and ask for the correct learning of the laws and their interpretation, as to find ways to make accountants think out of the box. In the study, Brewer et al. (2014) described "a shift in accountants' orientation from a support function to an enterprise performance management (EPM) role, which had enormous implications for defining the determinants of success within profession, the most important of, which involves becoming collaborators and integrated thinkers" (p. 30). Eleren and Kayahan (2007) indicated that accounting education, accounting profession and applications should be planned to be linked to current developments.

Results of great importance were that almost all accounting professionals ask for more interconnection between universities and workplaces and, going further, the permanent presence of professional accountants as a separate section in every accounting department of universities which would adapt any new changes in the accounting curricula. The last finding is very innovative and hopeful, nonetheless, due to the lack of any previous literature, there is no comparison on the results of such a venture. Consistent to Parker (2001), the conclusions highlighted the professional code of ethics as defined by the Economic Chamber of Greece which should be promoted officially by Greek universities. The results also emphasized the role of the educator as facilitator or mediator of learning, rather than as an instructor. Practically, the professional accountants ask for future developments in accounting profession to be reflected through interactive courses, case studies, workshops, continuous training and implementation of projects.

The previous results presented an unrealistic view of accounting education within an advancing business environment. To address this mismatch, and achieve greater alignment between accounting education and directions in accounting practice, the results showed that accounting professors are willing to cooperate with market stakeholders to define the content of the accounting curriculum and the learning mechanisms to integrate the new professional demands. This finding is consistent with the literature (Parker 2001) which emphasized on the user perspective of accounting in terms of subject content and improvements in the process and delivery of accounting education. However, inconsistent with the results of a study made by Rezaee et al. (2003), the accounting professors drew attention on many administrational issues in accounting education as the large number of students per class, the scant resources in terms of academic staff and financing and more flexibility from the ministry.

Practical Recommendations

The overall results indicate considerable shortfalls of accounting education in Greece in meeting the recent requirements of accounting profession and obvious potential to introduce further innovations in the content, delivery and assessment of a new accounting curriculum. Consistent with the primary aim of the study, the results provide both benchmark and performance implications against which accounting educators can compare, map and redevelop their curricula, reflect on their teaching practices and improve pedagogy in new or current accounting subjects.

In the investigation of the relation between accounting education and accounting profession in Greece, a particular focus was on how accounting professionals evaluated the accounting curricula and the teaching mechanisms in regards to the requirements of the accounting profession. In their own words, most professionals stated that accounting education in Greece provided only "the understanding of the basic accounting principles" and that "this was not sufficient enough to face the accounting jobs requirements". They asserted that to successfully manage the real requirements of the profession of accountant, "further executive studies and many professional seminars were necessary". There were a large proportion of responses classified as fully negative to define positive effects and a relatively high percentage of participants who criticized accounting curriculum and educators for not providing a full sense of professional identity, an appreciation of their ethical duties or an understanding of the profession's demands. All these indicated that the current accounting curriculum generally remains traditional in content and teaching methods, with a significant concentration on basic accounting principles as debits and credits, transaction analysis and recording. One implication of the prevalence of this perspective is that the orientation of accounting education continues to reflect a procedural bookkeeping and compliance-driven bias which is largely unsuited to meeting the needs of accounting majors, much less non-accounting majors.

Analysis of the survey data benchmarked the importance of the perceived benefits of restructuring accounting education in Greece on an ethical basis. Particularly, on average more than 80% of both accounting professionals and professors recognized the usefulness of such educational reform describing the benefits in the profession and the society. Characteristically, one of them pointed that "restructuring accounting education on an ethical basis is something necessary in Greece, as accountants would improve their profile to their customers' eyes", while another one stated that "Money transactions are the basis of the profession of every accountant. Your morality is tested extensively. Therefore, accountants should have strong and powerful personality oriented on business ethics". At the same time, almost all argued that there were many ethical lessons coming from the financial crisis in Greece regarding the accounting profession. Indeed, the majority of accounting professionals who work in private companies face ethical dilemmas very often, in contrast to low- or medium-level accountants who work in public organizations and are possessed by strict procedures that leave no space for ethical dilemmas. Moreover, more than 70% of the accounting professors had already considered altering the content of the accounting curricula or their teaching methods after the Greek crisis of 2009, while more than 80% of them believed that Greek universities should integrate new courses in their accounting curricula after crisis. One implication of the prevalence of this technical perspective is that there are many ethical issues among accountants who work in private sector in Greece, which in many times fuel the financial crisis by manipulating financial statements. For example, an accounting professional stated that "The recent financial crisis in Greece reinforced lack of liquidity and, hence, the unethical actions increased. Many times, when employers ask for financing from a bank, they usually hide some accounts". Another conclusion is that there is a belief among the accounting professionals and professors, ready to accept an educational reform which would be focused on ethical issues.

The survey results demonstrate new content on areas such as ethics, forensic accounting, auditing and green accounting. Specifically, the results foresee an increased future demand for ethics and auditing, while they consider ethics, forensic accounting and green accounting to be in high demand by the employers. Similarly, they reveal the intention from the professors to encourage students on career opportunities in forensic accounting and auditing in future. Consequently, the four examined areas are considered highly topical and should be included within the accounting curricula. However, modules as ethics, forensic accounting and green accounting are proved to be absent from the current content of the accounting curricula, while auditing course is the only of the four examined areas that is being offered frequently. One implication of the prevalence of this perspective is that the demand for more auditing courses is satisfied through the current content of accounting curricula as separate modules. Unlike auditing, the need for more ethics courses is partially satisfied mostly by integrating through other accounting courses, while the need for forensic accounting and green accounting is not supported at all by the current program. Another implication is that most accounting departments give more emphasis on integrating ethics and forensic accounting in the next five years rather on green accounting coverage.

A significant implication is that that the four examined courses should be offered at both the graduate and the undergraduate level.

Teaching delivery follows a traditional lecture and tutorial format, which tend to emphasize the role of the educator as instructor, rather than as a facilitator or mediator of learning. The results provide a clear indication that to a large extent Greek higher education follows a flat approach to learning knowledge across a broad range of subjects, which according to many researchers and professional boards is the root problem that accounting education faces. However, the study showed that some attempts were already made to introduce innovations in delivery, with a commonly cited example being e-learning and online resources, at issue here is that the utilization of information technology for teaching and learning does not necessarily address priorities for change in accounting education. Results also indicated that the most important learning mechanism in teaching ethics, forensic accounting, auditing and green accounting courses is the case studies and research projects. However, students who are more comfortable with numerical exercises and who learn through repetition and memorization are perhaps not best suited to the current demands of professional accounting practice. Hence, it may better match the above learning styles with guest speakers and textbooks which are also considered important teaching methods.

However, the study recognized that attempts to move to innovate and to better utilize learner-focused strategies for teaching ethics, forensic accounting, auditing and green accounting may be tempered by large class sizes, lack of financial resources or lack of faculty interest and less than ideal staff/student ratios. These problems may be beyond the control of individual educators, attributable instead to structural and resourcing constraints imposed by government, universities or the academic departments concerned.

The agenda for change in accounting education includes the need to improve students' soft skills, finding that this was a demand of modern, professional accounting practice. Indicatively, an accounting professional stated that "In our days, an accountant, beyond the excellent technical knowledge on the subject of accounting, should use modern tools of technology, should skillfully manage relations with his associates and should know the art of negotiation", while another one pointed that "The ongoing change on how businesses work in the new labor standards professionals with communicative virtues and group character. Teamwork and problem solving (case studies) help in this direction". Although the accounting professionals agreed that soft skills improve interpersonal relations and encourage team working as well as problem solving, there was little formal evidence of consideration given to soft skills development within accounting education in Greece. While this finding does not mean that soft skills development does not occur at all, the importance of these skills is not made explicit in formal learning objectives, topic lists or assessment activities in subject materials. Another implication of the survey is that an introductory accounting module would be necessary in shaping the perception of accounting studies, the profession of accountancy in general and thus it could create finest professionals. However, the current form of the introductory accounting modules in Greek universities mostly satisfies the need to partially teach the fundamental accounting terms and not to present an overall and realistic profile of the accountant.

An implication of the study results regarding the strategy which accounting education need to devise in the post-crisis era is that universities and companies need to build a harmonious and substantial relationship to meet the demands of the accounting profession. Accounting professionals and professors have to sit on the same table in order to reform accounting education. For example, an accounting professional stressed that "Every accounting department should contain a section composed of experienced accountants to adapt any new change in the accounting process in courses or workshops and extra seminars". Practically, this means to create a formal communication channel between them, which would integrate the latest developments of the accounting profession into the content of the curriculum and the teaching deliveries. Another important implication is that there is a need to satisfy the demand for interaction with other sciences, correct learning of the laws, promotion of the professional code of ethics as defined by the Economic Chamber of Greece and more use of interactive courses, case studies, workshops, continuous training and implementation of projects simulated to the real world. In other words, a participant argued that education should "find ways to make accountants think out of the box and not only as Debit/Credit". To successfully manage and accomplish the above enhancements, the recommended plan needs to include ways to overcome many administrational issues in accounting education as the large number of students per class, the scant resources in terms of academic staff and financing and more flexibility from the ministry.

Initially, the current study presented research in progress, aiming to investigate the compliance of the curricula and the teaching delivered by the relevant Greek higher education institutes with the emerging trends in accounting profession. The implications of the results identified many gaps and weaknesses of the current traditional curricula in regards to its correspondence to the real requirements of the accounting profession and to the perception about the work of accountant. This fact was reinforced during the global financial crisis of 2009, as it was proved that there were many lessons learnt for the accounting profession. Morality and ethics came to the foreground, as the study revealed many accounting omissions and manipulations in the accounting profession, mostly in the private sector and the high-level in the public sector, all of them based on unethical behavior (Brewer et al. 2014). Considering the results and the implications, it is now accepted both from professors and from professionals that the development of a new curriculum in accounting education is put forth. The survey results suggest a restructuring in accounting education according to the main research question: How could accounting educators alter the content and teaching methods in Greece in the post-crisis era? The proposed framework provides a tentative answer to this question. The framework was created based on the data analysis of the interviews and questionnaires, as well as the literature review and the benchmarking with other practical evaluation endeavors.

A brief description of the main components of the framework is provided below:

A. Ethics Module

Ethics modules should be included mandatorily both in undergraduate and in graduate level. The accounting curriculum in undergraduate level should include an initial course in ethics, rooted in philosophy and ethical reasoning, which would be should be a required course prior to taking a discipline-specific ethics or forensic accounting course in the basic curriculum. The discipline-specific ethics course in accounting should promote the professional code of ethics as defined by the Economic Chamber of Greece. Both subjects should be offered as separate modules and not through integration with other courses. The study also suggests integration of ethics into each accounting course throughout the curriculum for both graduate and undergraduate level, while during the graduate level a capstone course should be developed that deals with complex issues of business social responsibility and professional responsibility. Since study indicated interaction with other sciences, a professor of philosophy should teach the initial course of ethics, while the other ethics courses by professors of accounting. The proposed learning mechanisms for teaching ethics should be primarily offered by case studies and secondarily by research projects, guest speakers and textbooks.

B. Forensic Accounting Module

Forensic accounting would be a new module as almost no university offers such a course. The study showed that it is planned to be offered in two to five years in both undergraduate and graduate level. The study proposed that universities should offer two forensic accounting courses at the undergraduate level based on the expectation that graduating accounting students should have exposure to forensic accounting topics at the undergraduate level in order to be successful in the ethically challenging and practically scrutinized and regulated business environment. Since forensic accounting contains a lot of ethical and auditing elements, it is proposed to have as prerequisite the initial course in ethics and the auditing course. Moreover, both undergraduate forensic accounting courses should be mandatory and may be best placed toward the end of the undergraduate curriculum. The courses should be offered as a separate module and not through integration with other courses. Since study indicated interaction with law sciences, the initial course should be taught by a professor of law, while the basic course should by a professor of accounting. The proposed learning mechanisms in teaching forensic accounting are primarily through case studies and secondarily by research projects, guest speakers and fieldtrips.

C. Legal Terms

Using legal terms to teach ethics or forensic accounting may trigger strong negative feelings if many students have difficulties or past failures in social sciences or laws. The students may withdraw having a "self-concept shutdown" and blocking any new learning. The study recommends that altering such student's self-concept at the beginning of the learning process is very crucial step to knowledge. The student will not open up and learn until he or she believes that success is possible (Sousa 2006). Finding and solving the problems with necessary prior knowledge can make all the difference when it comes to learning.

D. Auditing Module

Auditing is not a new module as almost all universities offer it as separate course in both undergraduate and graduate level. The accounting curriculum in undergraduate level should include at least one mandatory auditing course, at the middle of the undergraduate studies, which would be a required course prior to taking the forensic accounting or the next auditing ones. Auditing should be offered as separate modules and not through integration with other courses. The proposed learning mechanisms in teaching auditing are primarily through case studies and secondarily by textbooks and research projects.

E. Green Accounting Module

Green accounting would be a new module as almost no university offers such a course. The professors reported that they are not planning to offer during the next three years in both undergraduate and graduate level. However, the study results showed that universities should offer a green accounting as an elective course or through integrating with other similar courses at the undergraduate level. This suggestion is based on the expectation that in the graduate level, this course would be offered as a new specialization to accounting students. The proposed learning mechanisms in teaching green accounting are primarily through case studies and secondarily by guest speakers.

F. Introductory Accounting Module

Introductory accounting is not a new module as almost all universities offer it as separate and mandatory course in the beginning of the undergraduate level. However, the content and the delivery stage of an introductory module need redesigning. Hence, the study suggests the introductory accounting to serve as a transition to university life and, hence, should be offered prior to accounting studies for a short period of one month. Moreover, both the study and literature propose an introductory accounting module, which would not only teach the fundamental accounting terms but also shape the perception of accounting studies, the profession of accountancy in general and thus create more conscious students. Particularly, this module should have two goals: "firstly, to provide information, assistance and guidance to general issues of transition and secondly discipline related requirements and study strategies" (Marangos 2006, p. 342). Consequently, the study recommends guest speakers and field trips as the main learning mechanisms for this module.

Along with the introduction of the new curriculum, this study showed that the following actions should be implemented:

A. Soft Skills Development

Opportunities for gaining particular soft skills, such as teamwork and oral communication competencies, should be offered through all courses of the accounting curriculum. To incorporate soft skills successfully into educational process, the study recommends educators to enrich the teaching mechanisms with group-based assignments, presentations and group learning activities. The study also indicates that in a technically focused accounting subject, soft skills can be developed by moving away from intellective (one right answer) class tasks and assessments to cognitive conflict activities. Within passive learning environments, experimental research also provides support for the notion that cooperative learning can build soft skills (such as teamwork) and improve student performance (Hwang et al. 2005).

B. Potential Obstacles

To mitigate potential obstacles in redesigning the accounting curriculum, such as teaching large classes, lack of financial resources and lack of students interest, the study suggests flexible teaching models in accounting combining face-to-face and electronic delivery, as opposed to conventional lecture/tutorial formats, yielding benefits similar to those of smaller classes in terms of student learning outcomes (Dowling et al. 2003). Moreover, covering fewer topics in greater detail and the use of more examples, especially real-life examples with which students can identify recall from their own past experiences, in shorter 20-minute time blocks can increase student learning and can provide students with the more profound understanding that accounting instructors seek (Simkins and Maier 2009). Enlarging the number of ways a new concept is presented to students, including the use of examples from other disciplines or interdisciplinary examples, increases the likelihood of linking the "new and known" patterns in elaborative rehearsal and strengthens understanding and the probability of retention (Sousa 2006). This generates deep learning and a level of understanding that is needed for the later application of new concepts, which is so desired by accounting instructors (Fogarty 2014).

C. Permanent Presence

The study adopts the professionals' demand for permanent presence of at least two accounting professionals as a separate section in every accounting department of universities. Their role would be to adapt current professional developments into the accounting curricula (Eleren and Kayahan 2007), to ensure interaction with other sciences and to cooperate with the accounting professors in order to find ways to make the new generations of accountants think out of the box. Both accounting professors and professionals should review the accounting curriculum in regular intervals to evaluate its effectiveness, to consider updates and to redefine the content and the learning mechanisms.

D. New Career Office's Role

The study also recommends that universities should upgrade the role of the careers office, which is placed within universities. The main role of the university careers offices' in Greece is to help students on employment services. Many university career services are already engaged in this work, but the study results showed new potential. The accounting professional body asks for a university careers office to collaborate to establish a "skills supply chain" between universities, Economic Chamber of Greece and local businesses, integrating placements and internships. Moreover, a career office should maintain a communication line with graduates along their careers in order to provide seminars and other advisory services.

CONCLUSION

This study acknowledged that accounting education is the key to successfully recognizing the causes of the recent financial crisis in Greece and to preventing future similar failures. Research has accumulated ample evidence demonstrating that considering certain changes in the accounting curriculum in tertiary education in Greece translates to production of finest and ethical professionals, which, in the long term, can restore the country's credibility and the quick exit of the country out of crisis (Zraa et al. 2011). It also examined a broad range of research work that relates to the accounting profession and education in Greece as well as to the available and current content and teaching methods in accounting education. Suggestions for improved constructive alignment, enhanced opportunities for accounting students to develop new competencies, to actively engage in the learning process and the need for increased innovation in delivery and assessment would not only redress the criticisms leveled at accounting education, but could contribute to the efforts made to limit the consequences of the financial crisis and to prevent a new one. Another implication in shifting from the apparently dominant traditional approaches to content, curriculum and delivery in new or restructured accounting program is the opportunity to promote deep, as opposed to surface, learning approaches in students. These improvements, including the reorientation of accounting education in regards to students' deliveries and learning approaches, have potential to benefit all accounting students, the future accounting professionals, the professional bodies, the employers of graduates and finally the society. Moreover, reshaping and enlivening the accounting curriculum, consistent with the benchmarks established and applied in this study, could encourage more students to major in accounting by providing a more accurate reflection of the nature of modern accounting work, having a potential flow-on effect in better meeting the needs of the professional bodies and the accounting profession, resisting in future financial crises and assisting to remedy the imbalance in the demand for and supply of conscious accountants.

REFERENCES

Allen, W., & Moessner, R. (2011). Banking crises and the international monetary system in the great depression and now. *Financial History Review, 18*, 1–20.

Arnold, P. (2009). Global financial crisis: The challenge to accounting research. *Accounting, Organizations and Society, 34*(6–7), 803–809.

Aspridis, G. M., Sdrolias, L., Blanas, N., Kyriakou, D., & Grigoriou, I. (2013). Economic crisis and the extroversion of the enterprises: An empirical approach. *Academic. Journal of Interdisciplinary Studies, 2*(9), 696.

Baralexis, S. (2004). Creative accounting in small advancing countries. *Managerial Auditing Journal, 19*(3), 440–461.

Bean, D., & Bernardi, R. (2005). Accounting ethics courses: A professional necessity. *The CPA Journal, 75*(12), 64–65.

Bekiaris, M., Efthymiou, T., & Koutoupis, G. (2013). Economic crisis impact on corporate governance and internal audit: The case of Greece. *Corporate Ownership & Control, 11*(1), 65–74.

Belias, D., & Koustelios, A. (2013). A pilot study of accounting teaching with LMS platform. *International Journal for e-Learning Security (IJeLS), 3*(1/2), 259–261.

Beresford, D. (2005). Accounting professionalism – Do we get it?. *American Accounting Association Annual Meeting*.

Brewer, P., Sorensen, J., & Stout, D. (2014). The future of accounting education: Addressing the competency crisis. *Strategic Finance, 96*(8), 29.

Buckhoff, T. A., & Schrader, R. W. (2000). The teaching of forensic accounting in the United States. *Journal of Forensic Accounting: Auditing, Fraud, & Taxation, 1*, 135–146.

Byrne, M., & Willis, P. (2005). Irish secondary students' perceptions of the work of an accountant and the accounting profession. *Accounting Education: An International Journal, 14*(4), 365–379.

Carroll, C. (2000). Why do the rich save so much? Does atlas shrug? The economic consequences of taxing the rich (ed. Joel B. Slemrod). Harvard University Press.

Creswell, J. (2007). *Research design: Qualitative, quantitative, and mixed methods.* Thousand Oaks, CA: Sage.

Dowling, C., Godfrey, J., & Gyles, N. (2003). Do hybrid flexible delivery teaching methods improve accounting students' learning outcomes? *Accounting Education, 12*(4), 373–391.

Eleren, A., & Kayahan, C. (2007). Evaluation of the accounting education in Afyon Kocatepe university student perspectives and have a vocational studies. *Accounting and Auditing Perspective Magazine*.

Farrell, A. (2005). *Ethical research with children.* Berkshire: Open University Press.

Feldmann, D., & Rupert, T. (2012). *Advances in accounting education: Teaching and curriculum innovations* (pp. 10–13). Bingley: Emerald.

Filos, J. (2010). Evaluation of corporate governance criteria set for business ethics award in Greece, based on perceptions of different stakeholders. 8th Corporate Governance and Internal Audit Conference, Chios, Greece.

Fogarty, M. (2014). How students learn economics and the importance of "real-life" examples. *Northeast Business & Economics Association*, 660–666.

Gabbin, A. L. (2002). The crisis in accounting education. *Journal of Accountancy, 193*, 81–86.

Green, B. P., & Calderon, T. G. (2005). Assessing student learning and growth through audit risk simulations. *Advances in Accounting Education, 7*, 1–25.

Hwang, N. R., Lui, G., & Tong, M. Y. (2005). An empirical test of cooperative learning in a passive learning environment. *Issues in Accounting Education, 20*(2), 151–165.

Jeffers, A. E. (2011). How Lehman Brothers used Repo 105 to manipulate their financial statements. *Journal of Leadership, Accountability & Ethics, 8*(5), 44–55.

Kermis, G., & Kermis, M. (2011). Professional presence and soft skills: A role for accounting education. *Journal of Instructional Pedagogies, 2,* 1–10.

Kouretas, G. P., & Vlamis, P. (2010). The Greek crisis: Causes and implications. *Panoeconomicus, 57*(4), 391–404.

Leone, M. (2008). IFRS requires a soft touch: If American companies plan on moving to IFRS, their financial statement preparers will require less technical training and more instruction on 'soft skills'. Retrieved November, 2008, from http://www.cfo.com/article.cfm/12626230

Livanos, L. (2010). The relationship between higher education and labour market in Greece; the weakest link? *Higher Education, 60*(5), 473–489.

Lockhart, J. A., & Mathews, M. R. (2000). Teaching environmental accounting: A four-part framework. *Advances in Accounting Education, 3,* 57–84.

Manganaris, P., & Spathis, C. (2012). Greek students' perceptions of an introductory accounting course and the accounting profession. *Advances in Accounting Education, 13,* 59–85.

Marangos, J. (2002). A survey of the value university students place on economics. *Economic Papers, 21*(3), 80–93.

Marangos, J. (2006). Changing students' perception of economics by facilitating their transition to university. *International Journal of Learning and Change, 1*(3), 329–344.

Marriott, N., & Marriott, P. (2003). Are we turning them on? A longitudinal study of undergraduate accounting students' attitudes towards accounting as a profession. *Accounting Education: An International Journal, 12*(2), 113–133.

Massey, D., & Van Hise, J. (2009). Walking the walk: Integrating lessons from multiple perspectives in the development of an accounting ethics course. *Issues in Accounting Education, 24*(4), 481–510.

Mintz, S. M. (1997). *Cases in accounting ethics & professionalism.* New York: McGraw Hill.

Olson, O. (2011). Research about financial crisis in the academic accounting literature the last 4 decades – A review of research published in the leading journals, Accounting Renaissance.

Parker, L. D. (2001). Back to the future: The broadening accounting trajectory. *The British Accounting Review, 33*(4), 421–432.

Pekdemir, I., & Pekdemir, R. (2013). High school teachers' perceptions and opinions on professional accountants: The Turkey case. Retrieved from http://ideas.repec.org/p/pra/mprapa/29865.html

Pimentel, J. R. C., Kuntz, J. R., & Detelin, S. E. (2010). Ethical decision-making: An integrative model for business practice. *European Business Review, 22*(4), 359–376.

Rada, D. (2014). Creative accounting and tax evasion. *Analele Universitatii 'Eftimie Murgu' Resita.* Fascicola II, p. 315.

Ravenscroft, S., & Williams, P. F. (2004). Considering accounting education in the USA post-Enron. *Accounting Education, 13*(1), 7–23.

Rezaee, Z., Crumbley, D., & Elmore, R. (2003). Forensic accounting education: A survey of academicians and practitioners. *Advances in Accounting Education Teaching and Curriculum Development, 6*, 193.

Santouridis, I., Tsifora, E., Trivellas, P., & Nikolopoulos, S. (2014). Revising Greek accounting & finance education in an economic crisis environment. *Procedia – Social and Behavioral Sciences, 148*, 428–436.

Simkins, S. P., & Maier, M. H. (2009). *Just in time teaching: Across the disciplines and across the academy.* Sterling, VA: Stylus Press/National Teaching and Learning Forum.

Smith, E. (2015). Young, gifted and Greek: Generation G – The world's biggest brain drain. Retrieved from http://www.theguardian.com/world/2015/jan/19/young-talented-greek-generation-g-worlds-biggest-brain-drain

Sousa, D. A. (2006). *How the brain learns* (3rd ed.). Thousand Oaks, CA: Corwin Press.

Spathis, C., Doumpos, M., & Zopounidis, C. (2004). A multicriteria discrimination approach to model qualified audit reports. Operational research. *An International Journal, 4*(3), 347–355.

Titard, P. L., Braun, R. L., & Meyer, M. J. (2004). Accounting education: Response to corporate scandals. *Journal of Accountancy, 198*(5), 59–65.

Venieris, G., & Cohen, S. (2004). Accounting reform in Greek universities: As low moving process. *Financial Accountability and Management, 20*(2), 183–204.

Xia, J., Caulfield, C., Baccarini, D. J., & Yeo, S. R. (2012). Simsoft: A game for teaching project risk management. In 21st teaching and learning forum, Perth, Murdoch University, Murdoch.

Zraa, W., Kavanagh, M., & Hartle, T. (2011, June 27–28). Teaching accounting in the new millennium. *Cambridge Business & Economics Conference (CBEC)*, Cambridge.

INDEX